A CRISIS OF DEMOCRATIC ACCOUNTABILITY

This book undertakes a comparative study of the public interest and political speech defences in defamation law, particularly from the perspective of the misuse of democratic free expression justifications. Specifically, it argues that the law and legal approaches taken by leading courts and legislatures in the UK, Australia, New Zealand, Canada, and the United States—five common law comparators—are undertheorised, lack adequate criteria for determining the correct form of the defence, and would benefit from a more precise understanding of 'democracy', 'accountability', and 'representation'. The book will be of great interest to scholars of free speech, defamation and public law.

A Crisis of Democratic Accountability

Public Libel Law and the Checking Function of the Press

Randall Stephenson

•HART•
OXFORD • LONDON • NEW YORK • NEW DELHI • SYDNEY

HART PUBLISHING
Bloomsbury Publishing Plc
Kemp House, Chawley Park, Cumnor Hill, Oxford, OX2 9PH, UK

HART PUBLISHING, the Hart/Stag logo, BLOOMSBURY and the Diana logo are trademarks of Bloomsbury Publishing Plc

First published in Great Britain 2018

A catalogue record for this book is available from the British Library.

Library of Congress Cataloging-in-Publication data

Names: Stephenson, Randall, 1971- author.

Title: A crisis of democratic accountability : public libel law and the checking function of the press / Randall Stephenson.

Description: Oxford, UK : Hart Publishing, 2018. | Based on author's thesis (doctoral—University of Oxford, 2017).

Identifiers: LCCN 2018010810 (print) | LCCN 2018011257 (ebook) | ISBN 9781509920822 (Epub) | ISBN9781509920815 (hardback)

Subjects: LCSH: Libel and slander—English-speaking countries.

Classification: LCC K930 (ebook) | LCC K930 .S74 2018 (print) | DDC 346.03/4—dc23

LC record available at https://lccn.loc.gov/2018010810

ISBN: HB: 978-1-50992-081-5
ePDF: 978-1-50992-083-9
ePub: 978-1-50992-082-2

Typeset by Compuscript Ltd, Shannon

CONTENTS

TABLE OF CASES

United States

European Court of Human Rights

United Kingdom

Canada

Australia

New Zealand

TABLE OF STATUTES

Australian Legislation

New Zealand Legislation

TABLES AND FIGURES

Tables

Figures

If the laws of each age were formulated systematically, no part of the legal system would be more instructive than the law relating to defamation. Since the law of defamation professes to protect personal character and public institutions from destructive attacks, without sacrificing freedom of thought and the benefit of public discussion, the estimate formed of the relative importance of these objects, and the degree of success attained in reconciling them, would be an admirable measure of the culture, liberality, and practical ability of each age. Unfortunately the English law of defamation is not the deliberate product of any period. It is a mass which has grown by aggregation, with very little intervention from legislation, and special and peculiar circumstances have from time to time shaped its varying course. The result is that perhaps no other branch of the law is as open to criticism for its doubts and difficulties, its meaningless and grotesque anomalies. It is, as a whole, absurd in theory, and very often mischievous in its practical operation.

Van Vechten Veeder, 1903

Introduction

Our opening passage raises timeless concerns with defamation principles and representative government, and what lies to be accomplished with future reform. For the comparatist, it also hints at the problems underlying this most 'devilishly difficult' of legal topics. Writing in the Columbia Law Review at the start of the twentieth century,[1] the distinguished New York City attorney (and later Federal Court Judge) Van Vechten Veeder could not have known how prophetic his critique of defamation law was to become. Besides the peculiarity of defamation law's three 'galloping presumptions' (ie falsity, malice, and damages), at the core of Veeder's concerns were the broader social effects of judicial efforts to 'optimally balance' free expression and reputation. Among the concerns prompting an eventual shift away from conventional strict liability principles, defamation law's restraining effects on newspapers were to play a vital role, both in America and abroad.

This liberalisation of defamation principles of course began with the US Supreme Court's seminal public libel decision in *New York Times v Sullivan*.[2] Adopting a categorical approach originating in English law,[3] a politician or public official was entitled to recover damages for defamatory statements of fact relevant to their public status only if the statement was made with 'actual malice', that is, with 'knowledge that it was false or with reckless disregard of whether it was false or not'.[4] Some 30 years later, courts in Australia, New Zealand, Britain, and Canada began revising qualified privilege principles to provide ostensive 'middle ground' solutions, aiming to split the difference between defamation law's strict liability framework and America's more press-friendly approach.

When observed from a broader comparative law perspective, a curious feature of this international judicial dialogue has been a universal rejection of the

[1] Van Vechten Veeder, 'The History and Theory of the Law of Defamation I' (1903) 3 *Columbia Law Review* 546, 546.

[2] 376 US 254 (1964). 'Public libel' refers to the use of defamation law in cases involving defamatory statements of fact on matters of public interest published to a mass audience, where the plaintiff is a politician, public official, or influential public figure or corporation.

[3] See *Wason v Walter* (1868) LR 4 QB 73; *Briggs v Garrett* 111 Pa St 404 (1886); *Jackson v Pittsburgh Times* 152 Pa 406 (1893); *Klos v Zahorik* 113 Ia 161 (1901); *Coleman v MacLennan* 78 Kan 711 (1908). For relevant commentary, see George Chase, 'Criticism of Public Officers and Candidates for Office' (1889) 23 *American Law Review* 346; Van Vechten Veeder, 'Freedom of Public Discussion' (1910) 23 *Harvard Law Review* 413; John E Hallen, 'Fair Comment' (1929) 8 *Texas Law Review* 41. See also Ian Loveland, *Political Libels: A Comparative Study* (Oxford, Hart Publishing, 2000).

[4] Sullivan (n 2) 279–80.

'actual malice' rule outside America.[5] What little scholarly attention has focussed on this outcome appears satisfied that such doctrinal heterogeneity simply reflects the natural incidents of cultural and political relativism, raising nothing more concerning than the comparatist's expectation of disagreement among common law jurisdictions attempting to solve similar problems through variations in legal doctrine and technique.[6] Indeed, Professor Mark Tushnet has detailed these multiple grounds for rejecting the 'actual malice' rule by identifying a broad range of 'principled' and 'institutional' (or strategic) accounts. Tushnet further subdivides these 'strategic' reasons into the following subgroups: country-specific; context-specific; institution-specific; cultural; and legal. Yet despite clarifying courts' apprehensions with the 'actual malice' rule, focussing on these descriptors invites a deeper and far more disquieting concern. That is, there would appear to be no principled standard or 'selection theory' for public libel doctrine *at all*.

Our present enquiry thus takes sharp leave of Professor Tushnet at this opening diagnostic moment. Organised around the importance of 'democratic accountability' and its current manifestation in free expression theory and institutions of representative government,[7] this comparative study is comprised of nine chapters structured around four interrelated themes. Part A introduces the problem of public libel law. Chapter one opens by reviewing defamation law's strict liability framework and the characteristic obstacles experienced by the press when reporting on public officials and pleading the defences of justification and qualified privilege. It then summarises the main sources and principles of public libel law. Despite unique institutional settings and doctrinal approaches, each of our comparators has proceeded by reflexively dismissing foreign decisions (principally *Sullivan*), and by undertheorising freedom of expression rationales. Significantly, where courts and legislatures have appealed to such rationales, they too often refer generically to 'democratic' theory, emphasising its least relevant features.

Chapter one therefore concludes by highlighting a more troubling concern for public libel jurisprudence than presently acknowledged in constitutional law scholarship. Namely, whether or not reasons are specified for rejecting the 'actual malice' rule, courts and legislators typically provide no justification for adopting

[5] See *Theophanous v Herald & Weekly Times Ltd* (1994) 182 CLR 104 (HCA) 135–38; *Lange v Atkinson and Australian Consolidated Press NZ Ltd* (1997) 2 NZLR 22 (HC) 36–37 (Elias J); *Hill v Church of Scientology* [1995] 2 SCR 1130 [127]–[131], [137]; *Grant v Torstar Corp* [2009] 3 SCR 640 [85]–[86]; *Reynolds v Times Newspapers Ltd* [2001] 2 AC 127 (HL) 201–03 (Lord Nicholls), 208–11 (Lord Steyn).

[6] See Mark Tushnet, '*New York Times v. Sullivan* Around the World' (2014) 66 *Alabama Law Review* 337. See also Paul Horwitz, 'Introduction: Still Learning from *New York Times v. Sullivan*' (2014) 66 *Alabama Law Review* 221.

[7] As developed in Part C, 'democratic accountability' refers to citizens' capability (as 'owners' of government) to hold to account their political representatives (who exercise powers of collective decision-making and action), public officials, and influential public figures and corporations, through a nation's multidimensional network of accountability mechanisms and extra-governmental institutions, particularly its institutional press.

doctrinal alternatives other than denying America's approach. Despite efforts by the Judicial Committee of the Privy Council and New Zealand courts to establish a practicable framework, results have been unconvincing, failing to synthesise a broad array of legal, constitutional, and media factors. Above all, no explanation has been provided for how such factors alone, or in combination, are meant to steer judges to 'optimal' and predictable doctrinal solutions. Providing another example of its richly-deserved reputation for aggregatory and anomalous growth, in simplest terms, this liberalisation of public libel law appears to have occurred without any external criteria or 'selection theory'.

Building on such introductory matters, chapter two identifies two methodological barriers to principled and effective public libel regulation. Both have operated behind the scenes to compromise our use and understanding of democratic theory. More precisely, widespread failures to marshal democratic theory are due (at least partially) to incomplete articulations of the 'core' justifications for free expression, and misguided efforts to subsume prevailing rationales under various single-valued approaches. Importantly, both developments have marginalised the *checking function of the press*—the free expression value most relevant to public libel cases and strengthening accountability mechanisms in representative systems. Chapter two therefore provides much-needed overviews of the two democratic models at the heart of our enquiry: Alexander Meiklejohn's democratic 'self-governance' rationale and Vincent Blasi's 'checking value' of the press.[8] As both models represent our point of departure for assessing democratic theorising in public libel jurisprudence, an early and precise understanding of their contrasting features is essential.

Shifting our attention to the latest instances of doctrinal confusion, Part B contains a comprehensive comparative law analysis of public libel doctrine across our five common law comparators. It details the theoretical and doctrinal errors of leading courts and legislatures, particularly their legal methodologies (eg ad hoc balancing, categoricalism), and their understanding and use of free expression justifications. This analysis reveals that the primary deficiency in public libel law is a persistent and widespread disregard of accountability concerns and the checking function of the press. Such undertheorising manifests in three distinct but interrelated forms, each the focus of its own chapter.

Chapter three begins by investigating the unusual doctrinal approaches endorsed by Australian and American courts. Following the US Supreme Court's adoption of the 'actual malice' rule in *Sullivan*, the High Court of Australia justified its novel 'responsible journalism' defence by appealing to an indeterminate implied rights doctrine based on an unsound transplantation of Canada's

[8] See Alexander Meiklejohn, 'Free Speech and its Relation to Self-Government' in *Political Freedom: The Constitutional Powers of the People* (New York, Harper & Row, 1948); Alexander Meiklejohn, 'The First Amendment is an Absolute' (1961) *Supreme Court Review* 245; Vincent Blasi, 'The Checking Value in First Amendment Theory' (1977) *American Bar Foundation Research Journal* 521.

pre-Charter jurisprudence. Most controversially, Australia's implied rights methodology purportedly rejects free expression theorising altogether. Considered together, American and Australian public libel doctrines provide a fitting introduction to our doctrinal analysis by emphasising the importance of employing a complete inventory of free expression values when regulating public libels, whether endorsing a categorical approach, or any form of ad hoc balancing.

Chapter four then examines the indifference of leading common law courts and legislatures to such imperfect references to democratic accountability and the checking function rationale as actually do exist in public libel jurisprudence. In particular, both the UK Supreme Court and the New Zealand Court of Appeal have discounted significant sources of domestic and international jurisprudence resonant with the checking function's fundamental premises and concerns. Along with New Zealand's disquieting judicial bias against the press, Britain's highest courts have essentially ignored important developments by the European Court of Human Rights in endorsing political criticism and the 'watchdog' role of the institutional press.[9]

Chapter five concludes Part B by examining the systematic and widespread conflation of the checking function with Meiklejohnian theory. As discussed in chapter two, despite their distinct emphases and assumptions, judges, legislators, and legal scholars have frequently construed these models as synonymous, showing little regard for their potentially sweeping implications for public libel doctrine and reform. Although this confusion is prevalent amongst all of our comparators, it is most instructively exhibited by UK authorities and the Supreme Court of Canada. In the case of Canadian public libel doctrine, an ambiguous understanding of 'democratic' theory has been methodologically embedded by omitting the checking function from the Court's inventory of free expression values. This has left Canadian courts little choice but to shoehorn accountability concerns into a Meiklejohnian framework and to appeal, awkwardly and unconvincingly, to less relevant theoretical justifications.

Part C signals an important shift in emphasis to 'system-building' by introducing a fresh approach for addressing the errors exposed in Parts A and B, and for reintroducing accountability and the checking function into public libel jurisprudence. Based on recent advances in public accountability theory, this revised framework is proposed as a workable 'selection theory' for the improved design and tailoring of public libel doctrine. Chapter six begins by arguing that the root of public libel law's undertheorising lies in the complex relationships between 'democracy', 'representation', and 'accountability'. At least since the publication of Hanna Pitkin's classic work on representation, the role of accountability in

[9] 'Institutional press' refers to only those print, broadcast, and digital news organisations and individuals—comprising well-organised, well-financed, professional critics—that are *independent*, *adversarial*, and *powerful* enough to serve as a worthy counterforce to government and influential private actors. See generally Part C; Blasi (n 8) 541.

representative government has called for greater clarity.[10] Yet despite the efforts of political theorists,[11] 'accountability' theory has been slow to establish its own tradition of academic analysis.

Aptly, a 'minimal conceptual consensus' has emerged in public accountability scholarship,[12] which reflects recent and widespread efforts to organise accountability research into a framework for systematic analysis. Besides clarifying the core meaning of accountability as a 'virtue' and 'mechanism', this conceptual stabilisation has also accentuated the multifaceted nature of 'accountability' and its overriding need for normative political criteria. Chapter six consequently examines the connections between accountability and 'neo-republicanism',[13] a political theory leveraging to a remarkable degree the implications of public accountability's emergent analytical framework. Along with offering a useful metacriteria for assessing the various mechanisms and regimes in accountability theory, this 'gas-and-water-works' republicanism benefits from the more rigorous analytical development found in public accountability scholarship and its implications for refining democratic institutional design.

Interposing public accountability theory with neo-republicanism also leads to a viable method for connecting public libel law and the institutional press to broader webs of accountability in representative systems. Chapter seven accordingly undertakes the task of formulating a revised analytical framework for public libel jurisprudence. Following an examination of accountability dysfunctions and the empirical evidence supporting the 'checking function' of the press, a revised framework is formulated by combining the effects of two sets of accountability mechanisms. The 'primary' set represents a jurisdiction's *fixed* elements of political and constitutional design, including its electoral structure, parliamentary/presidential structure, federal/unitary structure, mechanisms of legislative scrutiny, and specific form of judicial review. By contrast, the 'secondary' set represents those *dynamic* mechanisms supplementing a nation's basic accountability structure, including its government auditors, independent regulators, and direct public access mechanisms. Both sets of accountability mechanisms provide the aggregate background against which public libel doctrine must be matched.

Part D tests our revised analytical framework by applying it to the UK and its newly-updated public libel doctrine. Chapter eight's analysis of Britain's primary

[10] See Hanna Fenichel Pitkin, *The Concept of Representation* (California, University of California Press, 1967). See also Bernard Manin, *The Principles of Representative Government* (Cambridge, Cambridge University Press, 1997); Philip Pettit, 'Varieties of Public Representation' in Ian Shapiro and others (eds), *Political Representation* (Cambridge, Cambridge University Press, 2010).

[11] See, eg, Philippe C Schmitter and Terry Lynn Karl, 'What Democracy is … and is Not' (1991) 2(3) *Journal of Democracy* 75; Philippe C Schmitter, 'The Ambiguous Virtues of Accountability' (2004) 15(4) *Journal of Democracy* 47.

[12] See generally Mark Bovens and others (eds), *The Oxford Handbook of Public Accountability* (Oxford, Oxford University Press, 2014).

[13] See Philip Pettit, *Republicanism: A Theory of Freedom and Government* (Oxford, Oxford University Press, 1997); Philip Pettit, *On the People's Terms: A Republican Theory and Model of Democracy* (Cambridge, Cambridge University Press, 2012).

and secondary accountability mechanisms reveals the following. First, besides benefitting from alternative sources of political information generated by mechanisms of legislative scrutiny, the UK is still beset by general transparency concerns associated with its parliamentary-unitary structure and convention of ministerial responsibility. Second, this informational discrepancy between government and citizens is not fundamentally altered by Britain's secondary accountability mechanisms, ie its independent auditors, regulators, and direct public access mechanisms. Specifically, due to an attenuated bandwidth of audit inputs and effectiveness, the effects of restricted citizen access to the Parliamentary Ombudsman, and an expansive exemption regime undermining access to information under British legislation, there remains a strong need for auxiliary mechanisms to fill aggregate shortfalls in government transparency.

After outlining the UK's basic accountability profile, chapter nine then provides our project's main law reform recommendations. When judged against the under-theorised basis for Britain's public libel regime, the most appropriate doctrinal match for its accountability profile requires, at a minimum, adopting a generic qualified privilege similar in effect to the 'actual malice' rule. What is more, an absolute privilege for political speech cannot be ruled out. This is deeply ironic since, alongside a pattern of discounting accountability concerns in leading cases, Britain's public libel jurisprudence exhibits a firm reluctance to privilege political speech, which is further fueled by misunderstandings around categorical defences. Alternatively, Britain's new defence of 'Publication on Matter of Public Interest' can be reformed by introducing presumptions of 'public interest' and 'reasonable belief' rebuttable on 'clear and convincing' evidence in public libel cases involving plaintiff politicians, public officials, and influential public figures and corporations. As confirmed in Part B, such plaintiff-driven amendments are essential for ensuring suitable doctrinal footholds for the checking function and accountability concerns in free speech litigation involving media defendants.

Still, despite their logical and prescriptive force, such sweeping law reform proposals raise significant concerns with institutional competence and the need for further research and methodological refinement. Although the recommended approach to public libel doctrine benefits adjudication by placing the defamation inquiry—perhaps for the first time—on a more sophisticated and suitable theoretical foundation, the UK Parliament may be better equipped to refine Britain's public libel doctrine due to its greater resources and enlarged scope of review. After all, the more granular and extensive the analysis of accountability effects, the more clearly and confidently public libel doctrine can be matched to *actual* institutional settings.

Similarly, although our revised framework can identify gross mismanagement of public libel doctrine and establish justifiable ranges of possible alternatives, the analysis and results reported in Part D are unavoidably preliminary. As discussed in chapter seven, a more complete accountability assessment must also consider a jurisdiction's media structure and any relevant contextual factors affecting its accountability profile and embodiments of the checking function of the press.

Above all, an accountability assessment along these lines must still be balanced against a jurisdiction's commitment to 'reputation'. Such factors will invariably affect public libel doctrine in potentially drastic ways.

In the end, while much work remains in developing our public libel methodology, the theoretical repositioning required by our revised framework provides a long overdue and promising foundation for undertaking this process of methodological refinement. Although inspired by the Privy Council's conviction that comparative analysis helps to 'clarify and refine' issues and options in public libel jurisprudence, such innovative constitutional insights can only be transformed into a workable method by theoretically recasting and contextually reinstating the checking function of the press. While accountability concerns were arguably implicit in the New Zealand Court of Appeal's comparative law deliberations, its failure to explicitly reference public accountability theory not only constrained its identification of relevant accountability mechanisms, but, most critically, how they might *interrelate*, both with legal doctrine, and amongst themselves.

For instance, as revealed in chapter one, an unstated premise of the Court of Appeal's analysis was that New Zealand required a *more* press-friendly doctrinal approach than England or Australia because its accountability mechanisms were in fact stronger. By stark contrast, the prescriptions under our revised analytical framework necessitate a *less* press-friendly solution under such circumstances, the opposite of what the New Zealand Court of Appeal ultimately preferred. A more cautious assessment of the cumulative effects of accountability mechanisms at multiple levels of abstraction would appear to have been the missing piece of the puzzle all along. At last, while Van Vechten Veeder's opening critique must surely remain valid, it is hoped that at the conclusion of this comparative law study defamation law might be found less absurd in theory and perhaps even less mischievous in its practical operation.

Part A

Introduction to the Problem of Public Libel Law

Overview of Part A

Part A introduces public libel law's past and present difficulties. To situate its position amongst orthodox principles of tort liability, chapter one opens by reviewing defamation's strict liability framework, along with characteristic obstacles experienced by the press when reporting on public officials and pleading the defences of justification and qualified privilege. By placing recent law reform efforts into a broader historical and doctrinal perspective, these considerations explain much of the policy confusion and technical difficulties experienced by leading common law courts and legislatures.

Next, without probing too deeply into the theory-doctrine interface, chapter one summarises the main sources and principles of public libel jurisprudence in our five common law comparators. This brief overview not only identifies significant doctrinal discrepancies, but the reasons and justifications for selecting from a wide range of alternatives are not immediately clear, particularly as each jurisdiction proceeds from unique constitutional and institutional backgrounds. Closer analysis of leading public libel cases exposes two critical deficiencies.

First, public libel doctrine is significantly undertheorised, providing insufficient support for chosen doctrinal paths. Despite unique methodologies, each of our comparators has chosen its approach by reflexively dismissing foreign decisions (principally *Sullivan*), and by inadequately referencing freedom of expression justifications. Moreover, where courts and legislatures have referenced such justifications, they too often refer generically to 'democratic' theory, frequently stressing its least relevant aspects. Democratic accountability concerns most relevant to adjudicating public libel cases are routinely and inexplicably ignored.

Second, public libel doctrine is also unacceptably *acontextual*, failing to embrace comparative law analysis and the importance of 'local conditions' when adapting legal doctrine to institutional settings. Despite efforts by the Privy Council and New Zealand courts to establish an appropriate framework, results have been unconvincing, failing to synthesise a broad array of constitutional, media, and legal factors. Above all, no explanation has been provided for how such factors alone, or in combination, contribute to 'optimal' doctrinal solutions. As a result, there is effectively no external criteria for selecting public libel doctrine. To be clear, our concern is not to hold judges and legislators to unreasonably high standards of theorising, but to recognise that there must be *some* external criteria to support doctrinal choices. Likewise, if attempts are made to engage in free expression theorising, the rationales most relevant to adjudicating public libel cases must be prioritised and applied.

Building on such introductory matters, chapter two explores public libel law's principal methodological complications. Before undertaking our comparative law analysis in Part B, chapter two identifies two commonly overlooked barriers to principled and effective public libel regulation. Specifically, the failure of courts and legislatures to fully marshal democratic theory is due (at least partially) both to incomplete articulations of free expression's 'core' justifications, and efforts to subsume remaining rationales under various single-valued approaches. Both developments have disproportionately marginalised the checking function of the press, the free expression rationale most relevant to adjudicating public libel cases and strengthening accountability mechanisms in representative democracies.

Chapter two then reviews Alexander Meiklejohn's democratic 'self-governance' rationale and Vincent Blasi's 'checking value' of the press, the two democratic models anchoring our present study. As demonstrated in Part B, Meiklejohnian theory occupies a prominent but uncomfortable position amongst free speech justifications, having been uprooted from its native United States to Britain, Canada, and to a lesser extent, Australia and New Zealand. As both models represent our initial point of departure for assessing democratic theorising in public libel jurisprudence, a detailed understanding of their principal features is not only instructive, but necessary.

In the end, contemporary public libel law remains beleaguered by a missing 'selection theory'. This problem is intensified by the lack of a 'gold standard', or baseline, from which to assess doctrinal alternatives. Combined, these shortcomings have introduced substantial arbitrariness and incoherence into public libel doctrine, necessarily resulting in inadvertent under- and over-protection of speech and expression. Constructive efforts to place public libel jurisprudence on a more principled and secure footing must therefore begin in chapter one by chronicling the methodological, theoretical, and doctrinal background to these increasingly difficult problems.

1

Balancing Freedom of Expression and Reputation in Constitutional Context

I. Defamation's Moving Target: Balancing Free Expression and Reputation

Defamation is a strict liability tort.[1] But considerably unlike the rule in *Rylands v Fletcher*,[2] the core concern of defamation law is not the regulation of wild animals, explosives, or dangerous products, but the protection of *reputation*.[3] While libel and slander laws have a long history in English common law,[4] their overarching concern with safeguarding one's good name has inevitably conflicted with other socially-prized rights, values, and interests. Defamation law has above all struggled to balance freedom of expression and protection of reputation since at least Blackstone's Commentaries,[5] which has been aptly described as 'one of the law's perennial problems'.[6] Even modern-day libel reform continues to seek an

[1] See generally Alastair Mullis and Richard Parkes (eds), *Gatley on Libel and Slander*, 12th edn (London, Sweet & Maxwell, 2013).

[2] [1868] UKHL 1. Strict liability is typically concerned with activities involving extraordinary risk to others, either in the seriousness or frequency of the harm threatened. See John G Fleming, *The Law of Torts*, 9th edn (Sydney, Law Book Company Information Services, 1998) Ch 15.

[3] For a classic account of reputation and constitutional analysis, see Robert C Post, 'The Social Foundations of Defamation Law: Reputation and the Constitution' (1986) 74 *California Law Review* 691. See also Lawrence McNamara, *Reputation and Defamation* (Oxford, Oxford University Press, 2007); Bob Tarantino, 'Chasing Reputation: The Argument for Differential Treatment of "Public Figures" in Canadian Defamation Law' (2010) 48 *Osgoode Hall Law Journal* 595.

[4] See generally Van Vechten Veeder, 'The History and Theory of the Law of Defamation I' (1903) 3 *Columbia Law Review* 546; Van Vechten Veeder, 'The History and Theory of the Law of Defamation II' (1904) 4 *Columbia Law Review* 33; Paul Mitchell, *The Making of the Modern Law of Defamation* (Oxford, Hart Publishing, 2005).

[5] William Blackstone, *Commentaries on the Laws of England* (Oxford, 1765–1769) Vol 4, 150–53. See also Judge Edgerton of the Court of Appeals for the District of Columbia Circuit in *Sweeney v Patterson* 128 F2d 457, 458 (1942), who stated that '[w]hatever is added to the field of libel is taken from the field of free debate'.

[6] John Burrows, 'Lange v Atkinson 2000: *Analysis*' (2000) *New Zealand Law Reports* 389, 398.

'optimal balance', a point emphasised in the legislative history to Britain's Defamation Act 2013:[7]

> The law governing defamation is *crucial* to the proper functioning of any democratic society. It represents the dividing line between two established and powerful rights: freedom of expression on the one side; the right to reputation on the other. *Any slight shift in the balance* between these two competing rights and the procedures governing our legal system can have *far-reaching consequences* for the way in which we conduct public debate.[8]

As emphasised above, defamation law profoundly affects the informational needs of democratic states. As captured by Veeder's opening passage, the primary challenge in formulating and applying defamation principles involves reaching 'appropriate' accommodations between individual rights and social interests in both freedom of expression and reputation.[9] Predictably, doctrinal approaches have changed considerably over time and place. The concern for public libel doctrine now, as ever, is marshalling sufficient support to explain and justify the divergent approaches endorsed by leading common law jurisdictions.

A. Constituent Elements

Although there is no wholly satisfactory legal definition, 'defamation' is usually understood as any written or spoken statement, or any picture or representation, calculated to bring a person into hatred, contempt or ridicule, or to lower his or her reputation in the eyes of 'right-thinking' people in society.[10] Although falsity, malice, and damages are customarily presumed, a plaintiff must nonetheless establish that:[11]

1. The words were *defamatory*.[12]
   - This involves a statement about a person to their discredit.
   - Generally, such statements consist of words:
     i. Tending to cause a person to be hated or despised and to excite adverse opinions against him or her;

[7] Defamation Act 2013 (UK) c 26. The Act received Royal Assent on 25 April 2013. Section 4, which contains the defence of 'Publication on Matter of Public Interest', was proclaimed into force on 1 January 2014.

[8] Joint Committee on the Draft Defamation Bill, *Session 2010–12: Report, together with formal minutes* (HC 930–I, 19 October 2011) 15 (emphasis added) (citation omitted).

[9] For example, during first reading of New Zealand's draft Defamation Bill, introduced in August 1988, the Minister of Justice explained: 'It is the function of the law of defamation to find an acceptable balance between two competing principles. The first principle is the right of free speech, which has, of course, been hard won over the centuries. [...] The second principle is to protect a person's reputation against unjustifiable attack' (Rt Hon Geoffrey Palmer 491 NZPD 6369 (25 August 1988)), as quoted in New Zealand Law Commission, *Defaming Politicians: A Response to Lange v Atkinson* (Preliminary Paper 33, 1998) [9].

[10] *Gatley on Libel and Slander* (n 1) s 1.7.

[11] *Gatley on Libel and Slander* (n 1) s 1. English defamation law has been altered by the Defamation Act 2013, which establishes a further legal burden of 'serious harm'. See Defamation Act 2013 (n 7) s 1.

[12] *Gatley on Libel and Slander* (n 1) Ch 2.

   ii. Subjecting a person to ridicule;
   iii. Causing others to shun the plaintiff;
   iv. Imputing that a person is guilty in office;
   v. Tending to injure a person's reputation in business or trade, including his or her financial credit; or
   vi. Imputing immorality.
2. The words were *published.*[13]
   — Publication consists of making known or communicating the defamatory words or matter to a person or persons other than the plaintiff.
   — Publication can be accomplished by words, orally or in writing, radio, television, internet, cartoons, photographs, gestures, intonations, etc.
3. The *plaintiff* was personally defamed (the 'of and concerning' requirement).[14]
   — Defamation is a personal legal remedy, the object of which is to vindicate the plaintiff's reputation and to make reparation for private injury done by the publication to a third person or persons of false defamatory statements concerning the plaintiff.

B. Defences

Once a plaintiff establishes these elements on a balance of probabilities, a defendant may then rely on any of four traditional defences.[15] These defences provide the core doctrinal means of safeguarding free expression.[16]

1. Justification: The defence of justification or 'truth' is a complete defence to a defamation action, which requires the defendant to prove the truth of all material factual statements contained in a defamatory publication. The term 'justification' must not be understood in its ordinary sense of a person being morally or ethically 'justified' in making various assertions. It means, rather, that the defendant insists the defamatory words are true, and they intend to prove it. The rationale behind this defence is that a plaintiff is not entitled to a reputation that they do not possess. Although there may be damage accruing from publication, if the facts are true, defamation law gives no remedy by action.[17]
2. Fair Comment: 'Fair comment' is a defence when the words complained of are recognisably an expression of opinion, rather than fact. Fair criticism on a matter of public interest is not actionable as defamation. However, the underlying facts must be proved true to defend the defamatory statement,

[13] *Gatley on Libel and Slander* (n 1) Ch 6.
[14] *Gatley on Libel and Slander* (n 1) Ch 7.
[15] Additional defamation defences include consent, accord and satisfaction, limitations, *res judicata*, and various statutory defences. See *Gatley on Libel and Slander* (n 1) Ch 19.
[16] *Gatley on Libel and Slander* (n 1) chs 10–18.
[17] *Gatley on Libel and Slander* (n 1) Ch 11.

which is then protected provided the opinion is one that an honest person knowing those facts could hold. Although a defendant can rely on this objective honest belief test,[18] the comment must be made in good faith, since a plaintiff can defeat the defence by establishing subjective malice on the defendant's part.[19]

3. Absolute Privilege: On certain occasions, public policy requires that a person be free to publish defamatory words even though they cannot be proved true or defended as 'fair comment'. Words spoken or published on such occasions, even though spoken or published with full knowledge of their falsity and with intent to injure the plaintiff, are not actionable. These are said to be occasions of 'absolute privilege', which have been defined narrowly by courts and legislatures. Common examples include:
   a. Statements made in the course of judicial proceedings;
   b. Statements made in the course of quasi-judicial proceedings;
   c. Statements contained in documents made in judicial or quasi-judicial proceedings;
   d. Statements made by one state officer to another in the course of their official duties;
   e. Statements made in the course of parliamentary proceedings;
   f. Statements contained in parliamentary reports; and
   g. Fair and accurate contemporaneous reports in a 'newspaper' of proceedings publicly heard before courts exercising judicial authority.[20]
4. Qualified Privilege: On occasions of 'qualified privilege', a person may make false defamatory statements about another without incurring liability provided certain conditions are satisfied. Specifically, the speaker or author must have an interest or some legal, moral, or social duty in stating or writing what they believe to be true about another person to a listener or reader who has a corresponding duty or interest in receiving that information. Such a person is protected if they make the statement honestly and without any indirect or improper motive. The privilege is 'qualified' because protection is not absolute, depending upon the honesty of purpose with which the defamatory statement is made. Proof that the defendant published with malice or otherwise exceeded the scope of the protected occasion will defeat the defence. Since this defence is founded upon considerations of public policy and

[18] Many common law jurisdictions have only recently adopted an 'objective' honest belief test, which is more protective of freedom of expression. See *Channel Seven Adelaide Pty Ltd v Manock* [2007] HCA 60; *WIC Radio Ltd v Simpson* [2008] 2 SCR 420. Moreover, fair comment has been replaced in Britain by a statutory defence of 'honest opinion' under section 3 of the Defamation Act 2013. Among its changes, defendants no longer must prove that the defamatory statement was on a matter of public interest.

[19] *Gatley on Libel and Slander* (n 1) Ch 12.

[20] *Gatley on Libel and Slander* (n 1) Ch 13.

social convenience,[21] it involves consideration of what is 'necessary' for the general welfare of society. Thus, new occasions for its application will arise with changing social and political conditions.[22]

C. Publications to the 'World at Large'

As qualified privilege was restricted to narrow or 'private' publications,[23] it has seldom assisted the press. That is, it was until recently a strict requirement that defamatory statements not be 'shouted from the rooftops', but made only to interested parties.[24] Establishing a reciprocal duty or interest was essential.[25] Qualified privilege was therefore generally unavailable where the defendant was a newspaper or broadcaster, since it is rare that every reader or listener is an 'interested party' to statements published to the world at large.[26] This tension is best shown by examining superseded common law authorities denying qualified privilege for newspaper publications on matters of public interest.

In *Chapman v Ellesmere*,[27] a horse trainer brought suit in defamation for publications reporting on a post-race inquiry confirming the illegal doping of a racehorse under his care. The defamatory remarks were published in the local Jockey Club's 'Racing Calendar', and afterwards in *The Times*. The defendant newspaper pleaded justification and qualified privilege. After rejecting the newspaper's efforts to prove the truth of the disputed statements, the English Court of Appeal turned to qualified privilege. Since the Jockey Club's 'Racing Calendar' was the intended means of communication between the club's tribunal and the interested public sector, this much narrower publication was protected. The newspaper was not so lucky. Relying on a particularly guarded view of the institutional press, Lord Justice Romer stated:

> As regards the publication to and in the Times, and to the press agencies, the defence of privilege cannot, I think, prevail. So far as regards the stewards, such a publication seems to me to go beyond any duty that they owed to any one. So far as regards the Times Publishing Company, it may in one sense be true to say that they owe a duty to their readers to publish any and every item of news that may interest them. But this is *not* such a duty

[21] See *Toogood v Spyring* (1834) 1 CM & R 181, 193, where Parke B observed that the underlying justification for qualified privilege is that it serves 'the common convenience and welfare of society'.

[22] *Gatley on Libel and Slander* (n 1) chs 14, 15.

[23] *Gatley on Libel and Slander* (n 1) s 15.1.

[24] New Zealand Law Commission (n 9) [3].

[25] See *Adam v Ward* [1917] AC 309 (HL) 334, where Lord Atkinson instructed that the privileged occasion must be one 'where the person who makes [the] communication has an interest or a duty, legal, social or moral, to make it to the person to whom it is made, and the person to whom it is so made has a corresponding interest or duty to receive it'.

[26] A 'newspaper' has been judged permissible provided that the paper is effectively an enlarged circular restricted to the particular group sharing a legitimate common interest with the publisher. See *Morosi v Mirror Newspapers Ltd* [1977] 2 NSWLR 749 (CA) 779.

[27] [1932] 2 KB 431 (CA).

> as makes every communication in their paper relating to a matter of public interest a privileged one. *If it were, the power of the Press to libel public men with impunity would in the absence of malice be almost unlimited.*[28]

The Court notably provided no commentary on the theoretical grounds of the newspaper's privilege claim, or its own judgment.

This cautious assessment of the institutional press also influenced early decisions dismissing qualified privilege in public libel cases involving criticism of government and public officials. For example, in *Purcell v Sowler*,[29] the English Court of Appeal held that a Manchester newspaper's report of a board meeting of poor-law guardians, in which a union medical officer was described as neglecting to attend pauper patients, was not protected by qualified privilege. Although conceding that the article was 'a matter of public interest within the rule as to privileged publications',[30] Lord Chief Justice Cockburn avoided its application by categorising the board meeting as 'not necessarily public' and of 'very limited jurisdiction'.[31] Based on this strained factual construction, he concluded that 'there is no authority for [the] position' that qualified privilege attaches to meetings discretionarily opened to the public, the overriding concern being that 'unwise exercise of the discretion might expose a man to a publication otherwise libellous'.[32]

More concerning still were earlier pronouncements by Lord Chief Justice Denman in *Duncombe v Daniell*.[33] The plaintiff was a Parliamentary candidate when a concerned voter and barrister published two letters in *The Morning Post* reflecting poorly on him for late payment of debts. The defendant pleaded justification and qualified privilege. In rejecting both defences, Lord Denman CJ concluded that 'the occasion did not justify the present publication' because '[h]owever large the privilege of electors may be, it is extravagant to suppose that it can justify the publication to all the world of facts injurious to a person who happens to stand in the situation of a candidate'.[34] The plaintiff's status as a parliamentary hopeful had no legal purchase. Moreover, as in *Chapman*, no rationale was reported to justify this conservative doctrinal principle and result.

Therefore, based on these defamation authorities,[35] courts have traditionally insisted that publication methods not exceed what is reasonably appropriate for protecting the particular duty or interest asserted. Even where an occasion is prima facie privileged because of a common political or public interest, the selected

[28] ibid 475 (Romer LJ) (emphasis added).
[29] (1877) 2 CPD 215 (CA).
[30] ibid 218 (Cockburn LCJ).
[31] ibid 219 (Cockburn LCJ).
[32] ibid 220 (Cockburn LCJ).
[33] (1837) 8 C & P 223.
[34] ibid 229 (Lord Denman CJ).
[35] These authorities were reviewed by the Supreme Court of Canada in *Grant v Torstar Corp* [2009] 3 SCR 640 [34], where Chief Justice McLachlin acknowledged correctly that 'the defence of qualified privilege has seldom assisted media organizations'. See also *Douglas v Tucker* [1952] 1 SCR 275; *Globe and Mail Ltd v Boland* [1960] SCR 203; *Banks v Globe and Mail Ltd* [1961] SCR 474; *Jones v Bennett* [1969] SCR 277.

medium must reasonably ensure that defamatory statements are not circulated beyond those legitimately interested.[36] As a result, newspapers have operated without an effective defence for false defamatory statements of fact published to the world at large, or for defamatory statements that they were otherwise unable to prove to a court's satisfaction.

D. Politicians and Public Libels—The Resonance of Radical Whig Ideology

Besides difficulties associated with mass media publications, assessing the doctrinal implications of differing libel plaintiffs further complicates the task of balancing freedom of expression and reputation. As shown in *Duncombe*,[37] the most definitive example involves politicians and public officials attempting to use libel laws to remove the stain of 'false' defamatory statements of fact published in the press. Although freedom to criticise government and politicians has varied considerably over time and amongst jurisdictions, the use of libel law by government, elected officials, and even influential members of society raises vital concerns affecting a society's claims to democratic legitimacy.[38]

At its most extreme, defamation law has been used to stifle political debate and opposition through criminal prosecutions for seditious libel.[39] The law of seditious libel was most authoritatively pronounced in *Tuchin's* case.[40] As Lord Chief Justice John Holt directed at the time of Britain's newly-emergent parliamentary government, this offence left little room for criticising government bodies and public officials:

> If men should not be called to account for possessing the people with an ill opinion of the Government, no Government can subsist; for it is very necessary for *every* Government, that the people should have a good opinion of it. And *nothing can be worse to any Government, than to endeavour to procure animosities as to the management of it*. This has been *always* look'd upon as a crime, and *no* Government can be safe unless it is punished.[41]

From such inauspicious roots, defamation laws have responded to increasing demands for freedom of expression and the press. Among the most ardent supporters of press liberty were eighteenth-century radical Whigs,[42] who advanced

[36] *Gatley on Libel and Slander* (n 1) Ch 14, sub-s 3(e).

[37] *Duncombe* (n 33).

[38] See, eg, *Derbyshire CC v Times Newspapers Ltd* [1993] AC 534 (HL) 547, where it was held that to preserve 'uninhibited public criticism' of elected bodies, governments could not be suited in defamation.

[39] See, eg, An Act in Addition to the Act, Entitled 'An Act for the Punishment of Certain Crimes against the United States', ch 74, 1 Stat 596 (1798).

[40] [1704] Holt KB 424, 90 ER 1133.

[41] ibid 1133–34 (emphasis added).

[42] See generally John Trenchard and Thomas Gordon, *Cato's Letters*, 4 vols (London, 1723–24); John Wilkes, *The North Briton* (London, 1762); Father of Candor, *An Enquiry into the Doctrine Lately*

two significant but commonly-overlooked arguments resonant with democratic accountability: (1) that all governments (democratic or otherwise) have a tendency to aspire and destabilise due to unchecked ambition and power; and (2) that threats of publication by the press have a unique and decisive 'corrective effect' on the quality of governance and political corruption.

This notion of 'watchdog' journalism as an accountability mechanism was captured by the English lawyer and Foxite Whig Capel Lofft.[43] Emphasising the dangers of unchecked ambition and political instability, Lofft reasoned:

> In *every* civil establishment that has any Constitution to lose, there is an incessant tendency to decay; the causes which produce this, *power possessed and power to be acquired*, wage everlasting war against the Freedom of the Whole. To reduce the excess of power as low as possible; to make it circulate so that the holders of it may be ever mindful they have a deposit, not a property; to have no member of the Community who can say he is not a sharer in its political rights; *to have full information on constitutional franchises, and free investigation of public measures*;—this it is to be a FREE PEOPLE.[44]

American commentators proved similarly candid and rousing. Accepting Lofft's premise that '[a]ll Governments have an inevitable tendency to aspire',[45] republican theorist Tunis Wortman reaffirmed Lofft's concerns in a colourful passage worth quoting in full:

> It should always be remembered, that *Government possesses an evident advantage and superiority over every species of opposition*; it is a regular, disciplined, and organized corps; its moral and physical energies are concentrated and combined; it is capable of steady premeditation and continual design; it never loses sight of its object: but, with undeviating constancy, pursues its plans through the mazes of events, and in the midst of every obstacle. It is equally qualified to contrive and to execute: It perpetually exists, and slumbers not. Let it be added, it directs and commands all the resources of a State. *Unless,*

Propagated, Concerning Libels, Warrants, and the Seizure of Papers (London, 1764); *The Letters of Junius*, 2 vols (London, 1792). For a fuller account, see also Charles Blount, *A Just Vindication of Learning and the Liberty of the Press* (London, 1695); John Toland, *A Letter to a Member of Parliament, Shewing, That a Restraint on the Press is Inconsistent with the Protestant Religion, and Dangerous to the Liberties of the Nation* (London, 1698); Matthew Tindal, *Reasons Against Restraining the Press* (London, 1704); John Asgill, *An Essay for the Press* (London, 1712); Joseph Addison, *Thoughts of a Tory Author, Concerning the Press: With the Opinion of the Ancients and Moderns, About Freedom of Speech and Writing* (London, 1712); Capel Lofft, *An Essay on the Law of Libels* (London, 1785); James Adair, *Discussions of the Law of Libels as at Present Received, in Which its Authenticity is Examined* (London, 1785); Robert Hall, *An Apology for the Freedom of the Press, and for General Liberty* (London, 1793); Jean-Louis De Lolme, *The Constitution of England: In Which it is Compared Both with the Republican Form of Government, and the Other Monarchies in Europe* (London, 1822). For American republican theorists, see James Madison, *The Virginia Report of 1799–1800* in Gaillard Hunt (ed), *The Writings of James Madison*, 9 vols (New York, GP Putnam's Sons, 1900–1910); George Hay, *An Essay on the Liberty of the Press* (Philadelphia, 1799); Tunis Wortman, *A Treatise, Concerning Political Enquiry, and the Liberty of the Press* (New York, 1800).

[43] Lofft (n 42).
[44] Lofft (n 42) 60–61 (emphasis added).
[45] Wortman (n 42) 175.

> *therefore, some vigilant, powerful, and independent corrective is retained by Society, nothing can prevent its becoming the devoted victim of Despotism.*[46]

Given such threats to political liberty, radical Whigs sought equally strong tonics. In *The Constitution of England*,[47] Jean-Louis De Lolme nominated 'newspapers' as the 'vigilant, powerful, and independent corrective' for the political concerns shared by Lofft and Wortman, reassuring the British electorate that:

> As [public officials] are thereby made sensible that *all their actions are exposed to public view*, they dare not venture upon those acts of partiality, those secret connivances at the iniquities of particular persons, or those vexatious practices which the man in office is but too apt to be guilty of, when, exercising his office at a distance from the public eye, and, as it were, in a corner, he is satisfied that, provided he be cautious, he may dispense with being just.[48]

The influential Whig pamphleteer and theorist 'Father of Candor' also endorsed the press as a political accountability mechanism, counselling Britons that '[t]he liberty of exposing and opposing a bad administration by the pen is among the necessary privileges of a free people, and is perhaps the greatest benefit that can be derived from the liberty of the press'.[49] Press liberty is thus considered essential to democracy because '[...] it enables the people effectually to exert those means which the constitution has bestowed on them, of *influencing* the motions of the government'.[50]

As a result, using defamation laws to suppress or weaken public debate raises distinct challenges for representative democracies. While these concerns do not entail any specific doctrinal approach, radical Whig conceptions are powerful reminders to assess a nation's accountability requirements whilst rebalancing freedom of expression and reputation. Besides challenging traditional doctrinal restrictions on publishing to the world at large, early Whig conceptions of the press as a prized accountability mechanism would seem to prohibit the use of defamation law's strict liability principles by certain influential plaintiffs, above all government, politicians, and public officials.

E. Liberalising Media Defamation Defences

Responses to these 'perennial problems' have covered a wide range of doctrinal reforms. Following the repeal of seditious libel laws in Britain and America, the press has relied almost exclusively on the defence of justification, which raises discrete evidentiary problems and litigation risks.[51] Given the excessive costs

[46] Wortman (n 42) 175 (emphasis added).
[47] De Lolme (n 42).
[48] De Lolme (n 42) 176 (emphasis added).
[49] Father of Candor (n 42) 32.
[50] De Lolme (n 42) 178 (emphasis added).
[51] *Gatley on Libel and Slander* (n 1) chs 10–15.

and complications of proving the 'truth' of defamatory statements at trial, media defendants have understandably sought greater certainty and stronger legal protections. Yet despite recent attempts to modernise qualified privilege, success has been rare and uneven.[52] As noted above, reform efforts have been frustrated by strict application of its 'reciprocity requirement' (ie establishing a corresponding duty to receive the information), which conflicts with the objective of publishing matters of public interest widely without restriction.

But starting with the US Supreme Court's seminal public libel decision in *New York Times v Sullivan*,[53] leading common law courts have progressively acknowledged not only the realities and consequences of 'libel chill',[54] but the excessive costs, challenges, and uncertainties of pleading justification and qualified privilege.[55] Following *Sullivan*, appellate courts in Australia, New Zealand, Britain, and Canada have modified qualified privilege principles to provide 'middle ground' solutions, aiming for doctrinal accommodations between defamation's strict liability principles and America's more press-friendly approach.

The High Court of Australia proceeded first in 1994.[56] Canada was last to modernise its media defamation principles in 2009.[57] Together with New Zealand and the United Kingdom,[58] these leading common law jurisdictions have not only developed and endorsed different doctrinal options, but they have also provided intriguing methodological innovations. By balancing free expression and reputation differently, interesting and open questions are raised about the significance to public libel doctrine of variations in constitutional and political structure, human rights protections, and even the importance of 'local conditions' and variations in media ownership and structure.

II. Overview of Public Libel Doctrine

Before exploring public libel doctrine's specific problems, this section provides a brief jurisdictional summary of its defining legal principles and sources of freedom of expression.

[52] See, eg, earlier Canadian authorities cited at n 35. See also *Gatley on Libel and Slander* (n 1) s 14.1; *Morosi* (n 26) 772–92.

[53] 376 US 254 (1964).

[54] See Eric Barendt and others, *Libel and the Media: The Chilling Effect* (Oxford, Oxford University Press, 1997).

[55] *Sullivan* (n 53).

[56] See *Theophanous v Herald & Weekly Times Ltd* (1994) 182 CLR 104 (HCA); *Lange v Australian Broadcasting Corporation* (1997) 189 CLR 520 (HCA).

[57] *Grant* (n 35).

[58] *Lange v Atkinson* (1998) 3 NZLR 424 (CA) 468 (*Lange No 1*); *Lange v Atkinson* (2000) 3 NZLR 385 (CA) (*Lange No 2*); *Reynolds v Times Newspapers Ltd* [2001] 2 AC 127 (HL).

A. United States

i. First Amendment

Freedom of speech and the press are protected under the First Amendment to the United States Constitution, which reads:

> Congress *shall make no law* respecting an establishment of religion, or prohibiting the free exercise thereof; *or abridging the freedom of speech, or of the press*, or the right of the people peaceably to assemble, and to petition the Government for a redress of grievances.[59]

The First Amendment appears to provide unqualified protection of speech interests without requiring ad hoc balancing of competing rights, values, and interests.

ii. US Public Libel Doctrine

The principles of constitutional protection for defamatory statements of fact in the United States can be summarised as follows:

1. A *public official* or *public figure* can recover damages for a defamatory falsehood relating to conduct relevant to their public status only if the statement was made with 'actual malice', that is, with knowledge that it was false or with reckless disregard whether or not it was false.[60]
2. The standard of proof for establishing 'actual malice' is the heightened standard of 'convincing clarity', or proof by 'clear and convincing' evidence.[61]
3. States are free to define the standard of liability for media publications of defamatory falsehoods on matters of public concern injurious to *private* individuals, provided they do not impose liability without fault (ie strict liability).[62]
4. Absent a showing of 'actual malice', individuals cannot recover presumed or punitive damages from media defendants, and may only recover damages for actual injury.[63]
5. To recover damages in defamation actions involving matters of public concern, at least in cases involving media defendants, the plaintiff must show that the defamatory expression is one of fact, and false.[64]

[59] US Const Amend I (emphasis added).
[60] *Sullivan* (n 53) 278–80; *Curtis Publishing Co v Butts* 388 US 130, 164 (1967).
[61] *Sullivan* (n 53) 284–86.
[62] *Gertz v Robert Welch Inc* 418 US 323, 347 (1974).
[63] ibid 349–50.
[64] *Philadelphia Newspapers, Inc v Hepps* 475 US 767, 776–77 (1986).

B. Australia

i. Implied Right of Freedom of Communication

Australia has no bill of rights or federal statutory protection of individual rights.[65] Rather, its regulation of public libels is based uniquely on an implied right of 'freedom of communication'. This implied rights doctrine originated in a series of plurality and dissenting judgments by Justice Murphy of the High Court. Between 1977–86, a wide range of constitutional guarantees was implied under Australia's Constitution, from originally protecting 'freedom of movement of commercial goods', to later safeguarding 'freedom of speech and other communications'.[66] In time, Australia became the first common law jurisdiction to modernise its defamation laws post-*Sullivan*,[67] endorsing a qualified privilege for communications on 'political and government matters', which included an additional 'reasonableness' criterion for mass publications.

ii. Lange Defence

The Australian '*Lange* defence' may be summarised as follows:

1. Federal and State statutory and common law rules relating to defamation must conform to and be consistent with an implied constitutional guarantee of 'freedom of communication'.[68]
2. Whether a rule is consistent with this 'implied freedom of communication' depends on whether it effectively burdens that freedom (in terms, operation, or effect) and, if so, whether the rule is reasonably appropriate and adapted to serve a legitimate end compatible with Australia's constitutionally prescribed form of government.[69]
3. Where a publication involves information on 'governmental and political matters', there is a privilege to publish to a *mass audience* if the publication is 'reasonable' in the circumstances, and the publisher is not actuated by malice.[70]

[65] This is not to say that national human rights legislation has been uncontroversial. On 10 December 2008, the Labour Government of Kevin Rudd launched the National Human Rights Consultation. The Report of the National Human Rights Consultation Committee recommended a national statutory bill of rights similar to the New Zealand and UK models. This proposal was rejected in favour of the Human Rights (Parliamentary Scrutiny) Act 2011 No 186 (Cth), which adopted only political rights review.

[66] See *Buck v Bavone* (1976) 135 CLR 110 (HCA) 137 (Murphy J); *Ansett Transport Industries (Operations) Pty Ltd v The Commonwealth* (1977) 139 CLR 54 (HCA) 87–88 (Murphy J); *McGraw-Hinds (Aust) Pty Ltd v Smith* (1979) 144 CLR 633 (HCA) 667–70 (Murphy J); *Miller v TCN Channel Nine Pty Ltd* (1986) 161 CLR 556 (HCA) 582–83 (Murphy J).

[67] *Theophanous* (n 56); *Lange v Australian Broadcasting Corp* (n 56).

[68] *Lange v Australian Broadcasting Corp* (n 56) 560–63.

[69] *Lange v Australian Broadcasting Corp* (n 56) 568. See *Coleman v Power* (2004) 220 CLR 1 (HCA) [93].

[70] *Lange v Australian Broadcasting Corp* (n 56) 573–74.

4. 'Reasonableness' generally requires that the publisher have reasonable grounds for believing the defamatory imputation was true, and did not believe it was untrue; took appropriate steps where reasonably open to verify the accuracy of the material; and sought a response from the person who defamed and published it, except where the seeking or publication of a response was impracticable or unnecessary.[71]
5. Where the communication involving governmental and political matters is made to a smaller audience with an interest in the information, there is a common law privilege conditioned only on the absence of malice and not on the 'reasonableness' test.[72]
6. Express malice is defined as an improper motive, which must have existed on the privileged occasion and have actuated the publication. The motive necessary to defeat a qualified privilege involving publications of governmental or political matters does not include the purpose of destroying the election prospects of a candidate for public office, or to cause persons to think less of a person as a politician, or merely because of the vigour with which an attack is directed. But it may be shown by the communication of deliberate and knowing or reckless falsehoods.[73]
7. The governmental or political material must fall within the ambit of the privilege and be relevant to the occasion.[74]

C. New Zealand

i. New Zealand Bill of Rights Act 1990

New Zealand has no written constitution. But freedom of expression and the press are protected broadly under sections 13 and 14 of the New Zealand Bill of Rights Act 1990 (NZBRA 1990),[75] which provide (respectively):

> Everyone has the right to freedom of thought, conscience, religion, and belief, including the right to adopt and to hold opinions without interference.
>
> Everyone has the right to freedom of expression, including the freedom to seek, receive, and impart information and opinions of any kind in any form.[76]

[71] *Lange v Australian Broadcasting Corp* (n 56) 575.
[72] *Lange v Australian Broadcasting Corp* (n 56) 574.
[73] *Lange v Australian Broadcasting Corp* (n 56) 575.
[74] See *Nationwide News Pty Ltd v International Financing & Investment Pty Ltd* [1999] WASCA 95 [30]–[31].
[75] New Zealand Bill of Rights Act 1990 (NZ).
[76] ibid ss 13 and 14.

ii. Qualified Privilege for 'Political Expression'

New Zealand's qualified privilege for 'political expression' can be summarised as follows:

1. Where a statement published on a qualifying occasion involves information on matters of public concern about persons currently or formerly elected to Parliament, or aspiring to that office, directly affecting their ability and capacity to meet their public responsibilities, there is a common law privilege to publish that information to the public generally.[77]
2. In determining whether the occasion is privileged, the court will consider such matters as the publisher's identity, the content of the information, the publication context, and the likely audience to whom it is made.[78]
3. The defendant's motives will be closely scrutinised by the court and the privilege will be lost if the plaintiff shows the equivalent of common law malice that the defendant did not use the privilege responsibly but abused its purpose and took improper advantage of the occasion.[79]

D. United Kingdom

i. Human Rights Act 1998

Like New Zealand, the United Kingdom has no written constitution. Yet under the Human Rights Act 1998,[80] British courts have at least a limited obligation to develop defamation principles in line with the European Convention on Human Rights.[81] Not only must British courts '[…] have particular regard to the importance of the Convention right to freedom of expression […]' when granting injunctions,[82] they are also required more generally to '[…] *take into account* any—judgment, decision, declaration or advisory opinion of the European Court of Human Rights'.[83] Although uncertainty remains as to the extent to which British courts are required to endorse such decisions,[84] the UK Supreme Court

[77] *Lange No 2* (n 58) [10], [41]. See also *Lange No 1* (n 58) 467–68.
[78] *Lange No 2* (n 58) [13].
[79] *Lange No 2* (n 58) [42]–[49].
[80] Human Rights Act 1998 (UK) (HRA 1998).
[81] Convention for the Protection of Human Rights and Fundamental Freedoms 1950 (ECHR, as amended). The obligation to develop the common law in line with Convention rights stems from s 6 of the HRA 1998, which provides under sub-s 6(1): 'It is unlawful for a public authority to act in a way which is incompatible with a Convention right'. 'Public authority' is defined under sub-s 6(3) to include 'a court or tribunal'.
[82] HRA 1998 (n 80) s 12. See *Douglas v Hello! Ltd* [2001] QB 967; *Cream Holdings Ltd v Banerjee* [2004] UKHL 44.
[83] HRA 1998 (n 80) s 2 (emphasis added).
[84] For an excellent discussion of the application and effect of the HRA 1998 on UK private law, see generally David Hoffman (ed), *The Impact of the UK Human Rights Act on Private Law* (Cambridge, Cambridge University Press, 2011).

has indicated that it will follow a 'clear and consistent line' of Strasbourg Court authority, subject to a narrow range of exceptions.[85]

Freedom of expression and the press are protected under Article 10 of the Convention, which provides:

> 1. Everyone has the right to freedom of expression. This right shall include freedom to hold opinions and to receive and impart information and ideas without interference by public authority and regardless of frontiers. [...].
> 2. The exercise of these freedoms, since it carries with it duties and responsibilities, may be subject to such formalities, conditions, restrictions or penalties *as are prescribed by law and are necessary in a democratic society*, [...] for the *protection of the reputation or rights of others* [...].[86]

ii. Reynolds *Defence*

Until 1 January 2014, Britain's public libel doctrine was dictated by *Reynolds v Times Newspapers Ltd*,[87] which provided as follows:

1. A defence is available to the media and other comparable mediums of communications, independent of the privilege recognised at common law, to publish information on matters of public concern to a mass audience.[88]
2. The starting point as to whether a publication is in the public interest must be to ask whether the subject matter of the publication is a matter of public interest.[89]
3. The defence must be exercised responsibly and attaches to the communication, not the occasion.[90]
4. The defendant must show that the defence has been exercised *responsibly*. In deciding that question, the court will consider all the circumstances at the time of publication, including: the seriousness of the allegation, whether it is a matter of public concern, the degree to which the information already commands respect, the tone of the article, the timing and manner of the publication, the urgency of the information, the reliability of the source and the steps taken to verify it, including consultation with the plaintiff, and whether the plaintiff's view is presented.[91]

[85] In *Manchester City Council v Pinnock* [2010] UKSC 45 [48], Lord Neuberger summarised the law as follows: 'Where [...] there is a clear and constant line of decisions whose effect is not inconsistent with some fundamental substantive or procedural aspect of our law, and whose reasoning does not appear to overlook or misunderstand some argument or point of principle, we consider that it would be wrong for this court not to follow that line'. See also *R (on the application of Ullah) v Special Adjudicator* [2004] UKHL 26 [20]; *R v Horncastle* [2009] UKSC 14 [11].

[86] ECHR Art 10 (n 81) (emphasis added).

[87] *Reynolds* (n 58).

[88] *Flood v Times Newspapers Ltd* [2012] UKSC 11; *Seaga v Harper* [2008] UKPC 9 [11]; *Reynolds* (n 58).

[89] *Flood*, ibid [33].

[90] *Jameel v Wall Street Journal Europe* [2007] 1 AC 359 (HL) [46]; *Reynolds* (n 58); *Flood* (n 88). Recall that what is 'privileged' under traditional qualified privilege principles is the *occasion*, not the specific content.

[91] *Reynolds* (n 58) 205.

5. These criteria are to be applied in a flexible manner with due regard to practical realities. The overriding consideration in every case is whether the publisher acted fairly and responsibly in gathering and publishing the information.[92]
6. Once it has been established that the media has acted responsibly in the circumstances, there is little or no room for the issue of malice and the defendant will be protected.[93]

iii. Publication on Matter of Public Interest

On 1 January 2014, the *Reynolds* defence was abolished by the Defamation Act 2013.[94] Section 4 replaced it with a new defence of 'Publication on Matter of Public Interest', which provides:

1. It is a defence to an action for defamation for the defendant to show that:
   a. The statement complained of was, or formed part of, a statement on a matter of public interest; and
   b. The defendant reasonably believed that it was in the public interest to publish the impugned statement.
2. Subject to subsections (3) and (4), in determining whether the defendant has proven the matters mentioned in subsection (1), the court must consider all the circumstances of the case.
3. If the statement complained of was, or formed part of, an accurate and impartial account of a dispute to which the claimant was a party, in determining whether it was reasonable for the defendant to believe that publishing the statement was in the public interest, the court must disregard any omission of the defendant to take steps to verify the truth of the imputation conveyed by it.
4. In determining whether it was reasonable for the defendant to believe that publishing the impugned statement was in the public interest, the court must make such allowance for editorial judgment as it considers appropriate.
5. For the avoidance of doubt, the defence under this section may be relied upon irrespective of whether the impugned statement is a statement of fact or a statement of opinion.
6. The common law defence known as the *Reynolds* defence is abolished.[95]

The UK Parliament has indicated that it expects British courts to consult *Reynolds*, *Jameel*, and *Flood* when interpreting this new defence.[96]

[92] *Jameel* (n 90) [56].
[93] *Jameel* (n 90) [46].
[94] Defamation Act 2013 (n 7). The Act applies to England and Wales, and in limited measures to Scotland. Northern Ireland has refused to implement the Act.
[95] Defamation Act 2013 (n 7) s 4.
[96] Explanatory Notes to the Defamation Act 2013 [29].

E. Canada

i. Canadian Charter of Rights and Freedoms

Freedom of expression and the press are protected broadly under subsection 2(*b*) of the Canadian Charter of Rights and Freedoms, which guarantees (subject to s 1): 'freedom of thought, belief, opinion and expression, including *freedom of the press and other media of communication*'.[97]

ii. Responsible Communication on Matters of Public Interest

Canada's defence of 'Responsible Communication on Matters of Public Interest' may be summarised as follows:[98]

1. There is a new defence for those who establish that a defamatory publication of fact was made on a matter of *public interest* and that they acted *responsibly* in attempting to verify the allegation.[99]
2. The defence is not limited to print or broadcast media, but applies to publications originating in any 'medium'.[100]
3. The meaning of 'public interest' is not restricted to government matters, but applies to any subject matter inviting public attention, or about which the public has some substantial concern because it affects citizens' welfare, or to which considerable public notoriety or controversy is attached.[101]
4. Unlike qualified privilege, it is not the occasion that gives rise to the defence, but the subject matter of the statement.[102]
5. In determining 'responsible communication', the defence must be assessed as to the broad thrust of the publication in question. The defence applies where the publisher was diligent in trying to verify the allegation, having regard to: the seriousness of the allegation, the public importance and urgency of the matter, the status and reliability of the source, whether the plaintiff's view was sought and accurately reported, whether the inclusion of the defamatory statement was justifiable, whether the defamatory statement's public interest lay in the fact that it was made rather than its truth, and any other relevant circumstances.[103]

[97] Canadian Charter of Rights and Freedoms, Part I of the Constitution Act, 1982, being Schedule B to the Canada Act, 1982 (UK) c 11, sub-s 2(*b*) (emphasis added).

[98] *Grant* (n 35).

[99] *Grant* (n 35) [97]–[98].

[100] *Grant* (n 35) [73]; *Seaga* (n 88) [11].

[101] *Grant* (n 35) [105].

[102] *Grant* (n 35) [126].

[103] *Grant* (n 35) [126].

6. Once a judge determines that a defamatory statement relates to a matter of public interest, the jury decides whether the defence is established on the evidence.[104]
7. Once a statement is established as a responsible communication on a matter of public interest, the issue of malice is irrelevant.[105]

III. Continuum of Doctrinal Solutions

Given their heterogeneity, these doctrinal options can be charted on a continuum depicting their relative degrees of support for reputational interests or freedom of expression and the press. With different legal systems adopting a wide range of doctrinal approaches for regulating public libels, a 'one-size-fits-all' solution has proved both undesirable and impracticable.

Table 1: Continuum of Doctrinal Solutions

Protected Value	Doctrinal Solution	Scope	Jurisdiction/Decision
Freedom of Expression	Absolute Privilege	No distinction (at its most absolute; otherwise limited to official conduct)	United States (*Sullivan; Garrison*)[106] (Justices Black, Douglas, Goldberg)
	'Actual Malice' Rule	Public Officials Public Figures	United States (*Sullivan*) (Justice Brennan, for majority) United States (*Curtis*) (Chief Justice Warren, for majority)
▲	Qualified Privilege	Matters of public concern about former, current, or aspiring *parliamentary officials* published to world at large	New Zealand (*Lange No 2*) *Per Curiam*
	Gross Negligence	Public Figures	United States (*Curtis*) (Justice Harlan, plurality)
	Negligence	Private Individuals	United States (*Gertz*) (Justice Powell, for majority)

(*continued*)

[104] *Grant* (n 35) [128].
[105] *Grant* (n 35) [125].
[106] *Garrison v Louisiana* 379 US 64 (1964).

Table 1: (***Continued***)

Protected Value	Doctrinal Solution	Scope	Jurisdiction/Decision
	Publication on Matter of Public Interest	Information of public interest or concern	United Kingdom Defamation Act 2013 s 4
▼	Responsible Journalism 2	Information of public interest or concern	United Kingdom (*Flood*) (Lord Phillips P et al) Canada (*Grant*) (Chief Justice McLachlin, for majority)
	Responsible Journalism 1	Information on 'governmental and political matters' published to world at large	Australia (*Lange*) *Per Curiam*
Reputational Interests	Qualified Privilege	Information on 'governmental and political matters' not published to world at large	Australia (*Lange*) *Per Curiam*

As Table 1 reveals, not only are there significant doctrinal options for regulating public libels, but the reasons for choosing one approach over another are not clear, particularly as each jurisdiction proceeds from different constitutional and institutional contexts. Therefore, to better discern the nature and limitations of these doctrinal alternatives, it is necessary to critically examine their supporting reasons and justifications as proffered by leading appellate courts and legislatures. Closer analysis confirms that public libel jurisprudence is significantly undertheorised, acontextual, and bereft of an appropriate 'selection theory' for matching doctrinal alternatives to distinct institutional settings.

IV. Public Libel Law's Theory-Doctrine Rift

A. Universal Rejection of the 'Actual Malice' Rule

An important feature of the recent liberalisation of media defamation defences has been the universal rejection of the 'actual malice' rule endorsed by the US Supreme Court in *Sullivan*.[107] Disregarding both its earliest doctrinal roots in

[107] *Sullivan* (n 53). See Mark Tushnet, '*New York Times v. Sullivan* Around the World' (2014) 66 *Alabama Law Review* 337.

English common law, and its subsequent adoption by a minority of US states in the late nineteenth century,[108] appellate courts in Australia, New Zealand, England, and Canada have summarily rejected this doctrinal option for various 'principled' and 'institutional' reasons.[109] However, closer examination confirms more deeply-rooted problems. Specifically, no external criteria exists for selecting different approaches. Worse still, without a properly verified doctrinal 'gold standard', reflexive and cursory dismissals of the prevailing American standard have only frustrated the formulation of tailored solutions.[110]

For instance, in *Theophanous v Herald & Weekly Times Ltd*,[111] the High Court of Australia's earliest analysis of *Sullivan* proved rudimentary and unpersuasive. After rejecting absolute privilege and the 'actual malice' rule without appealing to free expression justifications, a majority of the Court attempted to justify its unprecedented expansion of qualified privilege principles by concluding imprecisely that '[t]he formula we favour redresses the balance *to some extent* in favour of the plaintiff; as much, in our view, as can *legitimately be achieved* without significantly interfering with free communication'.[112] Besides precipitously dismissing US doctrine, the High Court's reasons for judgment omitted any criteria by which this statement could be assessed.

New Zealand courts have also mishandled the 'actual malice' rule. Stating one-sidedly in *Lange v Atkinson*[113] that '[t]he United States approach has been criticised as "severe overkill"',[114] Justice Elias (at first instance) rejected *Sullivan* in the following derivative and disputable terms:

> There are difficulties in identifying when a plaintiff is a public figure. Concern has been expressed that the protection for free speech where statements are on matters of public interest has made vindication of reputation almost impossible for a public figure plaintiff and extremely difficult for a private figure plaintiff. There is a view that the public interest in true speech has been badly served by effectively removing a means for vindication of the truth and channelling the legal process instead into an examination of fault which focuses on media methods. The need to undertake inquiries into the reasonableness of media procedure is thought to have increased the costs of litigation.[115]

[108] See *Wason v Walter* (1868) LR 4 QB 73; *Briggs v Garrett* 111 Pa St 404 (1886); *Jackson v Pittsburgh Times* 152 Pa 406 (1893); *Klos v Zahorik* 113 Ia 161 (1901); *Coleman v MacLennan* 78 Kan 711 (1908). For relevant commentary, see George Chase, 'Criticism of Public Officers and Candidates for Office' (1889) 23 *American Law Review* 346; Van Vechten Veeder, 'Freedom of Public Discussion' (1910) 23 *Harvard Law Review* 413; John E Hallen, 'Fair Comment' (1929) 8 *Texas Law Review* 41. See also Ian Loveland, *Political Libels: A Comparative Study* (Oxford, Hart Publishing, 2000).

[109] See *Theophanous* (n 56) 135–38; *Lange v Atkinson and Australian Consolidated Press NZ Ltd* (1997) 2 NZLR 22 (HC) 36–37 (Elias J); *Hill v Church of Scientology* [1995] 2 SCR 1130 [127]–[131], [137]; *Grant* (n 35) [85]–[86]; *Reynolds* (n 58) 201–03 (Lord Nicholls), 208–11 (Lord Steyn). See also Tushnet (n 106).

[110] The UK Parliament has been no clearer in its justification for replacing *Reynolds*. See chapter five for an extended discussion of this point.

[111] *Theophanous* (n 56).

[112] *Theophanous* (n 56) 140 (emphasis added).

[113] *Lange v Atkinson and Australian Consolidated Press* (n 109).

[114] *Lange v Atkinson and Australian Consolidated Press* (n 109) 37.

[115] *Lange v Atkinson and Australian Consolidated Press* (n 109) 37, citing the Supreme Court of Canada's much-maligned assessment of the 'actual malice' rule in *Hill* (n 109) 1182–83.

Similar to Australian courts, no discernible criteria for preferring qualified privilege over the 'actual malice' rule (or any other doctrinal option) was reported. In other words, while the New Zealand High Court provided some reasons for rejecting the 'actual malice' rule, no reasons were provided for the test endorsed.

Similarly, despite reviewing leading authorities from Australia, Canada, the United States, Britain, and even the Strasbourg Court, the New Zealand Court of Appeal did not (ironically) *compare* doctrinal alternatives. Revealingly, although mentioning that 'the defendants in this case are not calling for the specific adoption of the *New York Times* rule [...]',[116] the Court's 'greater attention' to foreign jurisprudence appears not to have influenced its analysis beyond rejecting two poorly-understood extremes. Namely, in assessing 'international texts and comparative experience [...] *in a local context*',[117] the Court of Appeal rejected the 'actual malice' rule without considering its potential application to New Zealand. Evidencing a pattern initiated by the Australian High Court, whether or not reasons are specified for rejecting the 'actual malice' rule, there is ultimately no justification for adopting doctrinal substitutes other than their *not* being America's designated approach.

British courts have fared no better. In *Reynolds*,[118] the House of Lords rejected a generic qualified privilege inspired by the 'actual malice' rule in *Sullivan*. Besides relying on mischaracterisations of confidential source protection in English and American defamation law,[119] Lord Nicholls concluded unconvincingly that the newspaper's attempt to distinguish political discussion from other matters of public concern was 'unsound in principle',[120] and 'lack[ed] a coherent rationale'.[121] Lord Cooke similarly asserted that there was 'no good reason' why politicians and public officials should be subjected to greater risk of false allegations of fact in the media.[122] Importantly, these conclusions were unsupported by careful comparative law analysis or reflections on the doctrinal implications of pertinent freedom of expression justifications.

Equally concerning, the Supreme Court of Canada's constitutional analysis was articulated in just one short paragraph. Preferring a doctrinal 'middle road' bifurcating the 'actual malice' rule and qualified privilege, Chief Justice McLachlin concluded:

> In my view, the third option, buttressed by the argument from *Charter* principles advanced earlier, represents a *reasonable and proportionate response* to the need to protect reputation while sustaining the *public exchange of information that is vital to modern Canadian society*.[123]

[116] *Lange No 1* (n 58) 451.
[117] *Lange No 1* (n 58) 467 (emphasis added).
[118] *Reynolds* (n 58).
[119] *Reynolds* (n 58) 210 (Lord Steyn).
[120] *Reynolds* (n 58) 204 (Lord Nicholls).
[121] *Reynolds* (n 58) 203 (Lord Nicholls).
[122] *Reynolds* (n 58) 219 (Lord Cooke).
[123] *Grant* (n 35) [86] (emphasis added).

Besides incorporating a profoundly undertheorised 'argument from *Charter* principles',[124] the Supreme Court of Canada's legal analysis does not evidence the use of any evaluative criteria whatsoever.

On balance, whatever their contemporary influence and legal purchase, these constitutional analyses are presumptive and acontextual. After all, what is a 'reasonable and proportionate' doctrinal response when balancing freedom of expression against reputation? How much 'public exchange of information' is necessary for a modern democracy? Is there really no 'principled reason' to distinguish political discussion from other public concerns? How does the 'actual malice' rule (or any other doctrinal alternative) fit into these considerations? It seems clear that whatever else may be found wanting in public libel jurisprudence, it is most surely missing evaluative criteria for justifying doctrinal selections from a broad range of possible options.

i. Public Libel Law's Missing 'Gold Standard'

As we have seen, our comparators have chosen their doctrinal paths at least partially due to perceived limitations of the 'actual malice' rule. However, it is vital to emphasise that the US Supreme Court did not engage in comparative legal analysis in *Sullivan*. Much less did it examine how dissimilarities in constitutional structure and rights protection, among other potentially relevant factors, might affect and guide its doctrinal approach. Naturally, serious methodological concerns arise when foreign courts are materially influenced by a doctrinal alternative whose domestic suitability remains very much untested and unknown.

In fact, *Sullivan* was overwhelmingly focussed on domestic concerns, concentrating exclusively on the relationship of the First Amendment to defamation's strict liability framework. After citing an impressive line of authorities establishing 'a profound national commitment to the principle that debate on public issues should be uninhibited, robust, and wide-open [...]',[125] Justice Brennan appealed to the constitutional incongruities of the Sedition Act of 1798, and the dangers of 'libel chill' produced by defamation's traditional model. Concluding that the press' customary defence of justification unacceptably 'dampens the vigor and limits the variety of public debate',[126] Justice Brennan nonetheless adopted the 'actual malice' rule with minimal supporting analysis. Although he discussed briefly the rationale behind the 'actual malice' rule as formerly endorsed by US state courts,[127] at no time was a competing doctrinal alternative subjected to comparative law analysis based on any discernible criteria, including the option of 'absolute privilege' endorsed vigorously by Justices Black, Goldberg, and Douglas in dissent. Complicating matters further, *Sullivan* was driven primarily by pragmatic concerns with

[124] *Grant* (n 35) [57].
[125] *Sullivan* (n 53) 270.
[126] *Sullivan* (n 53) 279.
[127] *Sullivan* (n 53) 280, quoting *Coleman* (n 108).

'libel chill' and maintaining energetic public debate on political matters, both of which resonate strongly with competing democratic theories.[128]

Therefore, if the 'actual malice' rule functions as a 'gold standard' at all, it is one lacking proper methodological validation for its original application, which should cast considerable doubt on its use as a de facto gatekeeper and guide for doctrine selection in other jurisdictions.

B. Necessity for Expanded Comparative Law Framework

There is however a glimmer of hope amidst this confusion. An important clue for resolving public libel law's 'selection conundrum' lies in New Zealand's jurisprudence. While Australian, British, and Canadian courts have engaged in rudimentary comparative law analysis, New Zealand courts have displayed significant insight in this respect. Specifically, the New Zealand Court of Appeal has endorsed more sophisticated comparative law and interdisciplinary approaches, attempting to tailor public libel doctrine through complex value judgments informed by local circumstances and guided by constitutional and legal principles.

New Zealand's attentiveness to these concerns was prompted by a remarkable judgment at first instance in *Atkinson*,[129] where the High Court volunteered a more sophisticated methodology for evaluating public libels. Inviting deeper comparative law reflection, Elias J observed that defamation laws reflect changes in broader socio-political values, advising:

> The balances struck from time to time may be controversial. They are not set in concrete. The law has shifted to reflect the *changing needs of the societies* to which it applies [...]. Some shifts have occurred as a result of judicial reassessment, others as a result of legislative adjustment. In both cases, shifts necessarily reflect *judgments as to social values.*[130]

Justice Elias added that while '[...] the balance struck may vary from country to country', it is not an arbitrary exercise as '[t]he balance ultimately must be a value judgment *informed by local conditions* and *guided by principle*'.[131]

The New Zealand Court of Appeal upheld and further developed this innovative approach, endorsing a generic qualified privilege for 'political expression'.[132] Justice Blanchard (on behalf of the Court) advanced Justice Elias' more hesitant

[128] See Harry Kalven Jr , 'The *New York Times* Case: A Note on "The Central Meaning of the First Amendment"' (1964) *Supreme Court Review* 191; William J Brennan Jr , 'The Supreme Court and the Meiklejohn Interpretation of the First Amendment' (1965) 79 *Harvard Law Review* 1.

[129] *Lange v Atkinson and Australian Consolidated Press* (n 109).

[130] *Lange v Atkinson and Australian Consolidated Press* (n 109) 32 (emphasis added) (citation omitted). See also *Société TVA inc c Marcotte* [2015] QCCA 1118 [98], where the Québec Court of Appeal noted similarly that public libel doctrine varies according to 'the evolution of society', that is, in line with 'the legal traditions, constitutional guarantees and social norms in each country'.

[131] *Lange v Atkinson and Australian Consolidated Press* (n 109) 43 (emphasis added).

[132] *Lange No 1* (n 58).

designs by specifying the following constitutional and legislative features most germane to modifying New Zealand's public libel principles: (1) the acknowledged sovereignty of New Zealand's citizenry; (2) enhanced access to information under New Zealand's Official Information Act 1982; and (3) the pivotal legislative commitments to freedom of expression contained in the NZBRA 1990 and the Defamation Act 1992.[133]

On further appeal, the Judicial Committee of the Privy Council confirmed the importance of comparative law analysis, reaffirming the 'functionalist' tenet 'that different solutions may be reached in different jurisdictions without any faulty reasoning or misconception [...]'.[134] The Law Lords reassured New Zealanders that:

> [...] an appraisal of the English case law is an important part of the background against which the Courts in New Zealand are assessing the best way forward on this important and difficult point of the common law. This is not surprising. Even on issues of local public policy, *every jurisdiction can benefit from examinations of an issue undertaken by others*. Interaction between the jurisdictions can help to *clarify and refine the issues and the available options*, without prejudicing national autonomy.[135]

Proposing that this 'comparative constitutionalism' explore the legislative and structural differences between Britain, Australia, and New Zealand, Lord Nicholls instructed:

> [...] in the light of the comparative case law which has now emerged, including the clarification of the English common law in *Reynolds*, Their Lordships think it appropriate to give the New Zealand Court of Appeal the opportunity to reconsider the issue. After all, the three countries are all parliamentary democracies with a common origin. Whether the *differences in details of their constitutional structure and relevant statute law* have any truly significant bearing on the scope of qualified privilege for political discussion is among the aspects calling for consideration.[136]

Preferring its own path,[137] the New Zealand Court of Appeal nonetheless obliged the Privy Council's bid for expanded comparative law analysis, holding that New Zealand's legal, political, and social contexts were sufficiently different to merit separate doctrinal approaches. Starting from the general observation that '[t]he three countries share the *main relevant features* of a parliamentary democracy [...]',[138] the Court of Appeal began by referencing 'major differences in [their] electoral systems'.[139] More precisely, it contrasted New Zealand's voting

[133] *Lange No 1* (n 58) 463 (emphasis added). The Court restricted doctrinal modifications to those consistent with the 'functioning of representative and responsible government' (ibid 468), a highly abstract, non-specific criterion. See Part C for analysis of this point.

[134] *Lange v Atkinson* [2000] 1 NZLR 257 (PC) 263 (Lord Nicholls).

[135] ibid (emphasis added).

[136] ibid 263–64 (emphasis added).

[137] *Lange No 2* (n 58). The Court added a sixth constituent element in *Lange No 2*, requiring that '[t]o attract privilege the statement must be published on a qualifying occasion' (ibid [41]).

[138] *Lange No 2* (n 58) [26] (emphasis added).

[139] *Lange No 2* (n 58) [26].

on an 'equal nationwide basis' with the 'plurality, constituency-by-constituency' nature of UK general elections, and with Australia's slightly more proportional electoral systems which 'do not provide for voting on a national basis'.[140]

The second comparative law factor was New Zealand's freedom of information legislation. The Court of Appeal identified significant differences in legislative accountability between England and New Zealand, cautioning that

> United Kingdom law and practice relating to access to and release of information has yet to emphasise, in the way found here, the rights of citizens to participate in the process of policy and decision making and to call the government to account.[141]

As for Australia, the Court observed only that 'Australian state and federal legislation is closer to New Zealand's'.[142]

Lastly, the Court of Appeal stressed the following dissimilarities between British and New Zealand domestic human rights protections: (1) compared to the HRA 1998, the NZBRA 1990 'has a significantly narrower focus' on *public and political* processes; (2) the HRA 1998, '[...] unlike our Bill of Rights also expressly protects the *right to privacy*';[143] (3) the HRA 1998 'gives a particular direction to the Courts about how to approach freedom of expression matters',[144] requiring '[...] *a balancing exercise* in the light of the concrete facts of each case';[145] and (4) New Zealanders have pressed for 'the repeal, not matched apparently in the United Kingdom, of three criminal offences restricting public debate on political matters'.[146]

But despite the appearance of a more refined constitutional analysis, this is precisely where the New Zealand Court of Appeal foundered. Attempting to evaluate the meaning of this expanded array of factors, the Court proceeded to compare each jurisdiction's media practices and structure in an apparent bid to determine their 'democratic information requirements'.[147] However, despite drawing important distinctions on press ethics and practices, ownership structures, circulation figures, and the extent of media intrusion into citizens' daily lives, the Court of Appeal failed to integrate these factors into a comprehensive framework. That is, the Court left unspecified how such factors alone, or in combination, contribute to discerning 'optimal' doctrinal principles for New Zealand's (or any other jurisdiction's) institutional setting. In simplest terms, any underlying relationships implicit in this new analytical framework were left obscure.

[140] *Lange No 2* (n 58) [26].
[141] *Lange No 2* (n 58) [27].
[142] *Lange No 2* (n 58) [27].
[143] *Lange No 2* (n 58) [29] (emphasis added).
[144] *Lange No 2* (n 58) [30].
[145] *Lange No 2* (n 58) [30] (emphasis added).
[146] *Lange No 2* (n 58) [31].
[147] *Lange No 2* (n 58) [32]–[36].

V. Chapter Conclusion

In the end, despite such innovative and long-overdue advancements by the Privy Council and New Zealand courts, their methodological and theoretical challenges have not been taken up, let alone advanced, by other common law authorities. Public libel jurisprudence remains significantly compromised by a missing 'selection theory'.

Before specifying the nature and extent of public libel doctrine's undertheorising in Part B, chapter two examines two methodological barriers to public libel regulation. Specifically, the recurrent failure of courts and legislatures to properly engage democratic theory is embedded in both an incomplete articulation of freedom of expression's 'core' justifications, and misguided scholarly attempts to subsume separate rationales under various single-valued approaches. Both developments have necessarily and unduly marginalised the checking function of the press—the free expression theory most relevant to adjudicating public libel cases and strengthening accountability mechanisms in representative systems.

2

Methodological Barriers to Democratic Theorising

I. Overview

Before undertaking our comparative doctrinal analysis in Part B, chapter two identifies two methodological barriers to public libel regulation. Both devalue democratic accountability and the checking function of the press, the theoretical concerns most relevant to public libel cases.

The first methodological concern owes to incomplete articulations of freedom of expression's 'core' values. The most definitive account of free expression justifications dates back to Thomas Emerson's article 'Toward a General Theory of the First Amendment'.[1] Despite overlooking the checking function and vital notions of democratic accountability, Emerson's model has since defined a widely-accepted 'inventory' of free speech rationales, both within and outside America. As shown by the Supreme Court of Canada, unless courts are acquainted with such marginalised theories, there is every prospect that Emerson's model will function as a 'complete code'. Supplemental theories are then automatically disregarded as warranting no recognition in free speech jurisprudence. As further revealed in Part B, most often in public libel cases they are simply ignored.

A second methodological barrier to public libel regulation involves a much related concern. Following publication of Emerson's article, many legal scholars attempted to resolve perceptions of 'incoherence' in free speech jurisprudence by subsuming multi-valued classifications under various single-valued approaches. While not all were intended to be exclusionary (some theorists preferred to rank justifications by order of importance), even such 'lexically ordered hierarchies' necessarily marginalised lower-ranked theories. Besides subsuming Emerson's listed justifications, the most revealing example of this misguided practice was the mishandling of the checking function of the press. Forewarning widespread misuse of democratic theory in contemporary public libel law, the checking function was dismissed by single-valued theorists as merely 'derivative' of

[1] Thomas I Emerson, 'Toward a General Theory of the First Amendment' (1962) 72 *Yale Law Journal* 877.

Meiklejohnian theory. In this manner, the free speech justification most directly linked to accountability mechanisms in representative systems was significantly devalued.

Finally, given the apparent indifference of constitutional law scholarship to these distinctions, chapter two reviews Alexander Meiklejohn's democratic 'self-governance' rationale and Vincent Blasi's 'checking value' of the press, the two free speech models central to our enquiry. As demonstrated in Part B, Meiklejohnian theory occupies a prominent but uncomfortable position amongst free expression justifications, having been quickly and uncritically transplanted from its American constitutional context to each of our comparators. As both models represent our starting point for assessing misuse of democratic theory in public libel jurisprudence, a precise understanding of their contrasting features is essential.

II. Methodological Barrier I

A. Freedom of Expression's Incomplete 'Core'

Although defamation law has long recognised freedom of expression as a fundamental value,[2] its multiple and distinct grounds have only recently been recognised by common law courts and commentators. Despite seminal philosophical defences of free expression by John Milton and John Stuart Mill,[3] as well as important twentieth-century contributions by Justices Holmes and Brandeis of the US Supreme Court,[4] the current popularised core of free expression justifications originated with Thomas Emerson's 1962 article 'Toward a General Theory of the First Amendment'.[5] In his article, Professor Emerson explored the relationships between the First Amendment's philosophical rationales, general principles, and specific doctrines. Crucially, this American-borne analysis was supported by a far-reaching classification of four free speech rationales central to the modern 'liberal constitutional state'. Emerson instructed:

> The values sought by society in protecting the right to freedom of expression may be grouped into four broad categories. Maintenance of a system of free expression is necessary (1) as assuring individual self-fulfillment, (2) as a means of attaining the truth,

[2] See William Blackstone, *Commentaries on the Laws of England* (Oxford, 1765–1769) Vol 4, 150–53; George Chase, 'Criticism of Public Officers and Candidates for Office' (1889) 23 *American Law Review* 346; Hugh Fraser, 'The Privileges of the Press in Relation to the Law of Libel' (1891) 7 *Law Quarterly Review* 158; Van Vechten Veeder, 'Freedom of Public Discussion' (1910) 23 *Harvard Law Review* 413.

[3] See John Milton, *Areopagitica: A Speech of Mr. John Milton, for the Liberty of Unlicens'd Printing, to the Parliament of England* (London, 1644); John Stuart Mill, *On Liberty* (JW Parker and Son, 1859).

[4] See *Abrams v United States* 250 US 616 (1919); *Whitney v California* 274 US 357 (1927).

[5] Emerson (n 1).

(3) as a method of *securing participation* by the members of the society in social, including political, *decision-making*, and (4) as maintaining the balance between stability and change in the society.[6]

Evidencing a considerable intellectual debt to Alexander Meiklejohn's democratic 'self-governance' theory,[7] Emerson stated ambiguously that '[t]he crucial point, however, is not that freedom of expression is politically useful, but that it is *indispensable* to the operation of a *democratic* form of government'.[8] Stressing the American electorate's deliberative requirement for 'full freedom of expression both in forming individual judgments and in forming the common judgment',[9] Emerson's account of democracy's connection to freedom of expression ultimately owed very little (if anything) to equally fundamental notions of democratic accountability.

Although predating influential judgments and academic commentary endorsing 'watchdog' journalism and the institutional press,[10] Emerson's work has nevertheless assumed an authoritative status on free speech justifications, both within and (more remarkably) outside America.[11] Unfortunately, his free speech taxonomy was deficient from its inception, notably overlooking the checking function of the press, a freedom of expression rationale with profound links to democratic

[6] Emerson (n 1) 878–79 (emphasis added). For commentary on 'truth-seeking', see Stanley Ingber, 'The Marketplace of Ideas: A Legitimizing Myth' (1984) *Duke Law Journal* 1; Christopher T Wonnell, 'Truth and the Marketplace of Ideas' (1986) 19 *UC Davis Law Review* 669; William P Marshall, 'In Defense of the Search for Truth as a First Amendment Justification' (1995) 30 *Georgia Law Review* 1. For commentary on 'autonomy', see Brian C Murchison, 'Speech and the Self-Realization Value' (1998) 33 *Harvard Civil Rights-Civil Liberties Law Review* 443; C Edwin Baker, 'Autonomy and Free Speech' (2011) 27 *Constitutional Commentary* 251. For commentary on democratic 'self-governance', see Alexander Meiklejohn, 'Free Speech and its Relation to Self-Government' in *Political Freedom: The Constitutional Powers of the People* (New York, Harper & Row, 1948); Alexander Meiklejohn, 'The First Amendment is an Absolute' (1961) *Supreme Court Review* 245; Brian C Murchison, 'Speech and the Self-Governance Value' (2006) 14 *William & Mary Bill of Rights Journal* 1251; Robert Post, 'Participatory Democracy and Free Speech' (2011) 97 *Virginia Law Review* 477.

[7] See Meiklejohn, *Political Freedom* (n 6).

[8] Emerson (n 1) 883 (emphasis added).

[9] Emerson (n 1) 883.

[10] See *New York Times v Sullivan* 376 US 254 (1964); Potter Stewart, 'Or of the Press' (1975) 26 *Hastings Law Journal* 631; Vincent Blasi, 'The Checking Value in First Amendment Theory' (1977) *American Bar Foundation Research Journal* 521; Anthony Lewis, 'Keynote Address: The Right to Scrutinize Government: Toward a First Amendment Theory of Accountability' (1979) 34 *University of Miami Law Review* 793; Timothy W Gleason, *The Watchdog Concept: The Press and the Courts in Nineteenth-Century America* (Iowa State University Press, 1990).

[11] See, eg, *Ford v Québec (Attorney General)* [1988] 2 SCR 712, 764–65, where the Supreme Court of Canada adopted Emerson's 'traditional core' of free expression justifications as central to its constitutional methodology for litigating freedom of expression under the Charter. See also Stefan Braun, 'Freedom of Expression v. Obscenity Censorship: The Developing Canadian Jurisprudence' (1985–1986) 50 *Saskatchewan Law Review* 39, 42; Keith Dubick, 'The Theoretical Foundation for Protecting Freedom of Expression' (2001) 13 *National Journal of Constitutional Law* 1, 7; Robin Elliot, 'The Supreme Court's Understanding of the Democratic Self-Government, Advancement of Truth and Knowledge and Individual Self-Realization Rationales for Protecting Freedom of Expression: Part I—Taking Stock' (2012) 59 *Supreme Court Law Review* 435 [15].

accountability. Demonstrating the doctrinal implications of his 'closed' inventory of free expression values, Emerson advised:

> It is not within the scope of this article to demonstrate the *soundness of the traditional theory underlying freedom of expression*, or its viability under modern conditions. The writer believes that such a demonstration can be made. But the significant point here is that we as a nation are presently committed to the theory, *that alternative principles have no substantial support*, and that our system of freedom of expression must be based upon and designed for the realization of the fundamental propositions embodied in the traditional theory.[12]

Emerson's omission of accountability concerns was all the more surprising given his otherwise keen awareness of threats to political liberty resulting from technological advances in post-war America. Identifying the mounting impact of 'industrialization, urbanization and the proliferation of organization',[13] each gave rise in Emerson's view to increasing threats to freedom of expression:

> Large scale and pervasive government, operating on a new order of magnitude and function, poses greater and more subtle threats to individual rights. The government has become an overpowering antagonist in any clash between state and individual. The exercise of authority in many areas, imposing social controls which are acceptable in themselves, tends in actual operation also to circumscribe freedom of expression. Perhaps most important, *the danger of distorting legitimate powers for illegitimate purposes has become acute.*[14]

Building on this last point, Emerson noted significant political changes centring on 'the impact of mass public opinion'.[15] Sounding more like Herbert Marcuse and followers of the Frankfurt School than a liberal constitutional theorist, he observed that '[m]odern government strives to achieve unity and control more by the manipulation of public attitudes and opinion than by direct application of official sanctions'.[16] But rather than highlight the institutional press as a countervailing mechanism for such growing threats to free expression, Emerson appealed exclusively to the rule of law and judicial institutions for 'the maintenance of a system of freedom of expression'.[17] Therefore, despite laying out concerns that would have prompted radical Whig theorists into impassioned pleas for increased press liberty as a necessary check on increasing government powers, concerns with democratic accountability were neither formally embedded in Emerson's inventory of free expression justifications, nor acknowledged more generally. Little wonder that the checking function figures marginally (if at all) in contemporary public libel law.

12 Emerson (n 1) 886 (emphasis added).
13 Emerson (n 1) 901.
14 Emerson (n 1) 901–02 (emphasis added).
15 Emerson (n 1) 902.
16 Emerson (n 1) 903.
17 Emerson (n 1) 903.

As demonstrated in Part B, unless courts and legislatures are conversant with the underlying premises and concerns of the checking function, there is every prospect that Professor Emerson's inventory of 'core' justifications will function as a complete code, consigning supplemental theories to the proverbial 'dust bin' of philosophical curiosities. But before discussing the second methodological barrier, the need for expanded 'multi-valued' theorising, we must first introduce Meiklejohn's 'self-governance' rationale and Blasi's 'checking value' of the press.

III. Democratic Theorising in Public Libel Jurisprudence

A. Meiklejohn's 'Self-Governance' Rationale

Alexander Meiklejohn's democratic 'self-governance' rationale occupies a leading position among free expression justifications, having been quickly and uncritically transplanted from its original American constitutional context to Britain,[18] Canada,[19] and to a lesser extent, Australia[20] and New Zealand.[21] Yet despite its popularity, closer inspection reveals that Meiklejohnian theory is compromised not only by its signature absolutism and aspirational accounts of democratic citizenship and human nature, but by an unwavering reluctance to recognise

[18] See John Gardner, 'Freedom of Expression' in Christopher McCrudden and Gerald Chambers (eds), *Individual Rights and the Law in Britain* (Oxford, Oxford University Press, 1994); Ian Loveland, 'Reforming Libel Law: The Public Law Dimension' (1997) 46 *International and Comparative Law Quarterly* 561; Ian Loveland, *Political Libels: A Comparative Study* (Oxford, Hart Publishing, 2000); Eric Barendt, 'Freedom of Speech in the Media' in Eric Barendt, *Freedom of Speech*, 2nd edn (Oxford, Oxford University Press, 2007).

[19] See Clare F Beckton, 'Freedom of Expression in Canada—How Free?' (1983) 13 *Manitoba Law Journal* 583; Richard Moon, 'The Scope of Freedom of Expression' (1985) 23 *Osgoode Hall Law Journal* 331; A Wayne MacKay, 'Freedom of Expression: Is It All Just Talk?' (1989) 68 *Canadian Bar Review* 713; Dubick (n 11); Jamie Cameron, 'Does Section 2(*b*) Really Make a Difference? Part 1: Freedom of Expression, Defamation Law and the Journalist-Source Privilege' (2010) 51 *Supreme Court Law Review* 133; Benjamin Oliphant, 'Freedom of the Press as a Discrete Constitutional Guarantee' (2013) 59 *McGill Law Journal* 283.

[20] See Timothy H Jones, 'Freedom of Political Communication in Australia' (1996) 45 *International and Comparative Law Quarterly* 392; Michael Chesterman, 'Privileges and Freedoms for Defamatory Political Speech' (1997) 19 *Adelaide Law Review* 155; Adrienne Stone, 'Freedom of Political Communication, the Constitution and the Common Law' (1998) 26 *Federal Law Review* 219; Jack M Balkin, 'How Rights Change: Freedom of Speech in the Digital Era' (2004) 26 *Sydney Law Review* 5; William Buss, 'Alexander Meiklejohn, American Constitutional Law, and Australia's Implied Freedom of Political Communication' (2006) 34 *Federal Law Review* 421 (arguing that Meiklejohnian theory singly underlies the *Lange* defence).

[21] See New Zealand Law Commission, *Defaming Politicians: A Response to Lange v Atkinson* (Preliminary Paper 33, 1998); Guy Fiti Sinclair, 'Parliamentary Privilege and the Polarisation of Constitutional Discourse in New Zealand' (2006) 14 *Waikato Law Review* 80; New Zealand Law Commission, *Reforming the Law of Sedition* (Report 96, 2007) Ch 3.

humanity's shortcomings and the need for containing (politically or otherwise) its recurring abuses. Meiklejohnian theory therefore not only presents challenges as a practicable democratic model, but appears opposed to the philosophy and principles underlying the US Constitution.[22] Above all, Meiklejohn's model contributes remarkably little to our understanding of governmental accountability. The democratic theory most transferrable across our five comparators is thus conceivably not Meiklejohn's but the checking function of the press, despite the former's commanding grip on constitutional theorising and adjudication.

i. Meiklejohn's Theory of Democratic 'Self-Governance'

Writing in a post-war era of political conformity and suppression of 'dangerous' speech, Meiklejohn's primary target in his influential essay 'Free Speech and its Relation to Self-Government' was America's prevailing doctrine of 'clear and present danger'. Although originating in an earlier decision,[23] this doctrine was most famously applied by Justice Oliver Wendell Holmes Jr in his dissenting opinion in *Abrams v United States.*[24] Justice Holmes' theory was conveyed in one captivating passage, which set out his 'marketplace of ideas' metaphor and its underlying reasoning. Defending an alternative to persecuting dissent, Holmes pronounced:

> But when men have realized that time has upset many fighting faiths, they may come to believe even more than they believe the very foundations of their own conduct that the ultimate good desired is better reached by free trade in ideas-*that the best test of truth is the power of the thought to get itself accepted in the competition of the market*, and that truth is the only ground upon which their wishes safely can be carried out. That at any rate is the theory of our Constitution. It is an experiment, as all life is an experiment. Every year if not every day we have to wager our salvation upon some prophecy based upon imperfect knowledge. While that experiment is part of our system I think that we should be eternally vigilant against attempts to check the expression of opinions that we loathe and believe to be fraught with death, *unless they so imminently threaten immediate interference with the lawful and pressing purposes of the law that an immediate check is required to save the country.*[25]

Foremost among Meiklejohn's concerns was his rejection of Holmes' depiction of human nature. Convinced that, despite his literary eloquence and rhetorical power, '[...] the *thinking* of Mr. Holmes about the First Amendment [had] no such excellence',[26] Meiklejohn expressed grave doubt that the above passage was anything other than a 'partial insight'.[27] Alleging that excessive

22 See Alexander Hamilton and others, *The Federalist Papers* (edited by Lawrence Goldman) (Oxford, Oxford University Press, 2008) nos 10, 51.
23 *Schenck v United States* 249 US 47 (1919) (Holmes J per curiam).
24 *Abrams* (n 4).
25 *Abrams* (n 4) 630 (emphasis added).
26 Meiklejohn, *Political Freedom* (n 6) 61 (emphasis added).
27 Meiklejohn, *Political Freedom* (n 6) 73.

individualism and a pessimistic view of human nature would promote 'intellectual irresponsibility [...]',[28] Meiklejohn cautioned against the perils of Holmes' 'marketplace of ideas' metaphor, insisting that:

> Under its influence, there are no standards for determining the difference between the true and the false. *The truth is what a man or an interest or a nation can get away with.* That dependence upon intellectual laissez-faire, more than any other single factor, has *destroyed the foundations of our national education*, has robbed of their meaning such terms as 'reasonableness' and 'intelligence,' and 'devotion to the general welfare.' It has made intellectual freedom indistinguishable from intellectual license.[29]

Unpersuaded, Meiklejohn endorsed an aspirational counterpoint to Justice Holmes' bleak political outlook, arguing:

> As against the dogma of Mr. Holmes I would venture to assert the counterdogma that one cannot understand the basic purposes of our Constitution as a judge or a citizen should understand them, *unless one sees them as a good man*, a man who, in his political activities, is not merely fighting for what, under the law, he can get, but is *eagerly and generously serving the common welfare.*[30]

Reproaching Holmes' failure to recognise these 'sane and solid moral principles' upholding American democracy, Meiklejohn championed a fundamentally 'protective role' of the First Amendment:

> And his failure at this point is *crucial* for our argument because, whatever else it may mean, *the First Amendment is an expression of human goodness.* That amendment, in its own field, *stands guard over the general welfare of the community.* It protects men as they engage in the moral endeavor to advance that welfare. If that endeavor be reduced to meaninglessness it is little wonder that, in the same hands, the First Amendment has suffered the same fate.[31]

Contrastingly, Meiklejohn identified as the 'highest insight' of political freedom that 'truth-seeking' is essentially *instrumental* to promoting democratic deliberation and the general welfare. Meiklejohn reasoned:

> The First Amendment is not, primarily, a device for the winning of new truth, though that is very important. It is a device for *the sharing of whatever truth has been won.* Its purpose is to give to every voting member of the body politic *the fullest possible participation in the understanding* of those problems with which the citizens of a self-governing society must deal. [...] The primary purpose of the First Amendment is, then, that all the citizens shall, so far as possible, *understand* the issues which bear upon our common life.[32]

Contending that freedom of expression 'springs from the necessities of the program of self-government',[33] Meiklejohn construed the First Amendment

[28] Meiklejohn, *Political Freedom* (n 6) 73.
[29] Meiklejohn, *Political Freedom* (n 6) 74 (emphasis added).
[30] Meiklejohn, *Political Freedom* (n 6) 66 (emphasis added).
[31] Meiklejohn, *Political Freedom* (n 6) 68 (emphasis added).
[32] Meiklejohn, *Political Freedom* (n 6) 75 (emphasis added).
[33] Meiklejohn, *Political Freedom* (n 6) 27.

as '[...] a *deduction* from the basic American agreement that public issues shall be decided by universal suffrage'.[34] Besides the Preamble to the US Constitution,[35] Meiklejohn emphasised two constitutional provisions informing the First Amendment. First, the guarantee of parliamentary privilege in Article 1, Section 6 provided a 'prohibition against abridgment of the freedom of speech which is equally uncompromising, equally absolute, with that of the First Amendment'.[36] According to Meiklejohn, since parliamentary privilege is essential to representative government, public discussion requires the same protection. Meiklejohn instructed that '[t]he freedom which we grant to our representatives is merely a *derivative* of the prior freedom which belongs to us as voters'.[37]

Second, Meiklejohn claimed that the Fifth Amendment sheds considerable light on America's free speech commitments, which provides that 'no person within the jurisdiction of the laws of the United States may be "deprived of life, *liberty*, or property, without due process of law"'.[38] As the 'liberty' referenced in the Fifth Amendment includes 'liberty of speech',[39] Meiklejohn drew an important constitutional distinction. Namely, that both the First and Fifth Amendments recognise two radically different classes of utterances: 'private speech', which may be abridged subject to due process under the Fifth Amendment; and 'public speech' which, Meiklejohn insisted, under the First Amendment must receive absolute protection.

Defending this strict separation of 'public' and 'private' discourse,[40] Meiklejohn maintained then that the First Amendment '[...] was written to clear the way for thinking which *serves the general welfare*'.[41] Compared to Justice Holmes and Professor Chafee,[42] who defended the 'clear and present danger' doctrine by 'balancing' public safety against truth, Meiklejohn firmly rejected this approach, reminding Americans that:

> We have *decided* to be self-governed. We have *measured* the dangers and the values of the suppression of the freedom of public inquiry and debate. And, on the basis of that measurement, having regard for the public safety, *we have decided that the destruction of freedom is always unwise, that freedom is always expedient.* The conviction recorded by

[34] Meiklejohn, *Political Freedom* (n 6) 27 (emphasis added).

[35] US Const Preamble. Meiklejohn insisted that Americans had agreed to be self-governing, as evidenced by the Preamble to the US Constitution, which reads: 'We, the People of the United States, in order to form a more perfect Union, establish justice, insure domestic tranquillity, provide for the common defence, promote the general welfare, and secure the blessings of liberty to ourselves and our posterity, do ordain and establish this Constitution of the United States of America'.

[36] Meiklejohn, *Political Freedom* (n 6) 34–35.

[37] Meiklejohn, *Political Freedom* (n 6) 36 (emphasis added).

[38] Meiklejohn, *Political Freedom* (n 6) 36 (emphasis added).

[39] Meiklejohn, *Political Freedom* (n 6) 36.

[40] Meiklejohn, *Political Freedom* (n 6) 36.

[41] Meiklejohn, *Political Freedom* (n 6) 42 (emphasis added).

[42] See Zechariah Chafee Jr, *Free Speech in the United States* (Harvard, Harvard University Press, 1942).

> that decision is not a sentimental vagary about the 'natural rights' of individuals. *It is a reasoned and sober judgment as to the best available method of guarding the public safety.*[43]

Consequently, '[…] no idea may be suppressed because someone in office, or out of office, has judged it to be "dangerous"'.[44] Meiklejohn insisted that the First Amendment '[…] does not balance intellectual freedom against public safety. On the contrary, its great declaration is that intellectual freedom is the necessary bulwark of the public safety. That declaration admits of *no* exceptions'.[45]

Under this uncompromising model, individual Americans govern only insofar as their '[…] deliberate and informed judgment-making is equipped with the power which is needed to control and direct the pursuit of private interest in *whatever way the public welfare may require*'.[46] Besides unrestricted public discussion under the First Amendment, the act of voting assumed paramount significance for Meiklejohn, who insisted that 'we Americans are politically free *only* insofar as our voting is free'.[47] Contrasting sharply with modern-day voter apathy, public relations spin, and poor voter turn-outs, Meiklejohn's theory demands strictly that '[…] our judging of public issues, whether done separately or in groups, *must* be free and independent—*must* be our own […]'.[48]

These electoral expectations also imply substantial social responsibilities, including reinforcing education as the principal means of ensuring citizens' required levels of civic understanding. Meiklejohn insisted that '[w]e shall not understand the First Amendment unless we see that underlying it is the purpose that all the citizens of our self-governing society shall be "*equally*" educated'.[49] Accordingly, American democracy requires 'cultivating the general intelligence' of the people, a 'heavy and basic responsibility' that Congress must promote.[50] Idealising the pastoral town hall meeting as a model of free expression and self-government, Meiklejohn nonetheless stressed that his concern was not 'the words of the speakers, but the *minds* of the *hearers*. The final aim of the meeting is the *voting of wise decisions*'.[51] In public life, '[w]hat is essential is *not* that everyone shall speak, but that *everything worth saying shall be said*'.[52] Shared understanding and effective deliberation, not direct individual participation, are Meiklejohn's overriding political concerns.

For instance, prior to television and the proliferation of the Internet and social media, Meiklejohn criticised commercial radio in promoting public deliberation,

[43] Meiklejohn, *Political Freedom* (n 6) 57 (emphasis added).
[44] Meiklejohn, *Political Freedom* (n 6) 79.
[45] Meiklejohn, *Political Freedom* (n 6) 59 (emphasis added).
[46] Meiklejohn, *Political Freedom* (n 6) 163 (emphasis added).
[47] Meiklejohn, *Political Freedom* (n 6) 116 (emphasis added).
[48] Meiklejohn, *Political Freedom* (n 6) 117 (emphasis added).
[49] Meiklejohn, *Political Freedom* (n 6) 86 (emphasis added).
[50] Meiklejohn, *Political Freedom* (n 6) 20.
[51] Meiklejohn, *Political Freedom* (n 6) 26 (emphasis added).
[52] Meiklejohn, *Political Freedom* (n 6) 26 (emphasis added).

denouncing it as 'not engaged in the task of enlarging and enriching human communication', but rather, being solely 'engaged in making money'.[53] Meiklejohn lamented:

> The radio, as we now have it, is not cultivating those qualities of taste, of reasoned judgment, of integrity, of loyalty, of mutual understanding upon which the enterprise of self-government depends. *On the contrary, it is a mighty force for breaking them down.* It corrupts both our morals and our intelligence. And that catastrophe is significant for our inquiry, *because it reveals how hollow may be the victories of the freedom of speech when our acceptance of the principle is merely formalistic.*[54]

And here lies the defining but self-limiting element in Meiklejohnian theory. By focussing resolutely on underlying moral characteristics deemed essential for 'self-government', Meiklejohn disregarded the well-known and unrelenting shortfalls in human nature that prompted America's constitutional structure in the first place. At last, while Meiklejohn admirably embraced the ideals and possibilities of democratic rule, he contributed precious little to the political and constitutional prerequisites for effective democratic accountability, a seemingly inescapable conclusion after broadly comparing his theory with the checking function of the press.

B. Blasi's 'Checking Value' of the Press

Despite their importance to American society, the US Supreme Court has only recently defined the constitutional status of newspaper organisations and confronted the theoretical sources of freedom of the press.[55] Among the first commentators, Supreme Court Justice Potter Stewart published a powerful defence of the press' constitutional importance,[56] arguing that it '[...] has performed precisely the function it was intended to perform by those who wrote the First Amendment [...]'.[57] Nevertheless, legal scholars have since observed that the institutional press has struggled to achieve its intended place as an independent check on official misconduct.

The dominant authority on the checking function's failure to gain a foothold in constitutional theory is Professor Vincent Blasi. In a well-documented review published in the *American Bar Foundation Research Journal* in 1977,[58] Blasi advised that, along with traditionally expressed values underlying First Amendment theories, 'free expression is valuable in part because of the function it performs in

[53] Meiklejohn, *Political Freedom* (n 6) 87.

[54] Meiklejohn, *Political Freedom* (n 6) 87 (emphasis added).

[55] See *Sullivan* (n 10); *Garrison v Louisiana* 379 US 64 (1964); *Curtis Publishing Co v Butts* 388 US 130 (1967); *New York Times Co v United States* 403 US 713 (1971); *Gertz v Robert Welch Inc* 418 US 323 (1974).

[56] Stewart (n 10).

[57] Stewart (n 10) 631.

[58] Blasi (n 10).

checking the abuse of official power [...]'.[59] Similar to Emerson's earlier categorisation, Blasi instructed that First Amendment theories developed in the early-twentieth century emphasised three underlying values: (1) individual autonomy; (2) a commitment to 'truth-seeking' and diversity captured by the 'marketplace of ideas' metaphor;[60] and (3) self-government.[61] Nevertheless, Blasi observed that, in the 1960s and 1970s, significant change occurred in the free speech claims and claimants before the US Supreme Court. The value relevant to these newer claims was the Federalist-era concern of '[...] a free press [...] in checking the abuse of power by public officials'.[62]

i. Constitutive Premises and Philosophical Sources

Professor Blasi provided an authoritative definition of this checking function by classifying its five constitutive premises. Citing eighteenth-century radical Whigs such as Cato, Father of Candor, John Wilkes, and Junius,[63] along with American republican theorists James Madison, and Tunis Wortman[64]—all of whom advocated for a strong, independent press as a check on government power—Blasi sought to better understand the checking function by examining 'the sources of the value, the premises on which it rests, and the ways in which it differs from other values'.[65]

First, and most importantly, '[t]he central premise of the checking value is that the abuse of official power is an especially serious evil—more serious than the abuse of private power [...]'.[66] Blasi warned against democratic government's potentially imperious effects on individuals through its 'significant investigative

[59] Blasi (n 10) 528.

[60] See also Vincent Blasi, 'Holmes and the Marketplace of Ideas' (2004) *Supreme Court Review* 1.

[61] Blasi (n 10) 524; Meiklejohn, *Political Freedom* (n 6).

[62] Blasi (n 10) 527.

[63] See British theorists: John Trenchard and Thomas Gordon, *Cato's Letters*, 4 vols (London, 1723–24); John Wilkes, *The North Briton* (London, 1762); Father of Candor, *An Enquiry into the Doctrine Lately Propagated, Concerning Libels, Warrants, and the Seizure of Papers* (London, 1764); *The Letters of Junius*, 2 vols (London, 1792). For a fuller account, see also Charles Blount, *A Just Vindication of Learning and the Liberty of the Press* (London, 1695); John Toland, *A Letter to a Member of Parliament, Shewing, That a Restraint on the Press is Inconsistent with the Protestant Religion, and Dangerous to the Liberties of the Nation* (London, 1698); Matthew Tindal, *Reasons Against Restraining the Press* (London, 1704); John Asgill, *An Essay for the Press* (London, 1712); Joseph Addison, *Thoughts of a Tory Author, Concerning the Press: With the Opinion of the Ancients and Moderns, About Freedom of Speech and Writing* (London, 1712); Capel Lofft, *An Essay on the Law of Libels* (London, 1785); James Adair, *Discussions of the Law of Libels as at Present Received, in Which its Authenticity is Examined* (London, 1785); Robert Hall, *An Apology for the Freedom of the Press, and for General Liberty* (London, 1793); Jean-Louis De Lolme, *The Constitution of England: In Which it is Compared Both with the Republican Form of Government, and the Other Monarchies in Europe* (London, 1822).

[64] See American theorists: James Madison, *The Virginia Report of 1799–1800* in Gaillard Hunt (ed), *The Writings of James Madison*, 9 vols (New York, GP Putnam's Sons, 1900–1910); George Hay, *An Essay on the Liberty of the Press* (Philadelphia, 1799); Tunis Wortman, *A Treatise, Concerning Political Enquiry, and the Liberty of the Press* (New York, 1800).

[65] Blasi (n 10) 529.

[66] Blasi (n 10) 538.

capabilities', its ability to store and use 'vast accumulations of data', and its 'capacity to employ legitimized violence'.[67] Besides expressing concerns that the public '*want* to believe in the trustworthiness of [...] officials', he warned of public officials acquiring 'an inflated sense of self-importance', and of greater social costs when 'important expectations have been defeated' through official misconduct.[68]

The second premise of the checking function is a solemn acceptance of 'an essentially pessimistic view of human nature and human institutions'.[69] Professor Blasi observed correctly that '[h]uman beings have an unmistakable tendency to hurt each other, so much so that the prevention of man-made evil can be viewed as the most important task of all political arrangements'.[70] Although proponents of the checking function might value freedom of expression for other reasons, their primary concern will be encouraging its 'modest capacity to mitigate the human suffering that other humans cause', not the least of which is the greater human suffering 'caused by persons who hold public office'.[71]

Given the increasing size and complexity of modern government, a third premise posits a 'need for well-organized, well-financed, professional critics to serve as a *counterforce* to government [...]'.[72] This implies such critics are capable of 'acquiring enough information to pass judgment on the actions of government', and that they are 'capable of disseminating their information and judgments to the general public'.[73] Increasingly relevant to our era of digital mass communication and surveillance, Blasi cautioned that 'if modern government were ever to gain complete control of the channels of mass communication or to incapacitate its professional critics in some other way, there would be no effective check on official misconduct'.[74]

The checking function of the press also includes a fourth premise that 'the general populace must be the ultimate judge of the behavior of public officials'.[75] Although this implies that the checking function is connected significantly to democratic theory, Blasi rightly noted that 'it is the democratic theory of John Locke and Joseph Schumpeter, not that of Alexander Meiklejohn'.[76] While a proponent of the checking function might be a direct democrat, 'in the sense of favoring a significant participatory role for the ordinary citizen in day-to-day governance [...]',[77] Blasi surmised that he or she must 'be at least a Lockean democrat',[78] in that the general population define and enforce norms relating to official misconduct.

[67] Blasi (n 10) 538–39.
[68] Blasi (n 10) 540 (emphasis in original).
[69] Blasi (n 10) 541.
[70] Blasi (n 10) 541.
[71] Blasi (n 10) 541.
[72] Blasi (n 10) 541 (emphasis added).
[73] Blasi (n 10) 541.
[74] Blasi (n 10) 542.
[75] Blasi (n 10) 542.
[76] Blasi (n 10) 542.
[77] Blasi (n 10) 542.
[78] Blasi (n 10) 542.

Finally, the public's role in judging government officials implies a fifth premise 'that the concept of "misconduct" has meaning in the context of governmental decision-making'.[79] This implies 'violation by public officials of norms that transcend a wide spectrum of policy differences'.[80] Blasi offered the following examples: (1) fraudulent behaviour violating criminal laws, such as 'embezzlement or the acceptance of a bribe';[81] (2) behaviour adjudicated to be unconstitutional; (3) improper involvement in other nations' domestic affairs, including 'the deliberate bombing of civilians during wartime' and 'the assassination of foreign political figures';[82] (4) serious misrepresentations made to government institutions or the public;[83] and (5) using public office to augment one's private wealth.[84] All told, the checking function provides a valuable supplement to traditional freedom of expression justifications, particularly in light of the considerable gaps in Meiklejohnian theory.

ii. Distinguishing the Checking Function from Free Expression's Traditional Values

To further refine the checking function's significance for constitutional adjudication, Professor Blasi outlined its many dissimilarities to traditional free expression values. Committed to demonstrating its theoretical independence, he nonetheless insisted that the checking function '[...] could *never* replace the existing First Amendment value matrix but rather should be viewed as potentially a *vital additional component* in that constellation of interdependent values'.[85]

Blasi first observed that a proponent of the checking function 'views speech of a certain content as important because of its *consequences*: alerting the polity to the facts or implications of official behavior, presumably triggering responses that will mitigate the ill effects [...]'.[86] Proponents of the autonomy value are, by contrast, 'more concerned with the *process* of belief formation and communication; the value does not rest on any empirical propositions regarding the social effects of speech'.[87] Moreover, due to its 'largely irreducible' nature, constitutional claims based on autonomy 'tend to be absolute in nature'.[88] The checking function, by contrast, is more amenable to a 'balancing analysis' involving competing regulatory interests.[89] A final difference is that the checking function supports

79 Blasi (n 10) 542.
80 Blasi (n 10) 542.
81 Blasi (n 10) 543.
82 Blasi (n 10) 543.
83 Blasi (n 10) 543.
84 Blasi (n 10) 543.
85 Blasi (n 10) 548 (emphasis added).
86 Blasi (n 10) 546 (emphasis in original).
87 Blasi (n 10) 546 (emphasis in original).
88 Blasi (n 10) 547.
89 Blasi (n 10) 547.

doctrines that make constitutional protections a function of 'who is speaking and what is being said', suggesting '[…] a distinctive constitutional role for certain specialized countervailing forces in the society and certain specialized speech and press activities'.[90] Thus, 'a proponent of the checking value places a premium on, and […] may accord extraordinary constitutional protection to, speech […] concerning the behavior of public officials'.[91]

Second, although the checking and 'truth-seeking' values 'both support the protection of speech because of its social consequences rather than on the basis of […] intrinsic moral worth […]',[92] Blasi observed that the checking function focuses on a narrower concern. Namely, scrutinising public officials will produce more good—in the form of prevention or containment of misconduct—than harm, such as 'diminution in the efficiency of the public service or weakening of the trust that ultimately holds any political society together'.[93] Blasi noted that this narrower concern might lead to more focused priorities. Thus, '*exposing government misbehaviour* might be accorded a level of constitutional protection higher than that accorded other speech activities which have only the more general effect of enhancing diversity'.[94]

Professor Blasi also noted that while the checking and 'truth-seeking' values are similar in their focus on 'the interests of listeners and readers rather than speakers and writers', proponents of the checking function emphasise a narrower need for information about *what the government is doing*.[95] This informational need outweighs public advocacy, since for Blasi '[t]he moral and political implications of official behavior will often be apparent without extended public debate'.[96] Thus, '[t]he most important stage in the checking process is typically that during which the public is *first made aware of what is going on*'.[97] According to Blasi, acknowledging the checking function of the press as an independent free expression value should provide greater protection for 'speech activities which relate to the dissemination of information divorced from advocacy […]'.[98]

Of course, Blasi acknowledged that distinguishing Meiklejohnian theory 'requires the most extensive treatment'.[99] He observed that both theories focus on political consequences of speech and give special protection to communications relating to the political system; both emphasise the importance of communications to readers and listeners; and, both stem from democratic conceptions of sovereignty.[100] Of particular importance to our assessment of public libel doctrine,

90 Blasi (n 10) 547–48.
91 Blasi (n 10) 548.
92 Blasi (n 10) 551.
93 Blasi (n 10) 552.
94 Blasi (n 10) 552–53 (emphasis added).
95 Blasi (n 10) 553.
96 Blasi (n 10) 553.
97 Blasi (n 10) 553 (emphasis added).
98 Blasi (n 10) 554.
99 Blasi (n 10) 544.
100 Blasi (n 10) 557–58.

Blasi accepted that 'the checking value has the potential to influence First Amendment doctrine only insofar as it can be shown to have premises and implications significantly different from those of the self-government value'.[101]

According to Professor Blasi, the most obvious difference is that 'the checking value focuses on the particular problem of *misconduct by government officials*', whereas the self-government theory 'makes no such narrow ordering'.[102] In fact, Meiklejohn's theory provides absolute protection to 'all speech relevant to the process by which citizens decide how to vote'.[103] According to Blasi,

> [a] proponent of the checking value does not deny that myriad harms to the body politic may be forestalled by speech activities or that many goals of a democratic system of government may be served by [...] certain forms of communication.[104]

But since official misconduct is of a special order, '[...] its prevention and containment is a goal that takes precedence over all other goals of the political system'.[105]

Another important difference is that the checking function permits *balancing* the consequences of speech activities, whereas constitutional protection for 'self-governing' speech must be *unqualified*.[106] As discussed above, for Meiklejohn, 'any limitation imposed by the agents of the people on the self-governing speech of citizens is simply an impossible notion under our political compact'.[107] Although the checking function is consistent with private- or group-interest theories of politics, Blasi rightly observed that 'the [checking] value is especially important in a society characterized to a large degree by competition and the pursuit of private satisfaction'.[108]

Finally, Professor Blasi noted two differences of emphasis. First, due to its broader focus on the political process, Meiklejohn's theory places 'slightly more emphasis on argumentation [...] than does the checking value'.[109] The checking function, by contrast, emphasises *shortage of information* as the most serious issue relating to political problems.[110] Second, the two models place differing emphases on social and political elites. Blasi rightly noted that 'Meiklejohn [was] reluctant to assign a special role in the governmental system to any group of people [...]'.[111] Public officials were understood as only '*agents* of the collective political will'.[112] By contrast, since 'a proponent of the checking value sees political decision-making more as a product of *contending forces and counterforces*',[113] public officials are

101 Blasi (n 10) 558.
102 Blasi (n 10) 558–59 (emphasis added).
103 Blasi (n 10) 559.
104 Blasi (n 10) 558.
105 Blasi (n 10) 558.
106 Blasi (n 10) 559.
107 Blasi (n 10) 559.
108 Blasi (n 10) 563.
109 Blasi (n 10) 563.
110 Blasi (n 10) 563.
111 Blasi (n 10) 563.
112 Blasi (n 10) 563 (emphasis added).
113 Blasi (n 10) 563 (emphasis added).

seen more for their independence and as 'potential oppressors rather than as [...] agents'.[114] This view recognises that 'public officials are qualitatively different from ordinary voters' and that they can be 'effectively checked [...] by other elite groups with similarly specialized powers, skills, and attitudes'.[115] Besides organised political opposition, an obvious example of an elite counterforce is the institutional press. According to Blasi, only the checking function highlights this structural role and provides a compelling justification for treating journalists 'differently than ordinary citizens in determining what rights are guaranteed by the First Amendment'.[116]

In the end, the two models highlight very different facets of democratic governance. Where Meiklejohnian theory stresses deliberative democracy and the role of the press in facilitating electoral decision-making, the checking function focusses instead on political accountability and the liberal 'watchdog' function of the press. Combined, both models represent our conceptual basis for evaluating democratic theorising in public libel jurisprudence. But before probing these matters further in Part B, we must return to the second methodological barrier to public libel regulation. Alongside the mishandling of democratic theory by courts and legislatures, legal scholars have also muddied distinctions between Meiklejohnian theory and the checking function by intentionally conflating these two models.

IV. Methodological Barrier II

A. Necessity for 'Multi-Valued' Theorising

Besides concerns with free expression's incomplete inventory of 'core' justifications, another methodological barrier to public libel regulation must be considered. Following publication of Emerson's article, many legal scholars attempted to resolve perceptions of 'incoherence' in free speech jurisprudence by subsuming traditional justifications under various single-valued approaches.[117] Among the

114 Blasi (n 10) 564.

115 Blasi (n 10) 564.

116 Blasi (n 10) 564.

117 See, eg, Robert H Bork, 'Neutral Principles and Some First Amendment Problems' (1971) 47 *Indiana Law Journal* 1; Lillian R BeVier, 'The First Amendment and Political Speech: An Inquiry into the Substance and Limits of Principle' (1978) 30 *Stanford Law Review* 299; Lillian R BeVier, 'An Informed Public, an Informing Press: The Search for a Constitutional Principle' (1980) 68 *California Law Review* 482; Martin H Redish, 'The Value of Free Speech' (1982) 130 *University of Pennsylvania Law Review* 591; Michael J Perry, 'Freedom of Expression: An Essay on Theory and Doctrine' (1983) 78 *Northwestern University Law Review* 1137; Lawrence B Solum, 'Freedom of Communicative Action: A Theory of the First Amendment Freedom of Speech' (1989) 83 *Northwestern University Law Review* 54; Steven D Smith, 'Believing Persons, Personal Believings: The Neglected Center of the First Amendment' (2002) *University of Illinois Law Review* 1233; James Weinstein, 'Participatory Democracy as the Central Value of American Free Speech Doctrine' (2011) 97 *Virginia Law Review* 491.

theoretical aspirants were Meiklejohn's democratic 'self-governance' rationale,[118] 'self-realisation',[119] 'participatory democracy',[120] 'believing persons',[121] and even an adaptation of Habermas's theory of 'communicative action'.[122] Although not all single-valued approaches were exclusionary (some legal theorists preferred ranking justifications), even such 'lexically ordered hierarchies' necessarily marginalised lower-ranked rationales.

The most marginalised has surely been the checking function rationale. In a controversial 1982 article prophetically titled 'The Value of Free Speech', Professor Martin Redish argued that Emerson's classic free expression justifications were subsumed under the 'one true value' of 'individual self-realization'.[123] Claiming that traditional free expression justifications were '*in reality* subvalues of self-realization', Redish also took aim at 'multi-valued' approaches more generally, insisting that it was '*inaccurate* to suggest that "the commitment to free expression embodie[s] a complex of values"'.[124] After dismissing each of Emerson's 'core' justifications, Redish observed that 'Professor Blasi's "checking function" appear[ed] strikingly similar to the "democratic process" value of Meiklejohn'.[125] Relying unduly on formal logic, Redish dismissed the checking function as only a *derivative* of 'self-realisation', reasoning that '[b]ecause the checking function ultimately derives from the principle of democratic self-rule, and because that principle in turn follows from the self-realization value, the checking function is *merely one concrete manifestation* of the much broader self-realization value'.[126]

The difficulties with this overly reductionist, single-valued approach are many. First, as happens too often, Redish's interpretation of Professor Blasi's checking function was curt and dismissive, failing to engage with its clearly articulated 'constitutive premises' and Blasi's efforts to distinguish it from traditional free expression theories.[127] Second, Redish discussed the checking function of the press (as with all free expression values) in highly abstract terms, without the benefit of scrutinising its relationship to particular doctrinal issues, such as its potential role in public libel doctrine. Without setting his discussion amongst examples of official misconduct, it is difficult to appreciate how one might prefer 'self-realisation' or any other free expression justification over the checking function for factual relevance or exegetical power.

118 Bork, ibid; BeVier, 'The First Amendment and Political Speech', ibid.
119 Redish (n 117); Perry (n 117).
120 Weinstein (n 117).
121 Smith (n 117).
122 Solum (n 117).
123 Redish (n 117) 593.
124 Redish (n 117) 594 (emphasis added), quoting Blasi (n 10) 538.
125 Redish (n 117) 613, fn 77.
126 Redish (n 117) 615–16 (emphasis added).
127 With only a few exceptions (see Schauer and Greenawalt in the discussion below), legal scholars have cited the checking function rationale only long enough to conflate it with more highly abstract 'democratic' notions.

Lastly, Redish's argument minimised crucial distinctions between democratic 'self-governance' and the checking function that reveal themselves principally in the context of public libels. It is precisely the factual details of official misconduct and abuse of governmental power that ensure an accurate and credible balancing of free expression against reputation. That is, it matters greatly for public libel doctrine whether the freedom of expression side of the equation is properly weighted with relevant concerns. Epistemologically, Redish's argument races to progressively higher levels of abstraction at the expense of a sharper and more complete understanding of the checking function's contextual relevance and relationship to democratic theory. Simply put, as with all abstraction, it is in consequence most notable for *what it leaves out*.

Professor Michael Perry has also instructively dismissed the checking function by appealing to a simple mechanical criterion of whether a theoretical candidate adds any 'additional normative content' to freedom of expression.[128] In an illustrative example of this similarly misguided approach, Perry reasoned:

> The checking function, however, simply does not suggest normative content for freedom of expression *beyond that already indicated by the democratic value*. The democratic value calls for protecting information and ideas useful in evaluating public policy and performance. *Information about abuses of authority is plainly useful in evaluating public performance*. Nor is it surprising that the checking value does not suggest additional normative content: As my colleague Martin Redish has demonstrated, *the checking value is merely an aspect of the democratic value*.[129]

Perry's dismissal of the checking function is thus comprised of one simple, highly abstract statement regarding the potential overlap of information relevant to both values. This broad and undifferentiated understanding of Meiklejohnian theory and the checking function evidences the dangers of failing to consider carefully their differences in emphasis and relevance to *specific* factual contexts. With respect, what Professors Perry and Redish fail to explore is that the checking function might provide uniquely sound reasons to weigh freedom of expression more heavily in certain factual contexts, particularly in cases where governments, politicians, and certain public officials attempt to use defamation law to silence news organisations from publishing matters of public interest to mass audiences.

Fortunately, these methodological concerns have been addressed by other eminent constitutional law scholars.[130] The leading light on such matters is arguably

[128] Perry (n 117) 1159.

[129] Perry (n 117) 1152, fn 62 (emphasis added). For a Canadian example conflating both rationales, see David Fewer, Constitutionalizing Copyright: Freedom of Expression and the Limits of Copyright in Canada' (1997) 55 *University of Toronto Faculty of Law Review* 175 [29].

[130] See, eg, Frederick Schauer, 'Categories and the First Amendment: A Play in Three Acts' (1981) 34 *Vanderbilt Law Review* 265; Frederick Schauer, *Free Speech: A Philosophical Enquiry* (Cambridge, Cambridge University Press, 1982); Pierre J Schlag, 'An Attack on Categorical Approaches to Freedom of Speech' (1983) 30 *UCLA Law Review* 671; Steven Shiffrin, 'Liberalism, Radicalism, and Legal Scholarship' (1983) 30 *UCLA Law Review* 1103; Frederick Schauer, 'Must Speech be Special?' (1983) 78 *Northwestern University Law Review* 1284; Frederick Schauer, 'Public Figures' (1984) 25 *William and Mary Law Review* 905; Kent Greenawalt, 'Free Speech Justifications' (1989) 89 *Columbia Law Review* 119.

Professor Frederick Schauer who, in contrast to those crusading for one 'true' free expression theory, supports a seemingly less grand 'multi-valued' approach. Although advising that '[a]ttempting to apply the first amendment without some theoretical vision of free speech is *mere stumbling in the dark*',[131] Schauer has cautioned against the pitfalls of single-valued approaches endorsed by Professors Redish and Perry:

> [I]t is unlikely that any one theory can explain the concept of free speech, and no reason necessarily exists to suppose that it could. Freedom of speech need not have any one 'essential' feature. It is much more likely a bundle of interrelated principles sharing no common set of necessary and sufficient defining characteristics. [...]. *Any attempt to do so is likely to be both banal and to distort all of the principles involved.*[132]

Not long after, Professor Schauer concluded more definitively that:

> *To view the first amendment as being grounded in one and only one theoretical justification is a mistake.* Instead, there may be several theoretical foundations for the first amendment, occasionally mutually exclusive, but more often just compatibly different. If this is the case—*that the first amendment serves multiple purposes, and that those purposes are not congruent with each other*—then we should not be surprised to find that several of those purposes might coalesce around a particular grouping of circumstances. We also should not be surprised to find that, in other cases, only one of the justifications for the first amendment might apply.[133]

Professor Kent Greenawalt has also argued convincingly that single unifying justifications for freedom of expression risk either obscuring or oversimplifying its composite of interrelated rationales. In 'Free Speech Justifications',[134] Greenawalt posited a loose constellation of reasons, subjects, and subprinciples of free expression. Explaining the now familiar single-valued strategy of 'inclusion' used by Professor Redish,[135] whereby independent free expression values are subsumed under a broader theory, Greenawalt prudently advised:

> *[A]ny reason broad enough to yield a plausible claim that it includes everything else is bound to be extremely general and vague.* Such a reason will not provide a very helpful starting point for dealing with many actual social problems if citizens, legislators, and judges must descend quickly to the more specific 'subsidiary' reasons whose *implications are clearer.*[136]

Citing Blasi's 'checking value' as a rare and instructive example, Greenawalt thoughtfully resisted the single-valued temptations of Professors Redish and Perry, advising:

> No doubt, holding the government to account contributes to individual human fulfillment, but there may be other reasons, such as social justice, for responsible government.

131 Schauer, 'A Play in Three Acts', ibid 291–92, fn 124 (emphasis added).
132 Schauer, 'A Play in Three Acts', ibid 276–77 (emphasis added).
133 Schauer, 'Public Figures' (n 130) 930 (emphasis added).
134 Greenawalt (n 130).
135 The other single-valued strategy is 'elimination', whereby aspirant values are discarded for overlapping significantly with other values and interests (Greenawalt (n 130) 126).
136 Greenawalt (n 130) 126–27 (emphasis added).

> *The value of free speech for accountable government may be underestimated if only the relationship to individual fulfillment is addressed.* Putting the point more abstractly, the process of inclusion may distort the significance of more discrete reasons whose importance lies partly, but only partly, in what they contribute to the most general value.[137]

An orientation toward 'practical thought' is therefore paramount for Greenawalt, requiring a more 'bottom-up' and contextual approach to constitutional theorising. For example, when considering the checking function of the press as a free expression value of 'historical significance and central importance [...] powerfully developed by Vincent Blasi',[138] Greenawalt observed that it seemed '[c]losely linked to truth discovery and interests accommodation'.[139] However, demonstrating the power of his own prescriptions for preserving the checking function's theoretical independence, Greenawalt confessed:

> Perhaps the benefits of exposure and deterrence reach beyond anything neatly captured by truth discovery or interest accommodation. Apart from truths it actually reveals, and even when what its [*sic*] claims turns out to be inaccurate, a critical press affects how officials and citizens regard the exercise of government power, *subtly supporting the notion that government service is a responsibility, not an opportunity for personal advantage*'.[140]

In the end, given the corrupt and alarming behaviours that are too often emblematic of public libel cases, Professor Greenawalt's sensitivity to differing emphases of contending free expression theories seems a sensible approach worth preserving.

B. Structural Institutionalism, Categoricalism, and Ad Hoc Balancing

i. Structural Institutionalism

These prescriptions for 'multi-valued' theorising are also reinforced by recent constitutional law scholarship advocating a fundamental shift from acontextuality to 'institutionalism' in free expression jurisprudence. In *First Amendment Institutions*,[141] Paul Horwitz argues that First Amendment jurisprudence is in crisis, requiring a move away from applying acontextual rules and principles toward alternatives rooted in contextual realities and the unique characteristics of institutional actors. As Professor Horwitz instructs, a superior alternative to 'the standard way of carving up the world that lawyers and judges use' is to begin to see it

137 Greenawalt (n 130) 127 (emphasis added).
138 Greenawalt (n 130) 142.
139 Greenawalt (n 130) 142.
140 Greenawalt (n 130) 143 (emphasis added).
141 Paul Horwitz, *First Amendment Institutions* (Harvard, Harvard University Press, 2013). See also Frederick Schauer, 'Towards an Institutional First Amendment' (2005) 89 *Minnesota Law Review* 1256; Frederick Schauer, 'Is There a Right to Academic Freedom?' (2006) 77 *University of Colorado Law Review* 907; Frederick Schauer, 'Hohfeld's First Amendment' (2008) 76 *George Washington Law Review* 914.

'*as it is* and adjust the First Amendment to fit its framework'.[142] Besides being responsive to institutional context and changing social realities, Horwitz insists that the law should be developed from the bottom up. Structural institutionalism consequently seeks the possibility of 'doing law' in a more 'open-textured, participatory, [...] consensus-oriented, contextual, flexible, integrative, and pragmatic' manner.[143]

At least preliminarily, attempts to resuscitate the checking function as an independent free speech value fit easily into 'structural institutionalism's' theory and objectives. As Horwitz rightly observes, historically the 'free press' model 'conceived of the press as an independent, autonomous institution carrying out a "watchdog" or "checking" function with respect to government'.[144] Among the anticipated benefits of embracing Horwitz's 'institutional turn', '[a]n openly institutional treatment of the press would lead to more doctrinal coherence for the Press Clause and more stability and predictability for the press. [...] In particular, it would provide greater protection for journalism as an institutional *process*'.[145] Among the 'significant' and 'wide-ranging' doctrinal implications of structural institutionalism, Professor Horwitz would grant the press '[...] new constitutional privileges to conceal sources and to engage in newsgathering practices without legal interference'.[146] Focussing predominantly on *function* and not medium,

> an institutional approach would treat the press *as* the press. It would focus on whether a given entity was a journalistic entity engaging in the act of journalism, subject to the norms, traditions, and self-regulating practices that characterize the press.[147]

As examined in Parts C and D, evaluating public libel doctrine by appealing to public accountability theory and its focus on accountability mechanisms provides a fresh instantiation of Professor Horwitz's call for crafting legal principles and rules on the basis of 'contextual analysis' and the 'structural realities' of institutional settings. Therefore, not only is our aim of distinguishing the checking function from Meiklejohnian theory consistent with the 'multi-valued' views of Professors Schauer and Greenawalt, but a revised framework for public libel jurisprudence may yet explain how institutional settings and free expression justifications might optimally guide doctrinal selections.

ii. Categoricalism and Ad Hoc Balancing

A commitment to 'multi-valued' theorising also affects our understanding of public libel law's doctrinal architecture. Specifically, the traditionally opposed

142 Horwitz, ibid 68 (emphasis in original).

143 Horwitz, ibid 72, quoting Bradley C Karkkainen, '"New Governance" in Legal Thought and in the World: Some Splitting as Antidote to Overzealous Lumping' (2004) 89 *Minnesota Law Review* 471, 474.

144 Horwitz, ibid 149.

145 Horwitz, ibid 154–55 (emphasis in original).

146 Horwitz, ibid 10.

147 Horwitz, ibid 165 (emphasis in original).

methods of 'ad hoc balancing' and 'categoricalism' must equally account for all relevant rights, interests, and values in public libel cases. Once more, Professor Schauer has explained insightfully that a simple appeal to balancing invariably

> [...] masks questions about *who* should weigh competing values, the extent to which balancing should take place in more or less rigid rules or in the circumstances of the individual case [...], and the level of abstraction at which the competing values should be described and weighed.[148]

On the oft-confused issue of ad hoc balancing, Schauer instructs:

> It is by now hardly a novel observation that particularized balancing of interests by the judge in respect to the case at hand (ad hoc balancing) is not a technique with a monopoly on the weighing of interests. *We balance when we formulate rules for mechanical or categorical application. Nor is it a simple question of a choice between balancing at the rule-making level or at the level of application. There is a spectrum rather than a dichotomy.*[149]

On the precise nature of 'categorical' or generic rules, Schauer continued:

> When categorization is presented as a first amendment technique in opposition to balancing, *what is in fact being advocated is the establishment of rules leaving little if any discretion to the judge in the particular case.* The more a rule predetermines the outcome that flows from easily determinable facts, or the more a rule excludes certain facts from consideration by the judge, the less discretion is available to the judge and the more we can call the rule categorical.[150]

Given these methodological subtleties, Professor Schauer cautions against conflating free expression protection with heightened degrees of 'categoricalism', a particular concern for public libel law given its broad range of doctrinal options:

> In seeking answers to these questions pertaining to the appropriate blend of guidance and discretion, it is important to remember that *there is no necessary correlation between the approach employed and the strength of the first amendment protection.* Although ad hoc balancing has traditionally been associated with a puny first amendment and categorical rules with a powerful one, *it could have been and still could be otherwise.* It is possible, after all, to devise rigid rules that give little respect to free speech considerations.[151]

At a minimum, these threshold matters have the following implications for our examination of public libel jurisprudence in Part B. First, when applying ad hoc balancing in specific cases, courts and legislators must at the outset identify *all* relevant freedom of expression values, which only then can be aptly considered and applied to attain defensible outcomes. Second, even when considering a generic qualified privilege or more 'categorical' legal rule, one must still table, consider, and select from among the very same values before formulating such comparatively inflexible standards. While doubtless there remain other factors to consider

[148] Schauer, 'Must Speech be Special?' (n 130) 1285, fn 9 (emphasis in original).
[149] Schauer, 'A Play in Three Acts' (n 130) 299 (emphasis added) (citation omitted).
[150] Schauer, 'A Play in Three Acts' (n 130) 300 (emphasis added) (citations omitted).
[151] Schauer, 'A Play in Three Acts' (n 130) 303 (emphasis added) (citation omitted).

(as discussed in Part C), Professor Schauer persuasively shows that there is no escaping this difficult but necessary stage of constitutional analysis. Moreover, as emphasised collectively by Professors Schauer, Greenawalt, and Horwitz, free expression theorising is principally about maintaining an empirically-oriented perspective. As demonstrated by our comparative analysis in Part B, effective theorising is not about 'logical trickery' or adding further 'normative content', but about more carefully assessing and applying the theoretical justifications that already exist.

V. Moving Forward

Returning then to our main argument, public libel jurisprudence is beset by two principal deficiencies. First, to redress the undertheorising compromising media defamation law, its ultimate source must be identified and resolved. As confirmed in Part B, the primary source of undertheorising in public libel doctrine is a persistent and widespread disregard of democratic accountability concerns and the checking function of the press. The most prevalent example of this undertheorising is the conflation of the checking function with Meiklejohn's democratic 'self-governance' rationale. However, as the free expression theory most relevant in public libel cases, any omission of the checking function disrupts the delicate process of balancing free expression with reputation whilst selecting doctrinal alternatives. Systematic disregard of the checking function and accountability concerns represents *the* central problem in contemporary public libel jurisprudence.

Second, capitalising on the innovative contributions of the Privy Council and New Zealand courts, a suitable approach for evaluating public libel doctrine must both simplify and synthesise a broad range of constitutional, legal, and non-legal factors. As developed in Parts C and D, reconsidering the checking function's broader theoretical foundations suggests a dynamic and innovative approach to constructing a suitable framework. Drawing on recent advances in public accountability theory, this enquiry not only establishes that the checking function of the press is rooted in broader notions of accountability, but that selecting public libel doctrine must involve a contextual and aggregate assessment of interrelationships between various accountability mechanisms at multiple levels of abstraction. In the end, public libel doctrine must be adjusted to mitigate any accountability dysfunctions (deficits or overloads) characterising a jurisdiction's distinct institutional environment.

Part B

Undertheorising Democratic Accountability: Comparative Law Analysis of Public Libel Doctrine

Overview of Part B

Part B examines in detail the principal theoretical and doctrinal errors of leading public libel law authorities, particularly the legal methodologies (eg ad hoc balancing, categoricalism) that they endorse, and their understanding and application of free expression justifications. This comparative law enquiry reveals that the foremost deficiency in public libel jurisprudence is a persistent and widespread disregard of democratic accountability and the checking function of the press. Such undertheorising manifests in at least three distinct but interrelated problems.

As outlined in chapter three, both Australia and America have formulated unique doctrinal approaches, effectively downplaying the checking function rationale. Following the US Supreme Court's endorsement of the 'actual malice' rule in *Sullivan*, the High Court of Australia has justified its innovative 'responsible journalism' defence by appealing to an indeterminate implied rights doctrine based on an overly-mechanical transplantation of Canada's pre-Charter jurisprudence. Most controversially, Australia's implied rights methodology purportedly rejects free expression theorising altogether. The methodological peculiarities of Australian and American public libel doctrine provide a fitting start to our comparative doctrinal analysis by emphasising the importance of identifying and applying all relevant freedom of expression justifications when regulating public libels.

Chapter four then investigates the indifference of courts and legislatures to the imperfect references to the checking function pervading public libel jurisprudence. Both the UK Supreme Court and the New Zealand Court of Appeal have discounted significant sources of domestic and international law resonant with the checking function's central premises and concerns. Besides the disquieting bias against the institutional press evident in New Zealand jurisprudence, Britain's highest courts have essentially ignored the European Court of Human Rights' endorsement of political criticism and the 'watchdog' role of the press.

Lastly, chapter five documents the systematic and widespread conflation of the checking function with Meiklejohnian theory. As discussed in chapter two, despite their distinct emphases and assumptions, judges, legislators, and legal scholars have construed these models as synonymous, showing little regard for their potentially sweeping implications for public libel doctrine and reform. Although this theoretical confusion is shared amongst our five comparators, none has exhibited this tendency more instructively than the Supreme Court of Canada. Owing to confusion regarding the Court's pre-Charter 'implied right of political expression', the checking function has been systematically discounted as an independent justification. Specifically, an incomplete understanding of democratic theory has been methodologically entrenched by omitting the checking function from the Supreme Court's inventory of free expression values. This has left Canadian courts little choice but to shoehorn accountability concerns into a Meiklejohnian framework or to appeal, awkwardly and unconvincingly, to less relevant free expression justifications.

At the end of the day, the three cases of undertheorising examined in Part B evidence widespread misuse of democratic theorising in public libel jurisprudence. Essentially, vitally important concerns with accountability and the checking function of the press are being overlooked in favour of Meiklejohnian conceptions most resonant with deliberative democracy and the press' role as an 'information conduit' for electoral decision-making.

3

Indeterminate Balancing in Public Libel Doctrine: Generic Rules and 'Implied Rights'

I. United States

A close examination of the US Supreme Court's decisions on the application of the First Amendment to state libel laws reveals many deficiencies. First, as shown in *New York Times v Sullivan*, the Court's reasoning is characterised by significant undertheorising of the checking function of the press.[1] This undertheorising is particularly concerning for categorical, rule-based approaches—like the 'actual malice' rule—where the success of balancing free expression and reputation is contingent on the scope and quality of its initial legal analysis. Unlike ad hoc balancing, America's approach is unique in prohibiting judicial reassessment to resolve misalignment between theory and doctrine.

Second, this undertheorising is not only apparent from *Sullivan's* implicit and disordered references to the checking function and accountability concerns, but also from the Court's failure to interpret and apply it correctly in subsequent criminal and private libel cases. This has generated confusion and forced an apparent withdrawal from *Sullivan's* imperfect articulation of the checking function. Concerns of undertheorising have therefore intensified as the checking function of the press has neither been considered methodically from the outset, nor applied properly in subsequent cases.

Third, as discussed in chapter one, leading common law courts have selected their public libel doctrine at least partially in response to perceived limitations

[1] 376 US 254 (1964). Academic commentary attributes *Sullivan's* controlling rationale to Meiklejohn's 'self-governance' rationale. See Harry Kalven Jr, 'The *New York Times* Case: A Note on "The Central Meaning of the First Amendment"' (1964) *Supreme Court Review* 191; William J Brennan Jr, 'The Supreme Court and the Meiklejohn Interpretation of the First Amendment' (1965) 79 *Harvard Law Review* 1; Ian Loveland, *Political Libels: A Comparative Study* (Oxford, Hart Publishing, 2000); and Ian Loveland and Andrew Sharland, 'The Defamation Act 1996 and Political Libels' (1997) *Public Law* 113. Cf Anthony Lewis, '*New York Times v. Sullivan* Reconsidered: Time to Return to "The Central Meaning of the First Amendment"' (1983) 83 *Columbia Law Review* 603. Professor Kalven famously reported that Meiklejohn viewed *Sullivan* as 'an occasion for dancing in the streets' (Kalven Jr, ibid 221, fn 125).

of the 'actual malice' rule. However, the US Supreme Court did *not* engage in comparative law analysis. Much less did it examine how dissimilarities in constitutional structure and rights protection, among other factors, might guide its doctrinal approach. As a de facto gatekeeper for international public libel reform, the 'actual malice' rule has been used inappropriately as a 'gold standard' in lieu of a suitably robust 'selection theory'. As we shall see, its domestic suitability remains, in a very real sense, untested and unknown.

The primary consequence of this undertheorising is unintentional over and under protection of speech. Contrary to presumptions that America invariably 'overprotects' speech due to the 'unqualified wording' of the First Amendment,[2] the US Supreme Court has arguably underprotected instances of political speech subject to criminal prosecution.

A. Defamation Plaintiffs, Generic Rules, and Democratic Theory

i. Public Officials

Analysis of the undertheorising of the checking function in American public libel doctrine must begin with the Court's landmark decision in *Sullivan*.[3]

LB Sullivan was the Commissioner of Public Affairs for Montgomery, Alabama. He brought a defamation action against *The New York Times* in connection with a full-page, paid political advertisement sponsored by prominent civil rights advocates. It documented, with minor factual inaccuracies, significant incidents of political opposition, including an 'unprecedented wave of terror' by public officials against African American students engaged in non-violent demonstrations. It also sought financial support for the student movement, the struggle for black voting rights, and the legal defence of the movement's leader, Dr Martin Luther King Jr.

The advertisement alleged that the Montgomery police had 'ringed' the Alabama State College Campus, that the college dining hall was padlocked, and that Dr King's peaceful protests were met with personal assault, the bombing of his home, and spurious arrests.[4] Although Mr Sullivan was not named in the ad, he insisted readers would identify him as the Commissioner responsible for police supervision. Notably, out of a circulation of nearly 650,000, only 394 copies of *The New York Times* were distributed in Alabama, of which 35 reached Montgomery County.[5]

[2] This view is prevalent among UK legal scholars who have overlooked the 'actual malice' rule's English roots. See Eric Barendt, 'Case Comment: Libel and Freedom of Speech in English Law' (1993) *Public Law* 449, 452ff; Paul Mitchell, 'Book Review: Political Libels: A Comparative Study by Ian Loveland' (2000) *King's College Law Journal* 263; David Feldman, 'Publication Review: *Political Libels: A Comparative Study* by Ian Loveland' (2001) *Public Law* 432.

[3] *Sullivan* (n 1). See Anthony Lewis, *Make No Law: The Sullivan Case and the First Amendment* (New York, Vintage Books, 1991).

[4] *Sullivan* (n 1) 257.

[5] *Sullivan* (n 1) 260, fn 3.

Mr Sullivan predictably made no effort to prove special damages. The Circuit Court, Montgomery County, nonetheless entered judgment in his favour for $500,000, a considerable sum upheld on appeal. *The New York Times* was granted *certiorari* by the US Supreme Court.

The first evidence of undertheorising in *Sullivan* is revealed by the Supreme Court's overview of free speech arguments under the First Amendment. The Court's analysis began with the basic proposition that 'freedom of expression upon public questions is secured by the First Amendment [...]'.[6] This constitutional guarantee was supported by two arguments, one pragmatic, and the other based on the 'marketplace of ideas' metaphor. Appealing to the latter, Justice Brennan quoted Judge Learned Hand's ruling that the First Amendment

> presupposes that right conclusions are more likely to be gathered out of a multitude of tongues, than through any kind of authoritative selection. To many this is, and always will be, folly; but we have staked upon it our all.[7]

Founding the First Amendment also on civic virtue and stable government, Justice Brennan quoted Justice Brandeis' concurring opinion in *Whitney v California*:[8]

> Those who won our independence believed [...] that *public discussion is a political duty*; and that this should be a fundamental principle of the American government. [...] But they knew that order cannot be secured merely through fear of punishment for its infraction; that it is hazardous to discourage thought, hope and imagination; that fear breeds repression; that repression breeds hate; that hate menaces stable government; that *the path of safety lies in the opportunity to discuss freely supposed grievances and proposed remedies*; and that the fitting remedy for evil counsels is good ones [...].[9]

Yet despite relying on civic virtue, political stability, and the traditional 'truth-finding' justification, none of Justice Brennan's opening remarks foreshadowed his subsequent statements on the right of Americans to criticise public officials. Consequently, it was striking when, at its outset, his judgment affirmed the nation's commitment to freedom of expression in these celebrated words:

> Thus we consider this case against the background of a profound national commitment to the principle that debate on public issues should be *uninhibited, robust, and wide-open*, and that it may well include *vehement, caustic, and sometimes unpleasantly sharp attacks on government and public officials.*[10]

The US Supreme Court then considered whether the disputed advertisement 'forfeits that protection by the falsity of some of its factual statements and by its alleged defamation of respondent'.[11] In doing so, the Court implicitly referenced

[6] *Sullivan* (n 1) 269.
[7] *Sullivan* (n 1) 270, citing *United States v Associated Press* 52 F Supp 362, 372 (SDNY 1943).
[8] 274 US 357 (1927).
[9] *Sullivan* (n 1) 270 (emphasis added), citing *Whitney*, ibid 375–76.
[10] *Sullivan* (n 1) 270 (emphasis added).
[11] *Sullivan* (n 1) 271.

the checking function through a series of ad hoc arguments reflecting only a portion of its constitutive premises.

First addressing factual errors, Justice Brennan rejected the constraint of 'truth' (and implicitly the defence of justification) as a prerequisite for constitutional protection, accepting that 'erroneous statement is *inevitable* in free debate [...].[12] Calling to mind the perils of seditious libel upheld in *Tuchin's* case, Justice Brennan alternatively quoted Judge Edgerton of the Court of Appeal for the District of Columbia Circuit, who insisted that '[c]ases which impose liability for erroneous reports of the political conduct of officials reflect the obsolete doctrine that *the governed must not criticize their governors*'.[13]

The Court similarly held that reputational error '[...] affords no more warrant for repressing speech that would otherwise be free than does factual error'.[14] Justice Brennan analogised defamation actions to contempt of court proceedings, where 'concern for the dignity and reputation of the courts does not justify the punishment [...] of criticism of the judge or his decision [...]'.[15] But instead of relying on the 'clear and present danger' test to justify such censure,[16] Justice Brennan appealed to concerns broadly consistent with the checking function of the press, noting of America's judges that '[c]riticism of their official conduct does not lose its constitutional protection merely because it is effective criticism and hence diminishes their official reputations'.[17]

Most importantly, Justice Brennan concluded that the *combination* of factual and reputational error was insufficient 'to remove the constitutional shield from criticism of official conduct'.[18] Endorsing arguments in *The New York Times'* legal brief prepared by Columbia Law Professor Herbert Wechsler,[19] the Court summoned the spirit of the checking function by analogising Alabama's libel law to the Sedition Act of 1798. Justice Brennan quoted the Virginia Resolution of 1798, where the General Assembly denounced the Sedition Act as exercising a power '[...] which, more than any other, ought to produce universal alarm, because it is levelled against the right of freely examining *public characters and measures* [...]'.[20] Endorsing James Madison's argument that differences between British and American governments necessitated greater press liberty in the United States, Justice Brennan also approved his broad description of American press freedom: '[i]n every state, probably, in the Union, the press has exerted a freedom in canvassing the merits and measures of public men, [...] which has not been confined to the strict limits of the common law'.[21]

12 *Sullivan* (n 1) 271 (emphasis added).
13 *Sullivan* (n 1) 272 (emphasis added), citing *Sweeney v Patterson* 128 F2d 457, 458 (1942).
14 *Sullivan* (n 1) 272.
15 *Sullivan* (n 1) 272–73.
16 *Sullivan* (n 1) 273.
17 *Sullivan* (n 1) 273.
18 *Sullivan* (n 1) 273.
19 Brief for Petitioner at 45ff, 376 US 254 (1964) (WL 105891).
20 *Sullivan* (n 1) 274 (emphasis added).
21 *Sullivan* (n 1) 275.

The US Supreme Court therefore held that the fundamental basis of the First Amendment involved using the Sedition Act as a constitutional touchstone: '[w]hat a State may not constitutionally bring about by means of a criminal statute is likewise *beyond the reach of its civil law of libel*'.[22] In support, Justice Brennan correctly observed that common law damages 'may be markedly more inhibiting than the fear of prosecution under a criminal statute'.[23] Offering a convincing example, he emphasised that '[t]he judgment awarded in this case—without the need for any proof of actual pecuniary loss—was *one thousand times* greater than the maximum fine provided by the Alabama criminal statute, and *one hundred times* greater than that provided by the Sedition Act'.[24]

Perhaps the most compelling evidence of undertheorising in *Sullivan* was the Court's lack of theoretical support for its own doctrinal selection. Adopting a categorical, plaintiff-tailored approach founded in English common law and endorsed by a minority of US states in the late nineteenth century,[25] Justice Brennan declared a 'new' constitutional privilege prohibiting a public official from recovering damages for defamatory statements relating to official conduct 'unless he proves that the statement was made with "actual malice"—that is, with knowledge that it was false or with reckless disregard of whether it was false or not'.[26] Without such protection, '[i]t would give public servants an unjustified preference over the public they serve', due to the absolute privilege they enjoy 'within the outer perimeter' of their duties.[27] No analysis of doctrinal alternatives was provided by Justice Brennan's majority judgment.

Applying this enhanced constitutional protection for 'political speech' to the facts at hand, the Court accordingly rejected Mr Sullivan's attempt to satisfy defamation law's 'of and concerning' requirement by relying on his role as City Commissioner. Implicitly relying on the checking function rationale, Justice Brennan reproached:

> For good reason, 'no court of last resort in this country has ever held, or even suggested, that prosecutions for libel on government have any place in the American system of jurisprudence.' *The present proposition would sidestep this obstacle by transmuting criticism of government, however impersonal it may seem on its face, into personal criticism, and hence potential libel, of the officials of whom the government is composed.*[28]

Compared to the majority, the checking function was raised more explicitly in dissenting judgments by Justices Black and Goldberg.[29] From the outset, both

[22] *Sullivan* (n 1) 277 (emphasis added).
[23] *Sullivan* (n 1) 277.
[24] *Sullivan* (n 1) 277 (emphasis added).
[25] See George Chase, 'Criticism of Public Officers and Candidates for Office' (1889) 23 *American Law Review* 346; Van Vechten Veeder, 'Freedom of Public Discussion' (1910) 23 *Harvard Law Review* 413; John E Hallen, 'Fair Comment' (1929) 8 *Texas Law Review* 41. See also Loveland (n 1).
[26] *Sullivan* (n 1) 279–80.
[27] *Sullivan* (n 1) 282.
[28] *Sullivan* (n 1) 291–92 (emphasis added).
[29] Justices Black and Goldberg wrote concurring opinions in which Justice Douglas joined.

stressed the inevitability of underprotecting speech critical of public officials under the 'actual malice' rule. Justice Black voted to reverse because of his conviction that newspapers 'had an absolute, unconditional constitutional right to publish [...] their criticisms of the Montgomery agencies and officials'.[30] Describing the 'actual malice' rule as a 'stopgap measure',[31] he implored the Court to '[...] more faithfully interpret the First Amendment by holding that at the very least it leaves the people and the press free to criticize officials and discuss public affairs *with impunity*'.[32]

Justice Goldberg agreed, adding that '[i]n a democratic society, one who assumes to act for the citizens in an executive, legislative, *or judicial capacity* must expect that his official acts will be commented upon and criticized'.[33] He shared the Court's concern that if public servants enjoy absolute immunity, then citizens and the press 'should likewise be immune from libel actions for their criticism of official conduct'.[34] But in a clever forensic turn, Justice Goldberg supported an unconditional right to criticise public officials by equating government criticism with the officeholders themselves, stating:

> In a democratic society where men are free by ballots to remove those in power, *any statement critical of governmental action is necessarily 'of and concerning' the governors and any statement critical of the governors' official conduct is necessarily 'of and concerning' the government.* If the rule that libel on government has no place in our Constitution is to have real meaning, then libel on the *official conduct* of the governors likewise can have no place in our Constitution.[35]

In many ways, *Sullivan* was significant not so much for what the Court declared by announcing a constitutional standard for defamatory falsehoods of public officials, but what it did not say. Despite the importance of the Sedition Act of 1798 to the Court's reasoning, the underpinnings to Justice Brennan's opinion were comparatively meagre in a case of such massive doctrinal sweep. The majority's reluctance to answer Justices Black and Goldberg not only weakened the ratio, but raised the early spectre of underprotecting political speech, and confronted whether the outer limit of doctrinal accommodation for public libels was properly fixed with the 'actual malice' rule. Unfortunately, subsequent confusion in expanding *Sullivan* to criminal and private libels only further exposed the limitations in the Court's theoretical footing for the 'actual malice' rule, and cast further doubt on the checking function's notional role in *Sullivan*.[36]

[30] *Sullivan* (n 1) 293.
[31] *Sullivan* (n 1) 295.
[32] *Sullivan* (n 1) 296 (emphasis added).
[33] *Sullivan* (n 1) 299 (emphasis added).
[34] *Sullivan* (n 1) 304.
[35] *Sullivan* (n 1) 299 (emphasis added).
[36] In *Rosenblatt v Baer* 383 US 75 (1966), 'public officials' were defined as 'those among the hierarchy of government employees who have, or appear to the public to have, substantial responsibility for or control over the conduct of governmental affairs' (ibid 85). Notably, 'public officials' include political

ii. Criminal Libels

In *Garrison v Louisiana*,[37] the US Supreme Court held that the 'actual malice' rule '[...] also limits state power to impose *criminal sanctions* for criticism of the official conduct of public officials'.[38] *Garrison* not only provides strong evidence of undertheorising of the checking function, but implicitly weakens its case as *Sullivan's* controlling rationale.

Garrison involved the District Attorney of Orleans Parish, Louisiana, who was charged with criminal libel for disparaging public remarks directed at eight judges. Justice Brennan, for the majority, purported to rely on the *Sullivan* rationale, stating:

> The New York Times rule is not rendered inapplicable merely because an official's private reputation, as well as his public reputation, is harmed. *The public-official rule protects the paramount public interest in a free flow of information to the people concerning public officials, their servants.* To this end, anything which might touch on an official's fitness for office is relevant. Few personal attributes are more germane to fitness for office than *dishonesty, malfeasance, or improper motivation*, even though these characteristics may also affect the official's private character.[39]

But Justice Brennan soon afterwards misstepped, contending that '[t]he reasons which led us so to hold in New York Times [...] apply with no less force *merely because the remedy is criminal*'.[40] Without acknowledging the checking function's historical connection to criminal defamation cases, he concluded: '[w]here criticism of public officials is concerned, we see no merit in the argument that criminal libel statutes serve interests distinct from those secured by civil libel laws, and therefore should not be subject to the same limitations'.[41]

Focusing more convincingly on the checking function, Justice Black (concurring in the result) reminded Americans that '[f]ining men or sending them to jail for criticizing public officials not only jeopardizes the free, open public discussion which our Constitution guarantees, but can wholly stifle it'.[42] Properly associating criminal defamation laws with seditious libel, he insisted that 'under our Constitution there is absolutely no place [...] for the old, discredited English Star Chamber law of seditious criminal libel'.[43] Justice Douglas added that '[...] seditious libel was "entirely the creation of the Star Chamber." It is disquieting to know that one of its instruments of destruction is abroad in the land today'.[44] Justice Goldberg

candidates (*Monitor Patriot Co v Roy* 401 US 265 (1971)), and law enforcement officials (*Time, Incorporated v Pape* 401 US 279 (1971)).

37 379 US 64 (1964).
38 ibid 67 (emphasis added).
39 ibid 77 (emphasis added).
40 ibid 74 (citation omitted) (emphasis added).
41 ibid 67.
42 ibid 80.
43 ibid.
44 ibid 83 (citations omitted).

also concluded that applying civil or criminal sanctions to commentary about public officials violates the First Amendment.[45]

That the majority did not recognise the relevance of the '*Sullivan* rationale' to criminal libels is compelling evidence of undertheorising of the checking function of the press. By adopting the 'actual malice' rule without considering the checking function's broader historical context, *Garrison* potentially underprotects speech critical of public officials that is actionable under state criminal law. This confusion has only intensified when determining constitutional standards for 'public figures' and 'private individuals'.

iii. Public Figures

Undertheorising of the checking function was particularly evident in *Curtis Publishing Co v Butts*,[46] where the US Supreme Court missed significant opportunities to formulate distinct constitutional standards reflecting the degrees to which libel plaintiffs engage accountability concerns and the checking function of the press.

Curtis actually involved two actions. The first stemmed from a newspaper article accusing Wally Butts, the University of Georgia's athletic director, of fixing a college football game. Butts was employed by a private corporation, rather than by the state of Georgia. The United States Court of Appeals for the Fifth Circuit affirmed the trial Court's judgment for the plaintiff of $460,000. The second action arose from a news dispatch describing a riot at the University of Mississippi. The dispatch reported that retired Major General Edwin Walker had commanded a violent crowd and attacked federal marshals sent to enforce a court order to enrol an African American student. It also described Walker as encouraging violence and advising rioters on defending tear gas attacks. The Texas Court of Civil Appeals affirmed the trial Court's award of $500,000 damages for Walker.

The Court recognised in *Curtis* '[p]owerful arguments [...] for the extension of the *New York Times* rule in both cases'.[47] Although Justice Harlan announced the results, a fragmented majority agreed with Chief Justice Warren that the 'actual malice' rule applied to 'public figures'.[48] The diverse rationales expressed in *Curtis* suggest difficulties theorising and applying the checking function rationale. For instance, Justice Harlan struggled to reconcile the material facts with *Sullivan*, concluding that '[t]hese actions cannot be analogized to prosecutions for seditious libel'.[49] Endorsing a less onerous gross negligence standard, he restricted

[45] ibid 88.

[46] 388 US 130 (1967).

[47] ibid 146.

[48] Only three others accepted Justice Harlan's analysis (Justices Clark, Stewart, and Fortas). Justices White and Brennan agreed with Chief Justice Warren's application of *Sullivan* to 'public figures'. Justices Black and Douglas joined the Chief Justice's reasoning to assure a majority.

[49] *Curtis* (n 46) 154.

recoverability to '[...] a showing of highly unreasonable conduct constituting an extreme departure from the standards of investigation and reporting ordinarily adhered to by responsible publishers.[50]

Discarding Justice Harlan's approach, Chief Justice Warren maintained that 'differentiation between "public figures" and "public officials" and adoption of separate standards of proof for each have no basis in law, logic, or First Amendment policy'.[51] He reasoned that public figures' views and actions '[...] are often of as much concern to the citizen as the attitudes and behavior of "public officials" [...]'.[52] Although overstating matters at the outset, the Chief Justice provided a convincing rationale for treating at least *some* public figures the same as public officials in restricting recovery for defamatory falsehoods:

> *Increasingly in this country, the distinctions between governmental and private sectors are blurred.* [...] In many situations, policy determinations which traditionally were channeled through formal political institutions are now originated and implemented through a complex array of boards, committees, commissions, corporations, and associations, some only loosely connected with the Government. *This blending of positions and power has also occurred in the case of individuals* so that many who do not hold public office at the moment are nevertheless intimately involved in the resolution of important public questions or, by reason of their fame, shape events in areas of concern to society at large.[53]

Implicating concerns with democratic accountability and the checking function, Chief Justice Warren reasoned that

> [t]he fact that they are not amenable to the restraints of the political process only underscores the legitimate and substantial nature of the interest, since it means that *public opinion* may be the *only instrument* by which society can attempt to influence their conduct.[54]

The public accordingly has an interest in checking some 'public figures' that is potentially greater than for public officials.

While the Court endorsed the 'actual malice' rule by a narrow 5–4 majority,[55] this split was attributable to an unsophisticated and overbroad application of the checking function rationale. Where Justice Harlan recognised potential doctrinal incoherence for those public figures who do not analogise to 'government officials', Chief Justice Warren provided a convincing rationale (based on the checking function) for treating *some* public figures the same as public officials. However, by extending the 'actual malice' rule without reflecting these concerns in separate doctrinal approaches, *Curtis* arguably overprotects speech defamatory of 'public figures' who do not engage the same concerns about government corruption and misconduct as public officials do.

[50] *Curtis* (n 46) 155.
[51] *Curtis* (n 46) 163.
[52] *Curtis* (n 46) 162.
[53] *Curtis* (n 46) 163–64 (emphasis added).
[54] *Curtis* (n 46) 164 (emphasis added).
[55] *Curtis* (n 46) 165.

iv. Private Individuals

Division as to the meaning and scope of *Sullivan* deepened further when deciding the constitutional standard for private libels. The Court's first (and unsuccessful) attempt was in *Rosenbloom v Metromedia, Inc.*[56]

In *Rosenbloom*, a Philadelphia pornography merchant was arrested for selling obscene material. After police impounded his inventory, Mr Rosenbloom sought and obtained an injunction prohibiting further interference. He then brought suit against a radio station for its coverage of the police crackdown and the plaintiff's injunction proceedings, which described Rosenbloom as a 'girlie-book peddler' and reported on his involvement in the 'smut literature racket'. The District Court for the Eastern District of Pennsylvania held that *Sullivan* did not apply, and awarded $25,000 general damages and $250,000 punitive damages. The Court of Appeals for the Third Circuit held that *Sullivan* did apply, and reversed.

Although the US Supreme Court affirmed in a 5–3 decision, no controlling rationale emerged. Eight Justices wrote five opinions, none receiving more than three votes. The opinions differed not only in result, but methodologically. Each evidenced growing confusion over the relevance and application of the checking function, principally Justice Brennan's plurality opinion (Blackmun J and Burger CJ concurring) which, by further extending the 'actual malice' rule to private libels, effectively shielded the radio station from liability.

Justice Brennan's plurality opinion offered a novel gloss on *Sullivan* by guaranteeing constitutional protection to statements of 'general or public concern'. Subtly shifting theoretical emphasis, he stated: '[w]e honor the commitment to robust debate on *public issues*, [...] by extending constitutional protection to all discussion and communication involving matters of *public or general concern*, without regard to whether the persons involved are famous or anonymous'.[57] In support, Justice Brennan appealed indirectly to free expression rationales, noting that the issue of private libels '[...] must be answered against the background of *the functions* of the constitutional guarantees for freedom of expression'.[58]

Despite appealing to 'methodological rigour', Justice Brennan only confused matters by de-emphasising the checking function of the press, insisting that '[t]he guarantees for speech and press are not the preserve of political expression or comment upon public affairs'.[59] Distancing *Sullivan* from the Sedition Act of 1798, Justice Brennan insisted that press freedom was supported by rationales *other* than the checking function, including a conviction by the Founding Fathers '[...] that a free press would advance "truth, science, morality, and arts in general" as well as responsible government'.[60] According to this view, the First

[56] 403 US 29 (1971).
[57] ibid 43–44 (emphasis added).
[58] ibid 41 (emphasis added).
[59] ibid (citation omitted).
[60] ibid 42, quoting *Curtis* (n 46) 147.

Amendment extends to 'myriad matters of public interest' that '[...] cannot suddenly become less so merely because a private individual is involved'.[61]

Justice Harlan (dissenting), by contrast, sought greater legal protections for private individuals (including Mr Rosenbloom) by varying constitutional protection based on plaintiff status. Although finally acquiescing in the 'actual malice' rule for public figures, he insisted on a different legal rule for private libels. Appealing implicitly to the checking function, Justice Harlan reasoned that private individuals require greater constitutional protection because: (1) a 'public person has a greater likelihood of securing access to channels of communication sufficient to rebut falsehoods concerning him than do private individuals [...]'; and (2) 'public personalities [...] may be held to have *run the risk of publicly circulated falsehoods*' in a manner not shared by private individuals.[62] He accordingly concluded: '[...] States should be free to define for themselves the applicable standard of care so long as they do not impose liability without fault'.[63]

Justice Harlan also sought methodological rigour, advising: '[i]n analyzing these problems it is necessary to begin with a *general analytical framework* that defines those *competing interests* that must be reconciled'.[64] But instead of specifying recognised freedom of expression justifications, he obliquely referenced only 'First Amendment values',[65] 'special countervailing interests',[66] and an indefinite hope of '[a] more particularized inquiry into the nature of the competing interests involved [...]'.[67] Therefore, besides broader concerns with undertheorising and obscuring *Sullivan's* meaning and application, the Court's immediate problem after *Rosenbloom* was attaining consensus for its doctrinal approach to private libels.

The US Supreme Court returned to these problems in *Gertz v Robert Welch Inc*,[68] admitting it had 'struggled for nearly a decade to define the proper accommodation between the law of defamation and the freedoms of speech and press protected by the First Amendment'.[69] *Gertz* involved a murder trial of a Chicago policeman. The victim's family hired an attorney in civil proceedings against the accused. An article in the defendant's magazine alleged that the murder trial was part of a Communist conspiracy against local police, describing the attorney as a 'Communist-fronter', 'Leninist', and participant in 'Marxist' and 'Red' activities. The attorney sued for defamation. The US District Court for the Northern District of Illinois ruled that *Sullivan* applied even though the plaintiff was not a 'public figure', a decision affirmed by the Seventh Circuit Court of Appeals.

61 ibid 43.
62 ibid 70 (emphasis added).
63 ibid 64.
64 ibid 65 (emphasis added).
65 ibid 63, 66, 72.
66 ibid 67.
67 ibid 73.
68 418 US 323 (1974).
69 ibid 325.

Justice Powell delivered the majority opinion. Preferring a categorical rule to ad hoc balancing, he had 'no difficulty in distinguishing among defamation plaintiffs'.[70] Accepting that '[p]ublic officials and public figures usually enjoy significantly greater access to the channels of effective communication',[71] Justice Powell concluded that '[p]rivate individuals are therefore more vulnerable to injury, and the state interest in protecting them is correspondingly greater'.[72] Adopting Justice Harlan's reasoning in *Rosenbloom*, he also noted 'there is a compelling *normative* consideration underlying the distinction between public and private defamation plaintiffs'[73] as a public official or figure '[...] runs the risk of *closer public scrutiny* than might otherwise be the case'.[74]

While admitting that public figures might 'stand in a similar position' to public officials, the Court differentiated private individuals, who have '[...] a more compelling call on the courts for redress of injury inflicted by defamatory falsehood'.[75] Justice Powell accordingly rejected strict liability principles and endorsed the following standard: '[w]e hold that, so long as they do not impose *liability without fault*, the States may define for themselves the appropriate standard of liability for a publisher or broadcaster of defamatory falsehood injurious to a private individual'.[76] The Court favoured this compromise as '[i]t recognizes the strength of the legitimate state interest in compensating private individuals for wrongful injury to reputation, yet shields the press and broadcast media from the rigors of strict liability for defamation'.[77]

Although the checking function was implicit in Justice Powell's reasoning, his opinion exhibited significant undertheorising. Explaining his decision to impose a more demanding standard on publishers, Justice Powell noted:

> This conclusion is not based on a belief that *the considerations* which prompted the adoption of the *New York Times* privilege for defamation of public officials and its extension to public figures are *wholly inapplicable to the context of private individuals*. Rather, we endorse this approach in recognition of the strong and legitimate state interest in compensating private individuals for injury to reputation.[78]

However, omitted from the first sentence were 'the considerations' and their impact on offsetting reputation. Given the importance of the Sedition Act of 1798 to *Sullivan*, it arguably would have been more accurate to state that the different constitutional standard adopted for private individuals is justified precisely because the checking function was comparatively immaterial to private libels, resulting in reputation weighing more decisively in the choice of doctrinal approach.

[70] ibid 344.
[71] ibid.
[72] ibid.
[73] ibid (emphasis added).
[74] ibid (emphasis added).
[75] ibid 345.
[76] ibid 347 (emphasis added).
[77] ibid 348.
[78] ibid (emphasis added).

Dissenting opinions in *Gertz* displayed similar confusion. As in *Rosenbloom*, Justice Brennan insisted that *Sullivan* applied to private individuals involving events of 'public or general interest'. His primary disagreement with the majority was that Justice Powell's argument that private individuals do not invite increased defamation risk '[...] "bears little relationship either to *the values* protected by the First Amendment or to the nature of our society"'.[79] However, this statement neglects *Sullivan's* consistency with the checking function and otherwise makes little sense. By not as strongly engaging the checking function in private libels, the relationship of free expression values with reputational interests necessarily changes in favour of constitutional standards more protective of the latter. Moreover, the disquieting implication of Justice Brennan's criticism is the possibility that the checking function was never intended as *Sullivan's* defining free expression rationale. The more likely (and sensible) explanation is that Justice Brennan simply struggled with an undertheorised account of the checking function, and consequent doctrinal confusion as to the correct use of the 'actual malice' rule in distinct public and private libel contexts.

Justice Brennan's reasons for judgment in *Rosenbloom* further reveals this confusion, where he stated:

> [t]he *New York Times* standard was applied to libel of a public official or public figure to give effect to the [First] Amendment's function *to encourage ventilation of public issues*, not because the public official has any less interest in protecting his reputation than an individual in private life.[80]

With respect, Justice Brennan's conclusion to prioritise freedom of expression and the press more than the majority in private libel cases depends on *disregarding* the relative impact of the checking function in both contexts. As Justice Powell recognised, it is reasonable to adopt a less protective standard for publishers in private defamation cases precisely because of the relative insignificance of the checking function to the Court's task of balancing competing interests.

Similar theoretical confusion compromised Justice White's dissenting opinion. But where Justice Brennan overlooked the *context* of the checking function, Justice White analysed it too restrictively. Conceding that '[t]he central meaning of *New York Times* [...] is that seditious libel—criticism of government and public officials—falls beyond the police power of the State',[81] he struggled to comprehend the Court's rationale for the 'sweeping changes' that '[...] deprive the private citizen of his historic recourse to redress published falsehoods damaging to reputation [...]'.[82] Attributing this to the Court's readiness 'to sacrifice good sense to syllogism' and 'to find in the *New York Times* doctrine an infinite elasticity [...]',[83]

[79] ibid 364, quoting *Rosenbloom* (n 56) 47 (emphasis added).
[80] ibid 363 (citation omitted) (emphasis added).
[81] ibid 387.
[82] ibid.
[83] ibid 399, quoting Oliver Wendell Holmes Jr, *The Common Law* (Boston, Little, Brown 1881) 36.

Justice White failed to appreciate that concerns with 'self-censorship' and 'libel chill' also engage the checking function's more foundational aim of maintaining an independent and adversarial press. Simply because *Sullivan* underscored the press' role in checking official misconduct, it does not follow that balancing competing values in private libels cannot or should not include the checking function's more basic requirements and concerns.

B. Conclusion

At last, theoretical confusion persisting after *Sullivan* has not only left its underlying rationale and association with the checking function unclear, but also raises questions about whether the 'actual malice' rule is a sound doctrinal approach to public libels. As demonstrated by the Court's First Amendment libel decisions, speech will be unintentionally over and underprotected when the checking function is not precisely theorised, considered, and applied. This undertheorising demonstrates that the checking function is not performing its intended role, and hints as to why *Sullivan* has been summarily rejected around the world.

II. Australia

Australia was our first comparator to modernise its defamation laws post-*Sullivan* by expanding qualified privilege for communications regarding 'political and government matters', and by importing a 'reasonableness' criterion into its defence.[84] However, the theoretical foundation to its 'responsible journalism' defence remains unclear.[85] By discounting free expression justifications and purporting to derive implied freedoms from highly abstract constitutional principles such as the 'efficacious working of representative democracy', Australian courts have replaced longstanding theoretical justifications with a poorly articulated and methodologically questionable approach.

[84] See *Lange v Australian Broadcasting Corporation* (1997) 189 CLR 520 (HCA). Although the Australian High Court attributed importing its 'reasonableness' criterion to the Defamation Act 1974 No 18 (NSW) s 22, this idea was expressed earlier in the Defamation (Amendment) Act 1909 No 22 (NSW) s 6. I am indebted to Professor Eric Descheemaeker for explaining this during his lecture titled 'The *Reynolds* Privilege: Its Origins and Theoretical Significance' at Corpus Christi College, Oxford, on 23 May 2013.

[85] See generally Tom D Campbell, 'Democracy, Human Rights, and Positive Law' (1994) 16 *Sydney Law Review* 195; Andrew Fraser, 'False Hopes: Implied Rights and Popular Sovereignty in the Australian Constitution' (1994) 16 *Sydney Law Review* 213. See also Adrienne Stone, 'The Limits of Constitutional Text and Structure: Standards of Review and the Freedom of Political Communication' (1999) 23 *Melbourne University Law Review* 668; Dan Meagher, 'What is "Political Communication"? The Rationale and Scope of the Implied Freedom of Political Communication' (2004) 28 *Melbourne University Law Review* 438.

Most importantly, by overlooking the checking function of the press, Australia has underprotected media defendants and methodologically barred itself from tailoring public libel principles to its institutional setting. This outcome is intensified by the High Court's comparative law error of mechanically importing Canada's pre-Charter 'implied rights' jurisprudence. It thus remains an open question as to how long the High Court of Australia can persist in the misapprehension that its implied rights methodology is preferable to alternatives based on a comprehensive consideration of relevant free expression rationales.

A. Implied Rights: Disavowing Free Speech Theory

Australia's implied 'freedom of political expression' originated in a succession of interstate trade and commerce cases in the High Court, which developed from initially protecting 'freedom of movement of commercial goods', to later safeguarding 'freedom of speech and other communications'.[86]

Building on *Buck v Bavone*[87] and *Ansett Transport Industries (Operations) Pty Ltd v The Commonwealth*,[88] a suitably robust implied rights model was first conveyed in *McGraw-Hinds (Aust) Pty Ltd v Smith*.[89] *McGraw* involved a constitutional challenge to section 8 of Queensland's Unordered Goods and Services Act 1973, which targeted a well-known commercial fraud. The ruse involved distributing invoices asserting a right to payment for an unordered directory, or stated in misleading or deceptive terms calculated to trick recipients into believing such a right existed. The defendant imprudently sent such a document to the Queensland Government Tourist Bureau. Surprisingly (at least on the facts), the High Court of Australia granted the corporate defendant's appeal. But rather than invalidating the offence as an unjustified restraint on interstate commerce, Justice Murphy appealed to an implied 'freedom of communication' derived from the Australian Constitution and the Supreme Court of Canada's pre-Charter implied rights jurisprudence.

Insisting that '[t]he Australian Constitution does not express all that is intended by it: much of the greatest importance is implied',[90] Justice Murphy explained that '[b]ecause of the brevity of constitutions, implications are a prominent feature in the history of their interpretation'.[91] Along with responsible government, freedom of movement, the rule of law, and the prohibition of slavery or serfdom, 'freedom of communication' was added as an implied constitutional guarantee. Citing the

[86] See *Buck v Bavone* (1976) 135 CLR 110 (HCA); *Ansett Transport Industries (Operations) Pty Ltd v The Commonwealth* (1977) 139 CLR 54 (HCA); *McGraw-Hinds (Aust) Pty Ltd v Smith* (1979) 144 CLR 633 (HCA); *Miller v TCN Channel Nine Pty Ltd* (1986) 161 CLR 556 (HCA).

[87] *Buck*, ibid.

[88] *Ansett* (n 86).

[89] *McGraw* (n 86).

[90] *McGraw* (n 86) 667.

[91] *McGraw* (n 86) 667.

Supreme Court of Canada, Justice Murphy reasoned that '[...] from the nature of our society, reinforced by parts of the written text, an implication arises that there is to be freedom of movement and freedom of communication. [F]reedom of communication [is] indispensable to any free society'.[92] Although eventually recognising more precisely that '[t]he Constitution [...] contains implied guarantees of *freedom of speech and other communications*',[93] a distinct feature of Justice Murphy's implied rights doctrine was its disregard of free speech theory.

This theoretical indifference compromised the High Court's landmark decisions in *Nationwide News Pty Ltd v Wills*[94] and *Australian Capital Television (ACTV) Pty Ltd v The Commonwealth*,[95] where an implied right of 'free communication about matters relating to the Commonwealth government' was first recognised. In *Nationwide News*, a media defendant was charged, under subsection 299(1)(d)(ii) of Australia's Industrial Relations Act 1988, with disparaging a member of its Industrial Relations Commission. While not sounding in defamation, the right to criticise government and public officials was directly before the Court. Despite containing a disconcerting plurality of six judgments, as with earlier interstate trade and commerce cases, common to each was: (1) a lack of explicit consideration of free expression justifications; and (2) a failure to distinguish the checking function from Meiklejohnian theory.

Particularly illustrative was Justice Brennan's judgment. After briefly mentioning democratic accountability, which involved making 'both the legislative and executive branches [...] ultimately answerable to the Australian people',[96] concern shifted quickly to examining the 'legal incidents' of representative democracy. Quoting Justice McIntyre of the Supreme Court of Canada in *RWDSU, Local 580 v Dolphin Delivery*,[97] the checking function was effectively marginalised by adopting the following abstract passage exalting the relationship between democracy and free expression: '[r]epresentative democracy, as we know it today, which is in great part the product of *free expression and discussion of varying ideas*, depends upon its maintenance and protection'.[98] Shifting theoretical emphasis from accountability to deliberative concerns, this highly ambiguous statement all but guaranteed that the checking function would not feature in the High Court's analysis.

Confirming that 'there is no *right* to free discussion of government' under the Australian Constitution,[99] Justice Brennan nonetheless sought refuge in the Court's implied rights doctrine. Namely, that '[o]nce it is recognized that a representative democracy is constitutionally prescribed, *the freedom of discussion which is essential to sustain it* is as firmly entrenched in the Constitution as the system

92 *McGraw* (n 86) 670.
93 See *Miller* (n 86) 582 (Murphy J) (emphasis added).
94 (1992) 177 CLR 1 (HCA).
95 (1992) 177 CLR 106 (HCA).
96 *Nationwide News* (n 94) 47.
97 [1986] 2 SCR 573.
98 *Nationwide News* (n 94) 48 (emphasis added).
99 *Nationwide News* (n 94) 48 (emphasis in original).

of government which the Constitution expressly ordains'.[100] Although of intuitive appeal, this constitutional declaration again begged the question. No account of the relationship between 'representative democracy' and free expression was proffered.

Justice Brennan did, however, attempt to support Australia's implied 'freedom of communication' by citing the Supreme Court of Canada's decision in *Alberta Legislation*,[101] arguing analogically that 'the representative democracy ordained by our Constitution carries with it a comparable freedom for the Australian people [...]'.[102] Describing this implied freedom in distinctly Meiklejohnian terms, he added:

> [...] the Constitution prohibits any legislative or executive infringement of the freedom to discuss governments and governmental institutions and political matters *except to the extent necessary* to protect other legitimate interests and, in any event, not to an extent which substantially impairs the capacity of, or opportunity for, the Australian people *to form the political judgments required for the exercise of their constitutional functions.*[103]

Besides providing no evaluative criteria for determining what is 'necessary' for protecting these 'other legitimate interests', Justice Brennan's concern with 'political discussion' was expressed disproportionately in electoral terms.[104] More worrying still, after endorsing traditional defamation principles and criminal sedition laws without engaging in free speech theorising or appealing to any external criterion, Justice Brennan concluded implausibly that such dated regulatory methods '[...] *strike an appropriate balance* between the postulated freedom of discussion and the private or public interest which is protected by the curtailing of the freedom'.[105] If nothing else, a methodologically astounding result.

Such concerns were also reflected in the joint reasons for judgment of Justices Deane and Toohey. Both endorsed an inelegantly-phrased implied 'freedom of communication of information and opinions about matters relating to the government of the Commonwealth',[106] which was again captured in electoral terminology:

> *The actual discharge of the very function of voting in an election or referendum involves communication.* An ability to vote *intelligently* can exist only if the identity of the candidates for election or the content of a proposed law submitted for the decision of the people at a referendum can be communicated to the voter.[107]

[100] *Nationwide News* (n 94) 48–49 (emphasis added).
[101] *Nationwide News* (n 94) 49–52.
[102] *Nationwide News* (n 94) 50.
[103] *Nationwide News* (n 94) 50–51 (emphasis added).
[104] Justice Brennan later reiterated '*[t]he freedom relevant to this case* is a freedom among the governed to perform the function and to exercise the privileges possessed by the people in a representative democracy' (*Nationwide News* (n 94) 60) (emphasis added).
[105] *Nationwide News* (n 94) 52 (emphasis added).
[106] *Nationwide News* (n 94) 73.
[107] *Nationwide News* (n 94) 72 (emphasis added).

Joining issue with Justice Brennan, Deane and Toohey JJ also presumed that *Alberta Legislation* was '*equally applicable* to the working of the doctrine of representative government embodied in our Constitution'.[108] Quite aside from ignoring constitutional and institutional differences between Canada and Australia, no appeal to free expression justifications or external theorising was made.

These methodological concerns also beset *ACTV*,[109] which involved challenges to a federal statutory prohibition on political advertising. A majority of the High Court invalidated the legislation for infringing an implied 'freedom of communication on matters relevant to political discussion'.[110] Although the majority's analysis paralleled *Nationwide News*, Chief Justice Mason delivered an instructive concurring opinion. Perpetuating the same radically undertheorised approach, the Chief Justice accepted the media plaintiffs' argument that 'freedom of expression in relation to public and political affairs' must be implied from Australia's 'system of representative government',[111] advising:

> The very concept of representative government and representative democracy signifies government by the people through their representatives. Translated into constitutional terms, it denotes that *the sovereign power which resides in the people is exercised on their behalf by their representatives.* [...] And in the exercise of those powers the representatives of necessity are *accountable to the people for what they do* and have a responsibility to *take account of the views of the people* on whose behalf they act.[112]

Despite more capably engaging accountability concerns and the checking function rationale, the High Court's casual use of Canadian jurisprudence undermined the overall impact. Endorsing the highly abstract statement that freedom of expression was an 'essential feature of Canadian parliamentary democracy', Chief Justice Mason concluded his constitutional analysis with the following ambiguous statement: '[w]hat is presently significant is that the *implied freedom of speech and expression* in Canada is founded on the view that it is indispensable to the *efficacious working of Canadian representative parliamentary democracy*'.[113] Besides overlooking the checking function in Canada's pre-Charter implied rights jurisprudence (not to mention post-Charter developments), Chief Justice Mason's comparative law analysis in *ACTV* ultimately depended on generic references to democratic theory and an unconscious over-reliance on Meiklejohnian principles.

[108] *Nationwide News* (n 94) 74 (emphasis added).
[109] *ACTV* (n 95).
[110] See *ACTV* (n 95) 133 (Mason CJ), 149 (Brennan J), 168, 174 (Deane and Toohey JJ), 214–16ff (Gaudron J).
[111] *ACTV* (n 95) 136 (Mason CJ).
[112] *ACTV* (n 95) 138 (emphasis added).
[113] *ACTV* (n 95) 141 (emphasis added).

B. Defamation and Implied Freedoms

i. Theophanous v Herald & Weekly Times Ltd

The High Court's first attempt to evaluate defamation law against its implied freedoms doctrine was in *Theophanous v Herald & Weekly Times Ltd.*[114] Andrew Theophanous, an Australian MP, commenced a defamation action against a journalist and newspaper regarding a publication critical of his views on immigration. Along with defences of justification, fair comment, and qualified privilege, the newspaper pleaded an implied freedom to publish material on 'government and political matters'.

Theophanous was deficient in both analysis and result. The High Court held by a slim 4–3 majority that Victoria's defamation law was subject to an implied constitutional guarantee of 'political communication and discussion'. Chief Justice Mason, along with Justices Toohey and Gaudron (Joint Judgment), began by confirming that this implied freedom involved both communication between electors and the elected, and the electors themselves. Addressing the former, along with resultant notions of accountability and the checking function of the press, the Justices advised:

> [...] it is sufficient to say that 'political discussion' includes discussion of the *conduct, policies or fitness for office of government, political parties, public bodies, public officers and those seeking public office*. The concept also includes discussion of the political views and public conduct of persons who are engaged in activities that have become the subject of political debate [...].[115]

Focussing more revealingly on political communications amongst the electorate, the Joint Judgment endorsed Professor Eric Barendt's Meiklejohnian statement that '"political speech" refers to all speech relevant to the *development of public opinion* on the whole range of issues which an intelligent citizen should think about'.[116] The Justices even quoted Meiklejohn himself, who insisted that constitutional protection 'is assured only to speech which bears, directly or indirectly, upon issues with which voters have to deal—only, therefore, to the consideration of matters of public interest [...]'.[117] The Court's implied constitutional guarantee was accordingly supported notionally by both the checking function and Meiklejohnian theory.

Improving on previous efforts in *Nationwide News* and *ACTV*, the Joint Judgment also cautioned against the indiscriminate use of foreign jurisprudence.

[114] (1994) 182 CLR 104 (HCA).
[115] ibid 126 (emphasis added).
[116] ibid (emphasis added).
[117] ibid, quoting Alexander Meiklejohn, 'Free Speech and its Relation to Self-Government' in *Political Freedom: The Constitutional Powers of the People* (New York, Harper & Row, 1948) 79.

Noting that Canadian and American constitutional provisions '[…] are not the same as ours', the Justices insisted that Australia's implied freedom is significantly different from any 'unlimited freedom of expression' under the US Constitution or Canada's Charter of Rights and Freedoms.[118] Despite overlooking Canada's 'balancing mechanism' under section 1 of the Charter, the Justices clarified that '[…] *Nationwide News* and *Australian Capital Television* establish that [Australia's] implied freedom is a restriction on legislative and executive power'.[119] That is, '[i]f the Constitution, expressly or by implication, is at variance with a doctrine of the common law, the latter must yield to the former'.[120]

After concluding that traditional defamation principles infringed Australia's implied freedom of 'political communication and discussion', the High Court modified its public libel doctrine without engaging any free expression justifications. Specifically, it held that publications involving 'political discussion' will *not* be actionable if the defendant establishes that: (a) it was unaware of the falsity of the material published; (b) it did not publish the material recklessly, that is, not caring whether the material was true or false; and (c) the publication was *reasonable* in the circumstances.[121] The Court also confirmed that a media defendant's burden of proving 'reasonableness' would be discharged upon 'taking some steps to check the accuracy of the impugned material or by establishing that it was otherwise justified in publishing without taking such steps or steps which were adequate'.[122]

Evidencing substantial dislocation between this new doctrine and its underlying theoretical support, the *Theophanous* majority concluded that '[t]he formula we favour redresses the balance *to some extent* in favour of the plaintiff; as much, in our view, as can *legitimately* be achieved without significantly interfering with free communication'.[123]

ii. Lange v Australian Broadcasting Corporation

Australia's definitive authority on defamation law's compatibility with implied rights is *Lange v Australian Broadcasting Corporation*,[124] where the High Court re-examined public libel jurisprudence 'in order to settle both constitutional doctrine and the contemporary common law of Australia governing the defence

[118] ibid 127.

[119] ibid.

[120] ibid 128.

[121] ibid 139.

[122] ibid. Besides this new *constitutional* defence, the Court decided that defamatory statements published on political matters in a newspaper were protected by qualified privilege. This represented a more significant advance for freedom of expression and media interests than the constitutional defence, protecting non-malicious publications on matters relevant to democratic government, even when widely disseminated at significant cost to reputation(s).

[123] ibid 140 (emphasis added).

[124] *Lange* (n 84).

of qualified privilege […]'.[125] The primary issue in *Lange* was whether 'there is implied in the Constitution a defence to the publication of defamatory matter relating to *government and political matters* […]'.[126]

The facts in *Lange* were classically resonant with political accountability and the checking function rationale. The case was the first of multiple defamation actions brought by the former Prime Minister of New Zealand, David Lange. While a sitting MP and Minister of State, the Australian Broadcasting Corporation aired a 'Four Corners' television programme containing various derogatory statements. In particular, Lange complained of imputations that he was guilty of official misconduct and unfit to hold office. Also pleading qualified privilege, the media defendant relied on the constitutional defence ostensibly outlined in *Theophanous*. The plaintiff moved to strike out the defences prior to trial, alleging that they were 'bad' in law. The matter was removed to the High Court of Australia for consideration by the Full Court.

The High Court began by describing its implied 'freedom of communication' in highly abstract and indeterminate terms, stating that '[i]t is limited to what is necessary for the effective operation of that system of *representative and responsible government* provided for by the Constitution'.[127] Predictably, the Court's understanding of 'representative and responsible' government resonated with more deliberative aspects of Meiklejohnian theory.[128] Insisting that the implied freedom not be limited to elections, the Court observed tellingly that '[m]ost of the matters necessary to *enable "the people" to make an informed choice* will occur during the period between the holding of one, and the calling of the next, election'.[129] Evoking further concerns with deliberative democracy, the Court explained: '[i]f the freedom to receive and disseminate information were confined to election periods, the electors would be deprived of the greater part of the information necessary to make an effective choice at the election'.[130]

Moreover, even when citing Justice McHugh's dissent in *Stephens v West Australian Newspapers Ltd*,[131] which warned of 'the increasing integration of

125 *Lange* (n 84) 557.

126 *Lange* (n 84) 551 (emphasis added). Following *Lange*, the matter was remitted to the Supreme Court of New South Wales to allow the defendant to provide further particulars of the defence. The action was settled in December 1997.

127 *Lange* (n 84) 562 (emphasis added).

128 The secondary literature confirms that Meiklejohn's 'self-governance' rationale underlies the *Lange* defence. See Michael Chesterman, 'Privileges and Freedoms for Defamatory Political Speech' (1997) 19 *Adelaide Law Review* 155, 163; Adrienne Stone, 'Freedom of Political Communication, the Constitution and the Common Law' (1998) 26 *Federal Law Review* 219, 232ff, 255; Adrienne Stone, 'Rights, Personal Rights and Freedoms: The Nature of the Freedom of Political Communication' (2001) 25 *Melbourne University Law Review* 374, 392ff; William Buss, 'Alexander Meiklejohn, American Constitutional Law, and Australia's Implied Freedom of Political Communication' (2006) 34 *Federal Law Review* 421.

129 *Lange* (n 84) 562 (emphasis added).

130 *Lange* (n 84) 562.

131 (1994) 182 CLR 211 (HCA).

the social, economic and political life of Australia',[132] the High Court declared ambiguously that 'each member of the Australian community has an interest in disseminating and receiving information, opinions and arguments concerning government and political matters that affect the people of Australia'.[133] Reiterating this broadening of qualified privilege in Meiklejohnian terms, the Court advised:

> The duty to disseminate such information is simply the correlative of the interest in receiving it. The common convenience and welfare of Australian society are advanced by discussion—the *giving and receiving* of information—about government and political matters.[134]

As a result, despite the High Court's readiness to modify its public libel doctrine, the lack of explicit consideration of free expression theories necessarily led it astray by marginalising media interests and the checking function rationale. For example, although careful to emphasise that 'reasonableness of conduct is imported [...] *only* when the extended category of qualified privilege is invoked to protect a publication that would otherwise be held to have been made to too wide an audience',[135] the Court tabled and considered a remarkably limited number of factors. Despite Chief Justice Mason's judgment in *ACTV*, the Joint Judgment in *Theophanous*, and Justice McHugh's thoughtful dissent in *Stephens*[136]—all pointing to the checking function as a vital supplement to Meiklejohnian theory—the Court concluded simply that

> [h]aving regard to *the interest* that the members of the Australian community have in receiving information on government and political matters that affect them, the reputations of those defamed by widespread publications will be *adequately protected* by requiring the publisher to prove reasonableness of conduct.[137]

Entirely absent from the High Court's constitutional analysis was the free expression rationale most relevant to press and media interests—the checking function of the press.

At last, besides clarifying that Australia's Constitution provides no express right or protection for free speech or expression as held formerly in *Theophanous*, the High Court of Australia nonetheless confirmed that the text and structure of the Constitution require an implied protection for political communication based on traditional principles of qualified privilege. Specifically, applying equally to Federal and State statutory and common law rules, there is a privilege to publish information on 'governmental and political matters' provided the publication was 'reasonable' in the circumstances, and the publisher was not actuated by malice.

[132] ibid 265–66.
[133] *Lange* (n 84) 572.
[134] *Lange* (n 84) 572 (emphasis added).
[135] *Lange* (n 84) 574 (emphasis added).
[136] Justice McHugh proposed extending qualified privilege to those with 'special knowledge', including scientists, whistleblowers, and investigative journalists. See *Stephens* (n 131) 266.
[137] *Lange* (n 84) 575 (emphasis added).

C. Methodological Crisis in the High Court

Complications raised by the High Court's implied rights doctrine have intensified since *Lange*.[138] Although not sounding in defamation, recent High Court decisions have signalled a growing frustration with the implied 'freedom of political communication'. Its suggested reforms include: (1) reappraising the doctrine of implied freedoms; (2) capitulating to using free expression justifications when balancing implied freedoms against competing interests; and (3) appealing explicitly to differences in political and constitutional structure when considering doctrinal alternatives.

Following its refinement of the *Lange* test in *Coleman v Power*,[139] the High Court's undertheorising has continued to compromise public libel jurisprudence in cases involving criticism of government and public officials. For instance, in *Hogan v Hinch*,[140] a radio broadcaster was charged with violating suppression orders relating to disclosures of named sex offenders on his website and at a public rally. Hinch challenged Victoria's Serious Sex Offenders Monitoring Act 2005, arguing an infringement of the implied 'freedom of political communication' by inhibiting his ability: (a) to criticise legislation and its application in the courts; and (b) to seek legislative and constitutional changes and changes in court practice by public assembly and protest, and disseminating factual information concerning court proceedings.

Unanimously upholding the impugned legislation, Australia's High Court provided little supporting analysis. Despite raising issues of government accountability on the facts, the Court concluded incomprehensibly that:

> The burden upon political communication in any particular case will *vary* and depend upon the *scope* of the orders which the court makes under s 42(1), having *regard to the circumstances*. The offence created by s 42(3) is *not one of strict liability*.[141]

[138] See *Australian Broadcasting Corporation v Hanson* [1998] QCA 306 (media defendant's appeal of an injunction restraining the publication of statements defamatory of a Member of Parliament during a Federal election dismissed); *Herald & Weekly Times Ltd v Popovic* [2003] VSCA 161 (journalist's reliance on *Lange* for publishing an article critical of a local magistrate dismissed); *John Fairfax Publications Pty Ltd v O'Shane* [2005] NSWCA 164 (*Lange* defence dismissed in connection with the publication of an article critical of a local court magistrate); *Peek v Channel Seven Adelaide Pty Ltd* [2006] SASC 63 (*Lange* defence inapplicable to a defamatory television broadcast about a barrister representing a convicted sex offender). Most recently, a full bench of the Supreme Court of South Australia denied the *Lange* defence to a newspaper defendant on the basis that South Australia's general population would have 'no interest' in an article containing allegations of 'dishonest practices' in connection with elections to the state legislature. See *De Poi v Advertiser-News Weekend Publishing Company Pty Ltd* [2016] SASCFC 25 (15 March 2016) [72].

[139] (2004) 220 CLR 1 (HCA). For the latest authoritative High Court discussion of Australia's 'implied right of political communication of governmental and political matters', see *McCloy v New South Wales* [2015] HCA 34.

[140] (2011) 243 CLR 506 (HCA).

[141] ibid [98] (emphasis added).

It is worth pausing to consider the Court's methodology. Instead of applying free expression justifications to evaluate competing interests, the High Court appeared satisfied with technical considerations about whether statutory restrictions were couched in 'absolute terms'. By doing so, critically important policy rationales were disregarded in cases substantially similar to public libels. For example, the checking function's far-reaching emphasis on political accountability might have prevented the High Court's endorsement of the following troubling quote from Justice McHugh, who stated formerly:

> [C]ommunications concerning the *results of cases* or the *reasoning or conduct of the judges* who decide them are *not* ordinarily within the *Lange* freedom. In some exceptional cases, they may be. But when they are, it will be because in some way such communications also concern the acts or omissions of the *legislature or the Executive Government.*[142]

More recent High Court decisions indicate growing dissatisfaction with *Lange* and its implied freedoms methodology. In *Monis v The Queen*,[143] the High Court split 3–3 in a controversial case involving the delivery of letters to relatives of Australian soldiers killed in Afghanistan containing political criticisms of the Australian Government. The defendants were charged under section 471.12 of the Criminal Code 1995 for using the postal service for 'menacing, harassing or offensive' purposes. The defendants moved to quash the indictments for infringing the implied 'freedom of political communication'.

This growing dissension was perhaps best captured by Justice Heydon, who concluded (along with Justice Hayne and Chief Justice French) that 'it is beyond the legislative power of the Commonwealth to prohibit and punish conduct of the type underlying the charges in this case'.[144] Criticising the undertheorising and incoherence accompanying the Court's doctrine of implied freedoms, Justice Heydon observed:

> The implied freedom of political communication has *never been clear*. If there were a federal bill of rights, the implied freedom of communication about government and political matters would be listed. 'Bills of rights are not moral or even political philosophies. They are, at best, bullet points from such philosophies.' Like other philosophical bullet points, the *unclarity of the implied freedom* gives the courts *virtually untrammelled power* to make of it what each judge wills.[145]

Justice Heydon also lamented the High Court's increasingly imprecise definition of its implied freedoms doctrine, observing:

> Nor has the existence of the implied freedom enjoyed unanimous support. Its progenitor [Murphy J] was in a minority of one until after his death. From this point of view

[142] ibid [93] (emphasis added), quoting *APLA Ltd v Legal Services Commissioner (NSW)* (2005) 224 CLR 322 (HCA) [65] (McHugh J).
[143] [2013] HCA 4.
[144] ibid [236].
[145] ibid [244] (emphasis added) (footnote omitted). Cf ibid [124], where Justice Hayne remarked: '[...] the strength of the principles established in *Lange*, and of proportionality reasoning more generally, is the transparency that they bring to decision-making'.

> the provenance of the implied freedom has been viewed as unsatisfactory. It is notorious that there was *marked division of opinion* in the early cases. The statement of the implied freedom has *varied in each case* in which it has been considered—right up to the most recent case.[146]

Consequently, Justice Heydon invited a fundamental reconsideration of *Lange* and its implied rights methodology, advising that '[c]lose examination of the implied freedom of political communication would involve analysis of these issues. That examination may reveal that it is a noble and idealistic enterprise which has failed, is failing, and will go on failing'.[147]

Proving Justice Heydon's point, the High Court in *Monis* once more refrained from external theorising. In a disquietingly technical, anti-theoretical analysis, Justices Crennan, Kiefel and Bell concluded:

> The observations of Brennan J in *Nationwide News* are apposite. His Honour said with respect to the implied freedom that the Constitution may be taken to prohibit legislative or executive infringement of the freedom to discuss political matters, *except to the extent necessary to protect other legitimate interests.* It prohibits a restriction which substantially impairs the opportunity for the Australian people to form the necessary political judgments.
>
> Section 471.12 *does not impermissibly burden* the implied freedom. The *Lange* test is satisfied. Section 471.12 is valid.[148]

This methodological crisis has prompted two responses. First, the High Court is beginning to acknowledge comparative law perspectives and dissimilarities in constitutional and institutional contexts when assessing doctrinal options. For instance, emphasising the importance of constitutional structure and institutional settings in *Roberts v Bass*,[149] Justice Kirby observed:

> In Australia, as elsewhere, a number of considerations have affected such questions. They include the creation of a *distinct society with its own values*, the *changing nature and technology of communications* through which those values are commonly expressed and the *enactment of particular laws* that respond to such changes. *Transcending all of these factors is the Constitution*, establishing a particular kind of government for the nation. In the constitutional prescription are *important implications about the conduct of the representative democracy*, federal and State, for which the Constitution provides.[150]

Likewise, Justice Heydon has challenged the relevance of foreign indicators for Australian legal doctrine. Responding skeptically to the High Court's claim

[146] ibid [245] (emphasis added), citing *Wotton v Queensland* (2012) 246 CLR 1 [41], where Justice Heydon observed that '[a]lthough the *Lange* principles must be applied, they are fluid. They have been subject to change, or the possibility of change, since they were enunciated'.

[147] *Monis* (n 143) [251].

[148] *Monis* (n 143) [352]–[353] (emphasis added).

[149] [2002] HCA 57 [121]–[125] (Kirby J).

[150] ibid [123] (emphasis added).

that New Zealand's affairs throw light on Australian matters, Justice Heydon remarked:

> For the most part, Australians know nothing of New Zealand affairs. The information which the Australian public does possess of New Zealand affairs is more likely to generate great public boredom, not interest. And *what light can matters in a non-federal unicameral country throw on matters in a federal union of polities many of which are bicameral*?[151]

The second response is that High Court decisions have finally recognised the value of more traditional free expression theorising. In a revealing passage confirming the checking function's unique explicatory power, Chief Justice Gleeson thoughtfully enquired:

> If [...] there is one category of common law privilege relating to communications to thousands of electors in the course of an election, [...] and another category relating to communications to *the general public about political matters*, [...] then it seems clear that there is a substantial difference between them. *Why this should be so, as a matter of principle, is difficult to understand.* The law of defamation, including the law as to qualified privilege, strikes a balance between competing interests. *Those interests include the public interest in freedom of political debate, which is essential to the functioning of representative democracy.* Why should the balance that applies when a newspaper with a wide circulation publishes an article about the Prime Minister, or the Leader of the Opposition, differ from the balance that applies when someone distributes throughout an electorate a pamphlet urging electors to vote against the sitting member?[152]

These are first-rate questions, without doubt. Aptly, Justice Heydon has countered by advocating for explicit consideration of freedom of expression justifications. In *Attorney-General (SA) v Corporation of the City of Adelaide*,[153] the respondent council passed a by-law regulating road use by prohibiting preaching, canvassing, and haranguing, and the distribution of printed materials without written permission. Despite involving a blanket prohibition on freedom of political communication—the functional equivalent of a prior restraint—a majority of the High Court upheld the statutory restriction through yet another technical, anti-theoretical analysis. In a powerful dissenting opinion, Justice Heydon endorsed the following House of Lords description of the importance of free expression:

> Freedom of expression is, of course, intrinsically important: it is valued for its own sake. *But it is well recognised that it is also instrumentally important. It serves a number of broad objectives.* First, it promotes the self-fulfilment of individuals in society. Second, in the famous words of Holmes J (echoing John Stuart Mill), 'the best test of truth is the power of the thought to get itself accepted in the competition of the market'. Third, freedom of speech is the lifeblood of democracy. The free flow of information and ideas informs

[151] *Monis* (n 143) [249] (emphasis added).
[152] *Roberts* (n 149) [4] (Gleeson CJ) (emphasis added).
[153] [2013] HCA 3.

> political debate. [...] It acts as a *brake on the abuse of power by public officials*. It facilitates *the exposure of errors* in the governance and administration of justice of the country.[154]

Perhaps signifying a subtle shift in the High Court's public libel jurisprudence, although *Adelaide* was purportedly decided without appeal to external free expression theories, one of its majority judgments revealingly concluded that the disputed provision '*adequately balances* the competing interests in political communication [...]'.[155]

D. Conclusion

Australia's approach to regulating public libels is beset by serious methodological concerns. By discounting free expression rationales and purporting to derive implied freedoms from highly abstract constitutional principles such as the 'efficacious working of representative democracy', Australian courts have replaced longstanding theoretical justifications underlying defamation doctrine with a methodologically suspect approach that begs many questions. Of particular concern is the High Court's inability to explain its understanding of the link between freedom of expression and representative democracy.

Above all, by disregarding accountability concerns and the checking function of the press, Australia has underprotected media defendants and precluded the formulation of public libel principles tailored to its institutional setting. It thus remains an open question as to how long the High Court can persist in the misapprehension that its implied rights methodology is preferable to alternatives based on comprehensive consideration of relevant free expression rationales.

III. Chapter Conclusion

Chapter three has analysed methodological patterns of 'indeterminate balancing' in public libel doctrine. The United States and Australia have undertheorised the checking function rationale through incomplete articulations of its constitutive premises, or rejecting free expression theorising altogether. We now turn in chapter four to the equally disconcerting issue of discounting the extent of the checking function's limited jurisprudential foothold.

[154] ibid [151] (emphasis added), quoting Lord Steyn in *R v Home Secretary; Ex parte Simms* [2000] 2 AC 115 (HL) 131.

[155] ibid [141] (Hayne J) (emphasis added).

4

Overlooking the Checking Function of the Press

I. Overview

If a compelling ground exists for rejecting the 'actual malice' rule, it might be that such a 'radical' rebalancing of freedom of expression against reputation 'lacks a coherent rationale' or 'principled basis'. In *Reynolds v Times Newspapers Ltd*,[1] the House of Lords rejected a generic qualified privilege for political speech on precisely such grounds. However, the Law Lords disregarded a credible and principled foundation for political libels advanced by the European Court of Human Rights. Equally, the New Zealand Court of Appeal has disregarded strong domestic articulations of the checking function due to outmoded authorities evidencing bias against the institutional press. Both developments contribute significantly to present-day undertheorising of public libel doctrine.

II. Strasbourg Jurisprudence

A. Press Freedom and Political Expression under the European Convention

As outlined in chapter one, British courts are obliged under the Human Rights Act 1998 to 'take into account' judicial pronouncements of the European Court of Human Rights. As it happens, Strasbourg principles of freedom of expression and liberty of the press closely resemble the checking function's premises and concerns. Although Article 10 of the Convention does not reference 'the press', the Strasbourg Court has granted it exceptional status, based on many open references to the checking function. There is thus considerable evidence that it figures prominently in the Court's free expression jurisprudence.

[1] [2001] 2 AC 127 (HL).

This jurisprudence effectively originated with *Handyside v United Kingdom*,[2] where the Strasbourg Court endorsed free public discussion and government criticism, stressing that freedom of expression '[...] is applicable not only to "information" or "ideas" that are favourably received or regarded as inoffensive or as a matter of indifference, but also to those that *offend, shock or disturb the State* or any sector of the population'.[3] These principles were later applied in *Sunday Times v United Kingdom*,[4] where it was confirmed they '[...] are of particular importance as far as the press is concerned'.[5]

This adversarial view of the press was further clarified in *Barthold v Germany*,[6] where the Strasbourg Court first highlighted the press' role not only as an 'information purveyor' or conduit, but as a 'public watchdog'.[7] Similarly, freedom to criticise government and politicians was secured in *Lingens v Austria*,[8] where the Court attentively distinguished amongst libel plaintiffs, recognising a greater importance for protecting defamatory falsehoods of public officials than private individuals. In *Lingens*, a journalist was convicted of criminal defamation for criticising a politician for protecting former secret service members and accommodating Nazis. Relying on renowned dicta from US Supreme Court Justice Powell in *Gertz v Robert Welch Inc*,[9] the Court unanimously ruled:

> Freedom of the press [...] affords the public one of the best means of discovering and forming an opinion of the ideas and attitudes of political leaders. [...] *The limits of acceptable criticism are accordingly wider as regards a politician as such than as regards a private individual.* Unlike the latter, the former inevitably and knowingly lays himself open to close scrutiny of his every word and deed by both journalists and the public at large [...].[10]

Government criticism was further endorsed in *Oberschlick v Austria*,[11] *Observer and Guardian v United Kingdom*,[12] and *Castells v Spain*.[13] In *Observer and Guardian*, the Strasbourg Court acknowledged the 'special' checking function of the press, remarking that free expression '[...] is of special importance for the free press which has a legitimate interest in reporting on and drawing the public's attention to deficiencies in the operation of Government services, *including possible illegal activities*'.[14] Similarly, the *Castells* Court unanimously held that

[2] (1976) 1 EHRR 737.
[3] ibid [49] (emphasis added).
[4] (1979) 2 EHRR 245.
[5] ibid [65].
[6] (1985) 7 EHRR 383.
[7] ibid [58].
[8] (1986) 8 EHRR 407.
[9] 418 US 323, 344–46 (1974).
[10] *Lingens* (n 8) [42] (emphasis added).
[11] (1991) 19 EHRR 389 [57]–[60].
[12] (1992) 14 EHRR 153.
[13] App no 11798/85 (ECtHR, 23 April 1992).
[14] *Observer and Guardian* (n 12) [75] (emphasis added).

a senator's conviction for 'insulting the government' contravened Article 10, insisting that:

> The limits of permissible criticism are wider with regard to the Government than in relation to a private citizen, *or even a politician*. In a democratic system the actions or omissions of the Government *must* be subject to the close scrutiny not only of the legislative and judicial authorities *but also of the press and public opinion*.[15]

B. 'Responsible Journalism' and Judicial Censure

The Strasbourg Court has also acknowledged the checking function by providing a 'good faith' defence to media defendants that is (on balance) sympathetic to investigative journalism and the reporting of 'accountability news'.

In *Cumpana v Romania*,[16] two journalists were prosecuted for accusing a former civil servant of abusing her political office for personal gain. The journalists were sentenced to three months' imprisonment, disqualified from exercising certain civil rights, and prohibited from working for one year. Deciding unanimously that Article 10 was violated, the Strasbourg Court not only emphasised '[…] the *vital role of "public watchdog"* which the press performs in a democratic society',[17] but insisted that 'the role of investigative journalists is precisely to inform and alert the public about such undesirable phenomena in society *as soon as the relevant information comes into their possession*'.[18]

The Court also confirmed that Article 10 requires journalists to be '[…] acting in good faith in order to provide accurate and reliable information in accordance with the ethics of journalism'.[19] Namely, notwithstanding the press' obligation to expose political misconduct, 'the fact of directly accusing specified individuals by mentioning their names and positions placed the applicants under an obligation to provide a *sufficient factual basis for their assertions*'.[20] Nonetheless, despite the journalists having 'failed to adduce evidence at any stage of the proceedings to substantiate their allegations […]',[21] the Court held that the domestic court's sentence contravened Article 10, stressing that '[…] a prison sentence for a press offence will be compatible with journalists' freedom of expression […] *only in exceptional circumstances* […].[22] Although restricting the press while performing its 'special responsibilities', the Court emphasised that efforts to regulate free expression

[15] *Castells* (n 13) [46] (emphasis added). See also *Mondragon v Spain* (2015) 60 EHRR 7 [48]–[50].
[16] App no 33348/96 (ECtHR, 10 November 2004).
[17] ibid [93] (citations omitted) (emphasis added).
[18] ibid [96] (emphasis added).
[19] ibid [102].
[20] ibid [101] (emphasis added) (citations omitted).
[21] ibid [104].
[22] ibid [115] (emphasis added).

'[...] must *not* do so in a manner that unduly deters the media from fulfilling their role of alerting the public to *apparent or suspected misuse of public power*'.[23]

Since *Cumpana*, the Strasbourg Court has confirmed the following ancillary principles: (1) journalists are only required to make 'reasonable efforts' to verify defamatory statements of fact;[24] (2) the more serious the allegation, the more solid the factual basis should be;[25] (3) any requirement to prove a value judgment is generally impossible to fulfil and infringes Article 10;[26] (4) a requirement for journalists to prove (on a balance of probabilities) that a factual statement was substantially true does not contravene Article 10;[27] (5) journalists are entitled to rely on official documents when reporting on matters of public concern;[28] (6) journalists reporting on political or public matters have recourse to a degree of exaggeration or even provocation;[29] and (7) courts must not take an overly rigorous approach to assessing journalists' professional conduct, and must consider the likely impact of their rulings not only on individual cases before them, but also on the media in general.[30]

Despite supporting the institutional press' role in exposing political misconduct, the Strasbourg Court's free expression jurisprudence has been weakened by doctrinal inconsistency in its decisions on judicial criticism. As we shall see, this inconsistency seems most attributable to deficiencies in its underlying views of democratic sovereignty.[31]

In *Prager v Austria*,[32] two journalists and a publisher were convicted of criminal libel for criticising Austrian judges. In a controversial 5–4 decision, the Strasbourg Court held that Article 10 was *not* contravened. After recognising that '[t]he press is one of the means by which politicians and public opinion can *verify* that judges are discharging their heavy responsibilities [...]', it inexplicably declined to consider this issue, insisting that '[r]egard must [...] be had to the *special role* of the judiciary in society'.[33] Echoing *Tuchin's* case,[34] the Court insisted upon measured and reserved criticism of the judiciary, ruling that '[a]s the guarantor of justice, [...] it *must* enjoy public confidence if it is to be successful in carrying out its duties'.[35]

[23] ibid [113] (emphasis added).
[24] *Bozhkov v Bulgaria* App no 3316/04 (ECtHR, 19 April 2011) [47], [48].
[25] *Pedersen and Baadsgaard v Denmark* App no 49017/99 (ECtHR, 17 December 2004) [78].
[26] *Europapress Holding DOO v Croatia* App no 25333/06 (ECtHR, 22 October 2009) [54].
[27] ibid.
[28] *Gorelishvili v Georgia* App no 12979/04 (ECtHR, 5 June 2007) [41].
[29] *Dlugolecki v Poland* App no 23806/03 (ECtHR, 24 February 2009) [44].
[30] *Bozhkov* (n 24) [51].
[31] In *Perna v Italy* App no 48898/99 (ECtHR, 6 May 2003), the Court held there was no Article 10 violation in a case involving the intimidation of a journalist who accused a judge of aiding and abetting the Mafia.
[32] App no 15974/90 (ECtHR, 26 April 1995).
[33] ibid [34] (emphasis added).
[34] [1704] Holt KB 424, 90 ER 1133, 1133–34.
[35] *Prager* (n 32) [34] (emphasis added).

Not surprisingly, the Strasbourg Court held that the applicant had not adequately verified his allegations against the Viennese judges. Whether the defamatory accusations were 'treat[ing] each accused at the outset as if he had been convicted', or attributing to a particular judge an 'arrogant' and 'bullying' attitude, the Court concluded that they 'had thus not only damaged their reputation, but also *undermined public confidence* in the integrity of the judiciary [...]'.[36] The Court also rejected the applicant's 'good faith' defence, concluding that '[t]he research that he had undertaken does not appear adequate to substantiate such serious allegations'.[37]

That the checking function was significantly undertheorised in *Prager* was manifest from its two dissenting judgments. Both provided instructive counterpoints to the majority for whom the checking function operated only as a highly abstract principle, if at all. Remarking on international trends of exposing judiciaries to unrestricted media criticism, Judge Pettiti insisted:

> Journalistic investigation of the functioning of the system of justice is *indispensable* in ensuring verification of the protection of the rights of individuals in a democratic society. [...] Judges, whose status carries with it immunity and who in most member States are shielded from civil litigation, *must in return accept exposure to unrestricted criticism where it is made in good faith*.[38]

Enlarging on these concerns, Judge Martens examined the various deficiencies underlying the Court's disapproval of judicial criticism, expressing concern that it properly '[...] satisfy itself that the national authorities did apply standards which were in conformity with the principles embodied in Article 10 and, moreover, that they based themselves on an *acceptable assessment of the relevant facts*'.[39] Judge Martens began by critiquing the majority's review of Mr Prager's conviction and sentence, insisting that

> [...] to fulfil its task as the ultimate guarantor of freedom of expression, the European Court of Human Rights cannot confine itself to reviewing the national courts' balancing exercise, but *must necessarily* also—and firstly—examine their *interpretation and assessment* of the statements in question.[40]

Judge Martens cautioned that '[o]nly this double check enables the Court to satisfy itself that the right to freedom of expression has not been unduly curtailed'.[41]

Judge Martens' 'double check' revealed five deficiencies in the Austrian courts' reasoning for convicting Mr Prager. The first was that '[t]he Austrian courts only took into account five specific and isolated passages, ignoring [the] context'

[36] *Prager* (n 32) [36] (emphasis added).
[37] *Prager* (n 32) [37].
[38] *Prager* (n 32) 12 (Pettiti J, dissenting) (emphasis added).
[39] *Prager* (n 32) 15 [4] (Martens J, dissenting) (emphasis added), quoting *Jersild v Denmark* (1995) 19 EHRR 1 [31] (Grand Chamber).
[40] *Prager* (n 32) 15 [4] (emphasis added).
[41] *Prager* (n 32) 15 [4] (fn omitted).

of the article.[42] Recognising journalists' obligations to report on official misconduct, he noted that the article was published in a 'serious magazine for intellectual readers' on matters of 'considerable public concern', significant points disregarded by the Austrian courts.[43]

The second deficiency was that '[t]he Austrian courts interpreted these five passages [of the article] very one-sidedly'.[44] Judge Martens noted that, under German constitutional law, 'a judge who convicts a speaker or author whose utterance is objectively open to different interpretations, without giving convincing reasons for choosing the very interpretation which leads to conviction, violates the right to freedom of expression'.[45] Instead, the trial judge 'chose from two possible interpretations [...] without even bothering to make it clear that she had considered the other interpretation or to state her reasons for rejecting it'.[46]

The third deficiency concerned the applicant's inability to adduce evidence at trial. Judge Martens protested that the trial judge 'refused even to consider the (undisputed) fact that [the plaintiff judge] had once warned a defence lawyer to "keep it short" since he "had already reached his decision"',[47] which would have provided *some* evidence for his portrayal. A disturbing pattern consisted 'first [of] a non-reasoned interpretation which [was] (to put it mildly) not the most obvious but certainly the most unfavourable and then, on that basis, a refusal of Mr Prager's offer to prove the exceptio veritatis'.[48]

The fourth deficiency was that '[t]he above defects also affected the [...] court's decision on the due journalistic care issue'.[49] The trial judge reproached Mr Prager for 'glaring carelessness' based on her flawed interpretation of his article. Judge Martens explained that 'the Eisenstadt judge disregarded the article as a whole and, moreover, treated the two isolated sentences from the summary [...] as if they formed part of (the body of) an article devoted to Judge J only'.[50] He concluded that on a proper interpretation, 'the methods used by Mr Prager cannot *per se* be held to fall short of the standard of proper journalistic care'.[51]

The final deficiency was that Austria's malicious intent test infringed Article 10. Disregarding investigative journalists' obligation to report official misconduct, malicious intent was presumed by the trial judge because 'Mr Prager must have realised that the five passages concerning Judge J were very negative and would

[42] *Prager* (n 32) [16(a)].
[43] *Prager* (n 32) [8].
[44] *Prager* (n 32) [16(b)].
[45] *Prager* (n 32) [9].
[46] *Prager* (n 32) [9].
[47] *Prager* (n 32) [10].
[48] *Prager* (n 32) [12], [16(c)].
[49] *Prager* (n 32) [16(d)].
[50] *Prager* (n 32) [14].
[51] *Prager* (n 32) [14] (emphasis in original).

affect him accordingly'.[52] Judge Martens rejected this as 'incompatible with the right to freedom of expression',[53] proposing that 'the decisive test should be whether the impugned wording, however impudent, curt or uncouth, may still be found to derive from an honest opinion on the subject [...]'.[54] Unsurprisingly, the trial judge disregarded this approach, given that 'she intended to teach Mr Prager and his brother journalists a lesson'.[55]

C. Conclusion

Prager highlights numerous concerns compromising the Strasbourg Court's otherwise commendable use and understanding of the checking function of the press. First, justifiable 'balancing' of free expression values under Article 10 is '[...] obviously, only feasible when what has been expressed has been properly construed and assessed within its context'.[56] Second, the 'margin of appreciation' allowed to domestic authorities not only arbitrarily prohibits categoricalism, but is arguably too tolerant of encroachments on press independence. Notable examples include not only intolerance of judicial criticism, as in *Prager*, but the Court's frequent sanctioning of criminal libel. Third, absent a formal hierarchy of rights, government criticism is sure to be undervalued when, relative to other Convention interests, the checking function's preeminent concerns with exposing government misconduct and rectifying shortages of such information enjoy no theoretical or doctrinal priority. Finally, although the checking function has been recognised by the Strasbourg Court, for the reasons mentioned above, its free expression jurisprudence sheds little light on identifying specific solutions for individual jurisdictions.

Strasbourg jurisprudence nonetheless presents a reasonably clear and consistent representation of the press' role in checking government misconduct. Whether expressed as the press' 'public watchdog' role; its legitimate interest in reporting on 'deficiencies in the operation of Government services, including possible illegal activities'; the right to express ideas that 'offend, shock or disturb the State'; or insisting that state regulations not 'unduly deter [...] the media from fulfilling their role of alerting the public to apparent or suspected misuse of public power'; it seems clear that British courts should have little choice but to carefully consider these principles and the decisions in which they originated.

[52] *Prager* (n 32) [15].
[53] *Prager* (n 32) [15].
[54] *Prager* (n 32) [15].
[55] *Prager* (n 32) [17].
[56] *Prager* (n 32) [4] (Martens J, dissenting).

III. United Kingdom

Despite being obliged to consider any 'judgment, decision, declaration or advisory opinion' of the European Court of Human Rights,[57] the UK Supreme Court has regularly disregarded the checking function in its public libel jurisprudence. Remarkably, Britain's highest courts have overlooked public libel's most pertinent theoretical justification in two landmark decisions, most recently in *Flood v Times Newspapers Ltd*.[58] Besides undermining theoretical support for public libels, disregarding the Strasbourg Court's relatively clear description of the checking function has engendered numerous comparative law errors, including misuse of foreign libel laws (particularly US journalist confidentiality protections), and perfunctory and improper use of Strasbourg authorities. As a result, it is doubtful whether the checking function will ever be fully acknowledged in English law. The UK Supreme Court's public libel authorities provide only the slightest confidence.

A. Of 'Missing Rationales and Principles'

Despite its roots in English libertarian theory, the checking function has been routinely undertheorised by Britain's highest courts and disregarded entirely in two landmark cases involving investigative reporting of serious charges of political misconduct and corruption.

In *Reynolds v Times Newspapers Ltd*,[59] the Law Lords rejected a generic qualified privilege for publications on political matters, preferring a 'responsible journalism' defence involving ad hoc balancing of competing interests. The House of Lords based its preference largely on the perceived absence of a 'convincing rationale' for the newspapers' bid for greater protection for political speech.[60]

As it happens, the facts in *Reynolds* are particularly representative of the checking function rationale. The case involved the political crisis in Dublin in November 1994, in which the Irish Prime Minister Reynolds resigned amidst allegations of dishonesty in appointing a new President of the High Court. Mr Reynolds' resignation was of public interest because of his role in the Northern Ireland peace process. On 20 November 1994, the British mainland edition of *The Sunday Times* reported that Mr Reynolds had deliberately and dishonestly misled the Irish Parliament and his cabinet coalition colleagues by withholding sensitive information regarding the proposed High Court appointee. Mr Reynolds sued

[57] Human Rights Act 1998 (UK) (HRA 1998) s 2.

[58] [2012] UKSC 11.

[59] *Reynolds* (n 1).

[60] *Reynolds* (n 1) 203, 204 (Lord Nicholls), 219 (Lord Cooke).

the writer, editor, and newspaper for defamation. At trial, the jury returned a verdict for the plaintiff, but awarded only nominal damages (1p). The Court of Appeal reversed, ruling that the article was not protected by qualified privilege. The media defendants appealed to the House of Lords.

In reconciling free expression with reputational interests, the House of Lords reviewed foreign legal solutions, along with the HRA 1998 and Strasbourg authorities. Reflecting on this 'new legal landscape', the Law Lords recognised powerful policy arguments on either side. Lord Steyn expressed matters with appropriate seriousness by stating, '[t]here are at stake powerful competing arguments of policy. They pull in different directions. It is a hard case in which it is unrealistic to say that there is only one right answer'.[61] Likewise, Lord Nicholls admitted:

> This is a difficult problem. No answer is perfect. Every solution has its own advantages and disadvantages. Depending on local conditions, such as legal procedures and the traditions and power of the press, the solution preferred in one country may not be best suited to another country.[62]

Despite recognising these comparative law subtleties, the House of Lords' overall approach underscores the importance of precisely considering free expression justifications—particularly the checking function of the press—when balancing competing interests. The opinions of Lord Nicholls and Lord Steyn are particularly instructive.

Lord Nicholls delivered the leading speech,[63] insisting that there was '[...] *no need* to elaborate on the importance of the role discharged by the media in the expression and communication of information and comment on political matters'.[64] Accepting that '[t]he interest of a democratic society in ensuring a free press weighs heavily in the balance [...]',[65] Lord Nicholls nonetheless underplayed the press' role in checking official misconduct. His closest formulation was, when considering the 'contemporary' role of investigative journalism, he noted casually that '[t]his activity [...] is part of the *vital role* of the press and the media generally'.[66]

That the checking function was improperly theorised was evidenced most clearly by Lord Nicholls' response to the defendants' fallback position on appeal. Alternative to a categorical rule, the defendants proposed shifting the burden of proof to the plaintiff to demonstrate the newspaper's failure to exercise reasonable care. Lord Nicholls rejected this 'negligence-based' suggestion, stating he was 'troubled' it would '[...] turn the law of qualified privilege upside down'[67]

[61] *Reynolds* (n 1) 209.
[62] *Reynolds* (n 1) 201–02.
[63] Lord Cooke and Lord Hobhouse agreed fully with Lord Nicholls' speech. Lord Hope and Lord Steyn agreed with Lord Nicholls' rejection of categoricalism, but provided separate opinions.
[64] *Reynolds* (n 1) 200 (emphasis added).
[65] *Reynolds* (n 1) 200.
[66] *Reynolds* (n 1) 200 (emphasis added).
[67] *Reynolds* (n 1) 203.

and, most revealingly, that applying it to political information '[...] would *lack a coherent rationale*'.[68] Lord Cooke was similarly concerned, stating '[...] there is in my opinion *no good reason* why politicians should be subjected to a greater risk than other leading citizens, or for that matter *any other persons*, of false allegations of fact in the media'.[69] Both Law Lords plainly disregarded the checking function for distinguishing political matters from other information of public concern.

This undertheorising significantly narrowed the Court's consideration of doctrinal alternatives. After noting that free expression is subject to such Convention restrictions as are 'prescribed by law and are necessary in a democratic society for the protection of the reputations of others',[70] Lord Nicholls described his adjudicatory task as '[...] identifying the restrictions which are fairly and reasonably necessary for the protection of *reputation*'.[71] Assessing matters from this predisposition, Lord Nicholls cautioned that '[m]alice is notoriously difficult to prove', particularly where a '[...] newspaper is understandably unwilling to disclose its sources',[72] adding that '[u]nless the paper chose later to withdraw the allegations, the politician thus defamed would have no means of clearing his name, and the public would have no means of knowing where the truth lay'.[73] Besides overlooking doctrinal options, such worries are surely of secondary importance given Wortman's observations that '[g]overnment possesses an evident advantage and superiority over every species of opposition',[74] and that '[...] it directs and commands all the resources of a State'[75]—concerns especially relevant to Mr Reynolds and to late twentieth-century democracies generally.

Even so, Lord Nicholls declared the defence of qualified privilege to have the following methodological advantages over categorical approaches to public libels: (1) it facilitates considering 'all the circumstances when deciding whether the publication [...] was privileged because of its value to the public';[76] (2) it is highly elastic, being potentially 'applied [...] to all information published by a newspaper, whatever its source or origin';[77] and (3) it 'accords with the present state of [...] human rights jurisprudence'.[78] Consequently, Lord Nicholls formulated the

[68] *Reynolds* (n 1) 203 (emphasis added).
[69] *Reynolds* (n 1) 219 (emphasis added).
[70] *Reynolds* (n 1) 201.
[71] *Reynolds* (n 1) 201 (emphasis added).
[72] *Reynolds* (n 1) 201.
[73] *Reynolds* (n 1) 201.
[74] Tunis Wortman, *A Treatise, Concerning Political Enquiry, and the Liberty of the Press* (New York, 1800) 175.
[75] ibid. Compare *Derbyshire CC v Times Newspapers Ltd* [1993] AC 534 (HL) 550, where Lord Keith acknowledged, 'it is open to [a] controlling body to defend itself by public utterances and in debate in the council chamber'. See also *Dyuldin v Russia* App no 25968/02 (ECtHR, 31 July 2007) [45].
[76] *Reynolds* (n 1) 202.
[77] *Reynolds* (n 1) 202.
[78] *Reynolds* (n 1) 203.

following two-part defence. Once a publication was judged to be in the 'public interest', ten factors must be considered to determine whether it satisfied the requirements of 'responsible journalism'.[79] Noting that '[t]he weight to be given to these and any other relevant factors will vary from case to case',[80] Lord Nicholls hoped that '[o]ver time, a valuable corpus of case law will be built up'.[81]

Interestingly, Lord Nicholls' concluding remarks appeared undeniably supportive of the checking function of the press:

> Above all, the court should have particular regard to the importance of freedom of expression. The press discharges *vital functions as a bloodhound as well as a watchdog.* The court should be slow to conclude that a publication was not in the public interest and, therefore, the public had no right to know, especially when the information is in the field of political discussion. Any lingering doubts should be resolved in favour of publication.[82]

Lord Nicholls' reasons for rejecting a categorical privilege, however, tell a more complete story. Specifically, without fully theorising the checking function and concerns with democratic accountability, support for press freedom will be marginal at best. For instance, Lord Nicholls' rejection of categorical approaches followed his conviction that 'it would be *unsound in principle* to distinguish political discussion from discussion of other matters of serious public concern'.[83] Confounding matters further, Lord Nicholls' use of Strasbourg jurisprudence was perfunctory and unrepresentative of prevailing support for the checking function. Of the six cases he cited, two concerned statements of opinion, three involved no political discussion, and none were authority for the 'public watchdog' role of the press. This disregard of other more pertinent Strasbourg authorities also explains how Lord Cooke concluded that '[a]s the European case law stands at present, *no trace is to be found* of endorsement of a generic privilege in the political context'.[84]

Lord Steyn's opinion is also instructive. After conceding that '[t]he argument for addressing the chilling effect of our defamation law on political speech and for striking a better balance between freedom of speech and defamation is strong',[85] he then rejected a categorical approach for political speech on two grounds. The first was that domestic protections for journalist sources make it unacceptably difficult to prove 'reckless disregard of the truth'. The second was that a categorical defence was inconsistent with Strasbourg jurisprudence, 'which in cases of competing rights and interests requires a *balancing exercise* [...]'.[86] While

[79] *Reynolds* (n 1) 205.
[80] *Reynolds* (n 1) 205.
[81] *Reynolds* (n 1) 205.
[82] *Reynolds* (n 1) 205 (emphasis added).
[83] *Reynolds* (n 1) 204 (emphasis added).
[84] *Reynolds* (n 1) 223 (emphasis added).
[85] *Reynolds* (n 1) 210.
[86] *Reynolds* (n 1) 211 (emphasis added).

Lord Steyn's concerns anticipate significant methodological complications, they also evidence misunderstanding of US defamation laws, and highlight the importance of maintaining a complete inventory of free expression values when assessing doctrinal alternatives and differences in compositional balancing.[87]

Lord Steyn's first argument for rejecting categorical approaches was based on differences in protections for journalistic sources. Contrasting English and American authorities, Lord Steyn cited the US decision *Herbert v Lando*[88] for the proposition that 'a plaintiff in the United States is entitled to a pre-trial inquiry into the sources of the story and editorial decision-making'.[89] However, this attribution was incorrect. The Supreme Court held in *Lando* only that the press had no First Amendment or absolute privilege against pre-trial discovery of mental processes when determining whether 'actual malice' existed. Allowing plaintiffs to adduce direct and indirect evidence, the *direct* evidence sanctioned was '[...] the thoughts, opinions, and conclusions of the publisher',[90] *not* information from confidential sources.

What Lord Steyn missed was that American courts have since endorsed evidentiary privileges against disclosure of confidential sources, requiring plaintiffs to establish a need for confidential information.[91] And even if defendants were required to reveal sources as Lord Steyn presumed, various modifications to categorical approaches are possible (rather than outright dismissal), including shifting burdens of proof, reducing the standard of proof from 'convincing clarity', and using protective orders to limit disclosure of the source's identity to court and counsel only.[92] Relying on mischaracterisations of US law is not only an example of poor comparative legal analysis, but it is unpersuasive as a basis for rejecting stronger defamation defences more protective of media interests.

This confusion persisted alongside misapprehensions about 'balancing' in free expression jurisprudence. Lord Steyn's reasoning proceeded sensibly enough by noting that 'speech about political matters has a higher value than speech about private lives of politicians', and that it will 'always be necessary to take into account the dynamics of the role of the press'.[93] However, he concluded his defamation analysis with the following endorsement of the *Reynolds* defence, reflecting doctrinal prescriptions similarly vague to those endorsed by Australian and New Zealand courts: '[i]f the matter is approached *in this liberal*

[87] As Professor Schauer reminds us, '[...] the simple designation of "balancing" masks questions about who should weigh competing values, [and] the extent to which balancing should take place in more or less rigid rules or in the circumstances of the individual case [...]'. See Frederick Schauer, 'Must Speech be Special?' (1983) 78 *Northwestern University Law Review* 1284, 1285, fn 9.

[88] 441 US 153 (1979).

[89] *Reynolds* (n 1) 210.

[90] *Lando* (n 88) 170.

[91] See *Miller v Transamerican Press, Inc* 621 F2d 721 (5th Cir 1980).

[92] ibid 727.

[93] *Reynolds* (n 1) 215.

way the balance in our law between freedom of information and the right to reputation should fulfil the Convention requirement of being *necessary in a democracy*'.[94]

It is, however, difficult to accept Lord Steyn's conclusion when the Strasbourg Court's 'liberal' pronouncements on the institutional press' 'public watchdog' role were never acknowledged as a distinct free expression justification. Moreover, Lord Steyn's dismissal of categoricalism was influenced by an overly-simplistic, two-valued approach to 'balancing'. As Professor Schauer rightly notes, '[w]e balance when we formulate rules for mechanical *or* categorical application'.[95] Rather than dismissing categorical approaches as 'inconsistent' with Article 10, Lord Steyn and the Law Lords might have done better to appreciate that selecting doctrinal alternatives is not 'a simple question of a choice between balancing at the rulemaking level or at the level of application. There is a *spectrum* rather than a *dichotomy*'.[96] Given these methodological and theoretical limitations, whatever 'balance' was struck in future cases was bound to miss the mark.

The UK Supreme Court reconsidered the correct approach to the *Reynolds* defence most recently in *Flood*.[97] Superficially, the case is noteworthy for shifting power back to publishers in cases involving defamatory statements of fact on matters of public interest,[98] and by interpreting *Reynolds* through more sophisticated use of Strasbourg principles. However, besides the Court's continued silence on the nature of the *Reynolds* defence, the checking function was again undertheorised and inoperative in a case involving investigative reporting of serious corruption allegations.

Flood provided an exceptional opportunity to deliberate on facts consistent with the checking function of the press. The defendant newspaper was sued for defamation over an article containing allegations that Detective Sergeant Gary Flood had abused his position by accepting bribes in return for disclosing confidential information to forewarn wealthy Russian businessmen of extradition proceedings. The article was preceded by lengthy investigations by experienced journalists. It named Sergeant Flood and detailed the corruption allegations leading to internal police investigation. The article also contained a denial from Flood, via his lawyers, and a statement by the Metropolitan Police confirming that an investigation was underway. The trial judge held that *Reynolds* protected the newspaper. The Court of Appeal reversed. The newspaper appealed to the UK Supreme Court.

94 ibid (emphasis added).

95 Frederick Schauer, 'Categories and the First Amendment: A Play in Three Acts' (1981) 34 *Vanderbilt Law Review* 265, 299 (emphasis added).

96 ibid (emphasis added).

97 *Flood* (n 58).

98 'Reynolds' Triumphant Return' *The Lawyer* (London, 26 March 2012) 10.

Compared to its nominal use of Strasbourg jurisprudence in *Reynolds*, the Court undertook a more comprehensive analysis, most notably by Lord Mance. Citing the Strasbourg Court's acknowledgement of the press' role as 'social watchdogs',[99] Lord Mance reiterated that 'the bounds of press criticism admissible in respect of *politicians* and also, though not necessarily to the same extent, *officials* are larger than they are in relation to private individuals'.[100] He even added that '[t]he conduct of the judiciary [...] is likewise a legitimate subject of press scrutiny'.[101] But despite such plaintiff-centred corrections, very few informed the Court's opinions in a principled or consistent manner.

One could hope that the checking function would be used to rectify the Court's controversial errors in *Reynolds*, including its conclusion that it would be 'unsound in principle' to distinguish political expression, and that categorical approaches 'lack a coherent rationale'. But even the most charitable review of the Court's five opinions reveals no such penitent acts. Rather, undertheorising was evident from the outset of Lord Phillips P's leading speech. Emphasising 'matters that will often weigh conclusively *against* publication of details' of criminal accusations, Lord Phillips P quoted extensively from the Court of Appeal's prior judgment, which emphasised factual verification and protecting reputational interests.[102] Conspicuously absent from his 'public interest' analysis, therefore, were any references to free expression justifications, particularly the checking function of the press.

Such omissions were particularly concerning since Lord Phillips P initially observed that the article was of 'high public interest' not simply because it alleged corruption by Flood, but because '[w]hat was suggested was not merely a corrupt breach of confidentiality, but the *betrayal* of the *very object* of his employment by the police'.[103] He also accepted evidence that the journalists' primary motive was ensuring that the police investigation was underway.[104] Accordingly, he concluded that such a motive 'was relevant both because it constituted a *legitimate aim of publishing* [...], and because it was in the public interest to ensure that the investigation was carried out promptly [...]'.[105] Appealing (in effect) to the checking function's concern with exposing official misconduct, it was these factors, along with high public interest in the story, which justified publication.

Lord Phillips P's reasoning was then compromised by his assessment of naming Detective Sergeant Flood in the article. He expressed three concerns that, unfortunately, marginalised accountability concerns and the checking function of

[99] *Flood* (n 58) [138].
[100] *Flood* (n 58) [139] (emphasis added).
[101] *Flood* (n 58) [139]. Lord Mance cited neither *Prager* (n 32), nor *Perna* (n 31).
[102] *Flood* (n 58) [66] (emphasis added).
[103] *Flood* (n 58) [68] (emphasis added).
[104] *Flood* (n 58) [69].
[105] *Flood* (n 58) [69] (citations omitted) (emphasis added).

the press. The first was that it 'was impossible to publish the details of the Article without disclosing to those close to the respondent that he was the officer to whom it related'.[106] The second was Lord Phillips P's openness to the submission that if Flood had not been named, other Extradition Unit members might come under suspicion. The third—and most contentious—concern was his insistence that, since Flood was not a 'public figure', '[p]ublication of his name can have meant nothing to most readers, and any interest that it added to the article would not have outweighed the damage that it caused to his reputation'.[107]

Lord Phillips P's reasoning exposes major concerns with the Court's methodology in media defamation cases. By emphasising the corruption allegations against Flood and the journalists' motives, he advanced two concerns highly consistent with the checking function rationale. Exposing government corruption is, after all, the press' central objective under the checking function. But concerns with revealing Flood's identity and inviting suspicion among his fellow officers could have been disposed of more convincingly. Compared to predominant concerns with exposing official misconduct, proponents of the checking function will view such reputationally-sensitive matters as of meaningful, but secondary importance.

Likewise, considering Flood as a 'public figure' invited needless confusion and allowed Lord Phillips P to sidestep application of the checking function. Irrespective of whether Flood was a 'public figure', he was clearly a *public official* falling within the categories of individuals to whom the checking function classically applies.[108] Given the Court's ad hoc methodology, this factor might have been dispositive in another case. Thus, 'balancing' under *Reynolds* is being left to judges equipped with incomplete articulations of the checking function from Strasbourg jurisprudence, and limited methodological appreciation of free expression justifications when 'balancing' the freedom to publish statements defamatory of public servants and officials.

Similar concerns detract from the Court's deliberations on *Reynolds*' 'responsible journalism' test. Lord Phillips P observed that '[n]o [...] hard and fast principles can be applied when considering verification for the purpose of *Reynolds* privilege. They would impose too strict a fetter on freedom of expression'.[109] Similar to the Strasbourg Court in *Cumpana*, he insisted that '[...] journalists should be reasonably satisfied both that the "supporting facts" were true and that there was a serious possibility that Sergeant Flood had been guilty of the corruption of which he was suspected'.[110] But as Professor Blasi has

[106] *Flood* (n 58) [74].
[107] *Flood* (n 58) [73].
[108] Lord Brown described Sergeant Flood as a 'public officer' (*Flood* (n 58) [119]). Lord Mance revealingly sought protection for stories about public 'officials', versus politicians (*Flood* (n 58) [157]).
[109] *Flood* (n 58) [80].
[110] *Flood* (n 58) [81].

insisted, in cases involving official misconduct, the checking function provides a powerful rationale for allowing the press substantial freedom to investigate and report on political misconduct. If the concern is to avoid 'too strict a fetter on freedom of expression', the Court ironically might have benefitted from a closer analysis of the checking function's relevance and implications when considering this part of the *Reynolds* test.

B. Conclusion

Despite substantial Strasbourg jurisprudence emphasising the press' 'watchdog' role, *Reynolds* and *Flood* illustrate consistent undertheorising of the checking function in leading UK public libel cases. The primary consequence is a prima facie under protection of speech involving political matters.

IV. New Zealand

Unlike *Reynolds*, the New Zealand Court of Appeal has expanded qualified privilege to protect defamatory publications on matters of *political expression*. Yet despite liberalising its media defamation laws, concerns remain about their theoretical foundations. While New Zealand courts now evaluate media privilege claims in wider *social and constitutional contexts*, they have not consistently referenced free expression rationales. As in Britain, New Zealand courts have overlooked the checking function in paradigmatic cases of government and official misconduct. This oversight has compromised New Zealand's public libel principles, ultimately underprotecting media interests by adopting an artificially narrow view of 'political expression', and by promoting needlessly sharp distinctions between 'politicians', 'public servants', and 'public figures'. This undertheorising has ultimately weakened the Court of Appeal's relatively sophisticated comparative law framework for adapting public libel doctrine to distinct institutional settings.

A. Bias against the Press in the Court of Appeal

As with all of our comparators, New Zealand's public libel laws originated from English defamation principles. The New Zealand Court of Appeal's decision in *Truth (NZ) Limited v Holloway*[111] typified the Court's ready adoption of traditional English views on a newspaper's claim to qualified privilege. In *Holloway*,

[111] [1960] NZLR 69 (CA).

the defendant published articles implicating New Zealand's Minister of Industries and Commerce, the Honourable Philip North Holloway, in dishonest dealings connected with the issuance of import licences for fostering trade with Communist countries. At trial, the plaintiff was suited in defamation, the jury awarding £11,000 damages.

On appeal, the newspaper argued with ostensible 'boldness and originality' that the offending articles were published on privileged occasions. The New Zealand Court of Appeal unanimously rejected this claim of 'first instance', advising that 'the argument presented [...] loses sight of the distinction which requires to be drawn between *different functions* performed by newspapers'.[112] Noting that '[o]ne function is to provide its readers with fair and accurate reports of proceedings, judicial and otherwise [...]',[113] Justice North (on behalf of the Court) insisted that 'the right of a newspaper to carry out this task [...]'[114] was anchored only by New Zealand's Defamation Act 1954 and principles of qualified privilege.

Remarkably, among newspapers' many functions, the Court of Appeal made no mention of their role in reporting on government and official misconduct. Describing their journalistic responsibilities narrowly, it cautioned:

> [...] *there is no principle of law, and certainly no case that we know of*, which may be invoked in support of the contention that a newspaper can claim privilege if it publishes a defamatory statement of fact about an individual *merely because the general topic developed in the article is a matter of public interest*.[115]

Elaborating on this cynical view of New Zealand's institutional press, Justice North advised:

> The proprietor of a newspaper is in a difficulty if he begins to speak of a 'duty' to publish material, because such an assertion immediately provokes the kind of caustic answer given by Lord Macnaghten in *Macintosh v Dun* [...], where he said: 'Is it in the interest of the community, is it for the welfare of society, that the protection which the law throws around communications made in legitimate self-defence, or from a bona fide sense of duty, should be extended to communications made from motives of self-interest by persons who *trade for profit in the characters of other people*?'[116]

The Court accordingly confirmed that defamation 'does not recognize any special privilege as attaching to the profession of journalism', and that 'a journalist who obtains information reflecting on a public man or a public officer has *no more right than any other private citizen* to publish his assertions to the world at large'.[117]

[112] ibid 83 (emphasis added).
[113] ibid.
[114] ibid.
[115] ibid (emphasis added).
[116] ibid (emphasis added) (citations omitted).
[117] ibid (emphasis added).

This guarded view also influenced *Hyams v Peterson*,[118] a case involving allegations of property fraud and unlawful commercial activity by government employees. Dismissing the media defendants' appeal from a pretrial ruling refusing applications to strike the plaintiff's defamation claims, a unanimous Court of Appeal considered in dicta the balance struck between free expression and reputation in traditional defamation defences. Demonstrating the importance of marshalling a full complement of free expression rationales, Justice Cooke (on behalf of the Court) noted:

> [C]ounsel for the appellants made little attempt *to undertake the balancing exercise of showing why the media should be more free to publish untrue allegations then [sic] has been the case so far*. Assertions that public discussion should be unrestricted have a ready appeal. They may seem axiomatic. But the damage to reputations, through ineradicable but untrue smears, has to be weighed also. [...] The media have a big trade in reputations, and to some extent this must be acceptable in a democracy. *The question is where the line is to be drawn.*[119]

The Court of Appeal also reasonably suggested that '[i]f there is to be a change in the law, drawing the line in a different place in favour of the media, it should be made by way of *extending* the defences of qualified privilege or fair comment'.[120]

Readjusting principles of qualified privilege might never have occurred if the only facts before the Court of Appeal had been those in *Television New Zealand Limited (TVNZ) v Quinn*.[121] *Quinn* involved shoddy investigative reporting by federal broadcasters into allegations of illegal drug doping and financial irregularities in the corrupt world of New Zealand harness racing. At trial, the jury awarded damages of $400,000 and $1,100,000 in respect of two publications, each founding a separate claim. These awards were the largest in New Zealand history.

Upholding the first award and overturning the second, the Court of Appeal was plainly swayed by the substandard journalism. For instance, among TVNZ's submissions was that the 'chilling effect' of the awards was detrimental to investigative journalism. Showing little sympathy, Lord Cooke (Richardson and Gault JJ concurring) summoned only the following reproving words: '[i]f [...] what was done in this case were a fair sample of investigative journalism, I do not think that concern would need to be felt about any tendency to discourage it'.[122] The broadcaster's practices also tainted the Court's views on freedom of expression and the press more generally, Lord Cooke urging:

> The threat of 'going to the papers' or to programmes like the 'Holmes' one can be *oppressive and unfair*, especially with the *power of modern mass media*. Of course such a threat

[118] [1991] 3 NZLR 648 (CA).
[119] ibid 657 (emphasis added).
[120] ibid (emphasis added).
[121] [1996] 3 NZLR 24 (CA).
[122] ibid 31.

> may be in the public interest, as in some cases of whistle-blowing. Still, in my opinion *the risk of abuse* is among the factors telling against changing the present balance of the law about freedom of speech.[123]

Consequently, as illustrated in *Holloway*, *Hyams*, and *Quinn*, the Court of Appeal's early application of public libel principles was influenced by both a negative perception of media practices, and an undertheorised view of the checking function of the press. Following Australian law reforms, the New Zealand Court of Appeal later expanded the defence of qualified privilege for media publications on matters of political expression. Neither of the above deficiencies was resolved.

B. 'Drawing the Line': Theoretical Disjunctions and Public Libel Reform

New Zealand's public libel reform was precipitated by a rare combination of clever lawyering and material facts involving a former Prime Minister. In *Lange v Atkinson* (*Lange No 2*),[124] the Court of Appeal provided a qualified privilege defence for media publications respecting the actions and qualities of those currently or formerly in Parliament (including candidates), provided those factors directly affected their capacity to meet their public responsibilities.[125] The Court also confirmed that public concern would justify the extent of publication, and that the statement must be published on a qualifying occasion.[126]

The facts resonated strongly with the checking function rationale. The plaintiff, David Russell Lange, was a former Prime Minister and leader of the New Zealand Labour Party. At the time of the defamatory publication, he was MP for the Mangere electorate and a senior member of the parliamentary opposition. The first defendant, Joe Atkinson, was a political studies lecturer at the University of Auckland and a columnist for the magazine *North & South*. The magazine's publisher was the second media defendant. *North & South* published an article by Mr Atkinson critical of the plaintiff's performance and leadership in office. The article was accompanied by a satirical political cartoon. The plaintiff sued the author and publisher for defamation, complaining he was conveyed as irresponsible, dishonest, insincere, manipulative, and lazy. The plaintiff applied to strike parts of the Statement of Defence pleading a novel 'Political Expression' defence, along with qualified privilege. The High Court dismissed the plaintiff's application, ruling that '[...] it is for the "common convenience and

[123] ibid 38 (emphasis added).
[124] (2000) 3 NZLR 385 (CA).
[125] ibid [10].
[126] ibid [38], [41].

welfare" of New Zealand society that the common law defence of qualified privilege should apply to claims for damages for defamation arising out of *political discussion*'.[127]

i. Lange No 1

The plaintiff's appeal was first heard by a five-member panel of the New Zealand Court of Appeal, which upheld the lower court's ruling.[128] Significantly, the Court of Appeal provided additional support for expanding qualified privilege by considering freedom of expression within its 'wider theoretical perspective'.[129]

After consulting authorities in Canada, the United States, Britain, and the Strasbourg Court, Justice Blanchard (Richardson P, Keith and Henry JJ concurring) acknowledged their collective doctrinal complexity, observing that '[t]hey reflect the proposition that however fundamental freedom of expression may be in the culture, law and politics of the jurisdictions in issue it will be given *varying degrees of importance* when it collides with other rights and interests'.[130] To better enhance the Court's application of free expression principles, Justice Blanchard examined their 'wider political and social context [...]',[131] which included many references to traditional free speech justifications. Unfortunately, despite attempts to enlarge freedom of expression's theoretical foundation, the Court's sole reference was to the considerably less relevant 'truth-seeking' rationale.[132]

For example, after referencing celebrated free speech passages by John Milton and John Stuart Mill,[133] the Court left such concerns in favour of ideas and sources more clearly aligned with public libels and the checking function. Quoting JF Stephen in a passage resonant with political concerns shared by Cato and Father of Candor over a century earlier, Justice Blanchard advised:

> Two different views may be taken of the *relation between rulers and their subjects*. If the ruler is regarded as the *superior* of the subject, as being by the nature of his position presumably wise and good, the rightful ruler and guide of the whole population, *it must necessarily follow* that it is wrong to censure him openly [...].

[127] *Lange v Atkinson and Australian Consolidated Press NZ Ltd* (1997) 2 NZLR 22 (HC) 46 (emphasis added).

[128] *Lange v Atkinson* (1998) 3 NZLR 424 (CA) (*Lange No 1*). The leading judgment was provided by Justice Blanchard (Richardson P, Keith and Henry JJ concurring). Justice Tipping wrote a separate concurring judgment.

[129] For criticism of the Court of Appeal's analysis, see New Zealand Law Commission, *Defaming Politicians: A Response to Lange v Atkinson* (Preliminary Paper 33, 1998) [15]–[16]. Ironically, the Commission's critique also overlooked the checking function.

[130] *Lange No 1* (n 128) 459 (emphasis added).

[131] *Lange No 1* (n 128) 460.

[132] See New Zealand Law Commission (n 129) [15], where the Law Commission properly dismissed the Court's references to Milton and Mill.

[133] *Lange No 1* (n 128) 460.

> If on the other hand the ruler is regarded as the *agent and servant*, and the subject as the wise and good master who is obliged to *delegate his power to the so-called ruler* because being a multitude he cannot use it himself, it is obvious that this sentiment *must be reversed*. […] To those who hold this view fully and carry it out to all its consequences *there can be no such offence as sedition*.[134]

Strangely, instead of emphasising democratic accountability and the checking function rationale, the above passages were referenced only because they '[…] suggest the *relative and contingent character* of areas of law like the present'.[135] Rather than supporting the press' role in checking government misconduct, Justice Blanchard claimed such remarks '[…] may better be seen as indicating a movement over the centuries […] of *basic changes in the constitution*, […] which had led by the late nineteenth century to *much greater* freedom of political speech'.[136] Therefore, despite the checking function's greater relevance, only the 'truth-seeking' rationale was effectively operative, which significantly undercut support for the Court of Appeal's doctrinal approach. Following remittance by the Privy Council,[137] this undertheorising compromised the doctrinal clarity otherwise promised by its more comprehensive comparative law analysis.

ii. Lange No 2

In *Lange No 2*,[138] the Court of Appeal again downplayed free expression justifications, neglecting theoretical analysis altogether. Without the checking function as a focal point, the Court's comparative legal analysis was unavoidably influenced by excessive and fragmented description, with little appreciation of how, specifically, differences among various institutions and defamation principles affect the press' ability to check misuse of government power. Much less could it discern how courts might tailor public libel doctrine to different institutional settings.

Although the Court avoided free speech theorising, it did explore New Zealand's local political and social conditions, including the responsibility and vulnerability of its institutional press.[139] Particularly significant was the unique relationship of New Zealanders to their government. Citing the general report of the Committee on Official Information, the Court stressed the Committee's expectations of 'popular participation in the making and administration of laws and policies, the promotion of *the accountability of those in office* and the government's need for public understanding and support to get its policies

[134] *Lange No 1* (n 128) 461 (emphasis added), quoting James Fitzjames Stephen, *A History of the Criminal Law of England* (London, Macmillan, 1883) Vol 2, 299–300.

[135] *Lange No 1* (n 128) 461 (emphasis added).

[136] *Lange No 1* (n 128) 461 (emphasis added).

[137] *Lange v Atkinson* [2000] 1 NZLR 257 (PC).

[138] *Lange No 2* (n 124).

[139] *Lange No 2* (n 124) [32]–[36].

carried out [...]'.[140] Besides promoting Meiklejohnian theory and democratic accountability, the Court also adopted the Committee's liberal characterisation of New Zealand's institutional press, observing:

> New Zealand is a small country. The Government has a *pervasive involvement in our everyday national life*. This involvement is not only felt, but it is also sought, by New Zealanders, who have tended to *view successive Governments as their agents*, and have expected them to act as such. [...] Our social support systems also rely heavily on central government. History and circumstances give New Zealanders *special reason for wanting to know what their Government is doing and why*.[141]

Despite describing New Zealand democracy in a manner consistent with the checking function, the Court's failure to adequately theorise free expression rationales greatly inhibited its ability to track the doctrinal implications and general significance of its otherwise astute observations. For instance, after noting the Privy Council's mention of the importance to public libel principles of differing press structures, the Court stated revealingly that 'this material is of limited significance since this case is *less* about the press and rather more about the constitutional right of all New Zealanders to *participate in the discussion and evaluation of their own political leaders*'.[142] Rather than consider the press' role in reporting on abuses of official power—the above quotes do on balance resonate most with Meiklejohnian notions—the Court sharply distinguished *Reynolds* and the Australian *Lange* case, noting in an overly-technical manner that '[t]he plaintiffs in those two cases were *foreign politicians* and accordingly would not fall within the conclusions this Court stated in 1998 [*Lange No 1*]'.[143]

At last, without appealing to the checking function and exploring its institutional requirements, it is difficult to accept the Court of Appeal's reasoning for defending either its chosen doctrinal approach, or its laudable efforts to 'fine-tune' qualified privilege principles to New Zealand's institutional context.

C. Enlarging the Scope of Qualified Privilege

New Zealand's *Lange* decisions have complicated expanding qualified privilege beyond its original application. Central to these complications has been the Court of Appeal's negative conceptions of the press. While the scope of qualified privilege has been challenged recently in *Dooley v Smith*[144]—*Dooley* is significant for

[140] *Lange No 2* (n 124) [32] (emphasis added), citing Committee on Official Information, *Towards Open Government: General Report* (Wellington, 1980) (Danks Committee Report).

[141] *Lange No 2* (n 124) [32] (emphasis added), citing Danks Committee Report, ibid [21].

[142] *Lange No 2* (n 124) [33] (emphasis added).

[143] *Lange No 2* (n 124) [33] (emphasis added).

[144] [2012] NZHC 529. See also *Karam v Parker* [2014] NZHC 737, where the High Court recently rejected an extension of the *Lange* defence.

suggesting that the *Lange* defence is available for defamatory statements about a locally-elected trustee—continued disregard of free expression justifications has, on balance, prevented principled expansion of New Zealand's public libel principles.

Undertheorising of the checking function first resurfaced in *Vickery v McLean*.[145] Though no media figures were impleaded, *Vickery* involved classic checking function concerns of fraud and political corruption allegations published by the press. The three plaintiffs were officers of the Papakura District Council. The defendant Mr Vickery, a local Papakuran resident and Chairman of its Ratepayers Association, objected to a political proposal for outsourcing and franchising Papakura's provision of water and waste water services. Concerned that the prospective franchisee was involved in corruption scandals overseas, Mr Vickery distributed a document alleging procedural irregularities and international corruption. The defendant forwarded his concerns to three newspapers, including *The New Zealand Herald*. After the Serious Fraud Office informed Mr Vickery that available evidence discredited his accusations, the Mayor of Papakura requested an apology. Mr Vickery declined. At trial, the publications were described as 'political expressions' in unsuccessful attempts to rely on the *Lange* defence. The jury awarded the three plaintiffs a total of $55,000 damages.

On appeal, a unanimous Court of Appeal dismissed the submission that the *Lange* defence 'should logically be extended to cover local body as well as national politicians'.[146] The Court concluded unconvincingly that '*[t]he rationale* for the *Lange* privilege cannot be regarded as applying to the present circumstances'.[147] Relying on an excessively narrow reading of 'political discussion', Justice Tipping (on behalf of the Court) reasoned:

> It is of major moment to notice that those who have been defamed are *not* politicians, whether national or local. They are *paid servants of a local body*. They may contribute to policy making but they are *not* the ultimate policy makers. The subject matter of Mr Vickery's publications *cannot sensibly be regarded as political discussion*, much less political discussion of a kind contemplated by *Lange No. 2* or *any rational extension* of that decision.[148]

Insisting that Mr Vickery 'establish his asserted privilege by reference to first principles',[149] the Court offered the following ironic commentary on the defendant's 'futile' position, advising:

> It is, in our view, *demonstrably not in the public interest* to have criminal allegations, even if bona fide and responsibly made, *ventilated through the news media*. That could

145 [2000] NZCA 338.
146 ibid [13].
147 ibid [15] (emphasis added).
148 ibid [17] (emphasis added).
149 ibid [18].

> *only* encourage trial by media and associated developments which would be inimical to criminal justice processes. *Society has mechanisms for investigating crime and determining guilt or innocence. It is not in the public interest that these mechanisms be bypassed or subverted.*[150]

Illustrative of deficiencies in the Court's public libel analysis was its disregard of free expression justifications. Of particular relevance to *Vickery's* reasoning and outcome were accountability concerns and the checking function of the press. For instance, the Court's remarkably obtuse distinction between 'politicians' and 'paid servants of a local body',[151] would be difficult (if not impossible) to uphold had its focus been on democratic accountability and New Zealanders' well-documented need to 'know what their government is doing'. The checking function also vitiates the Court's concern that 'paid servants of a local body' were not 'the ultimate policy makers'.[152] Misconduct at the hands of either group is sufficiently important to warrant mass publication and condemnation. Most importantly, a fundamental role of the press in any democracy is *investigative journalism*, which surely qualifies as a legitimate 'mechanism for investigating crime'. Justice Tipping's reasoning that 'previous perceptions of the public interest' had not changed sufficiently to permit expanding qualified privilege beyond the strict ratio in *Lange No 2* is, in the end, wholly contingent on the Court of Appeal's theoretical enquiry. Overlooking the checking function in *Vickery* contributed to an undertheorised conception of freedom of expression that greatly undermined its reasoning and results.

Despite the Court of Appeal's adherence to *Lange's* original formulation, New Zealand's lower courts have begun challenging the notion that qualified privilege must remain narrowly restricted to publications involving only MPs or candidates for office. In *Dooley*,[153] Justice Lang suggested in dicta that defamatory statements about a locally-elected trustee potentially attract the *Lange* defence. While the press was not directly involved, *Dooley* involved serious allegations of government misconduct characteristic of public libel cases.

The plaintiff Dooley was a trustee of Development West Coast (DWC), a registered charitable trust. He was also DWC's Chairman. DWC was established to manage $92 million allocated to the wider West Coast region for economic development. DWC's activities attracted the news media's attention, along with community residents and ratepayers. The defamatory statements were made by two of Dooley's fellow trustees, Mr Smith and Mr Shahadat, to journalists at the *Greymouth Star*. The statements alleged Dooley's interference with appointments to DWC's Board of Trustees, and his denial of such meddling. These allegations formed the basis of a front-page article in the *Greymouth Star*, which

150 ibid [19] (emphasis added).
151 ibid [17].
152 ibid.
153 *Dooley* (n 144).

was reproduced by the *Westport News*. Although the self-represented defendants sought to rely on qualified privilege, neither referenced *Lange* or *Vickery* in their submissions.

Despite this oversight, Justice Lang outlined in dicta why the *Lange* defence was available to the *Dooley* defendants. Although defeated by overriding motives of hostility attributed to the defendants (thereby constituting 'malice'), the defence of qualified privilege was nonetheless subjected to searching and extensive review. Justice Lang began by acknowledging the 'tightly defined' subject matter of the privilege as being 'limited to those elected or seeking election to Parliament'.[154] Nevertheless, the High Court was emboldened in its approach by *Vickery*. As 'the only other case since *Lange* in which the Court of Appeal has been required to consider the application of the principles enunciated in the *Lange* judgments',[155] Justice Lang insisted that 'the Court did *not* deal with the issue of whether those principles might apply to elected officials other than members of Parliament'.[156] Distinguishing *Vickery* on the basis that more serious criminal wrongdoings were alleged in *Dooley*, Justice Lang preferred a more liberal reading of the *Lange* defence, stating:

> [...] the Court of Appeal did not take the opportunity in *Vickery* to say that qualified privilege of the type identified in *Lange* was restricted exclusively to defamatory statements made in respect of elected members of Parliament. It appears to have left open the possibility that the defence *might extend to other elected officials in circumstances where the principles that the Court identified indicate that it should apply*.[157]

Implicitly warning of a 'blending of position and power' observed earlier by US Supreme Court Chief Justice Warren in *Curtis Publishing Co v Butts*,[158] Justice Lang reasoned:

> I see no logical reason why the principles enunciated in *Lange* should be restricted exclusively to statements made about [...] elected members of Parliament. Members of the public may have an *equally legitimate interest* in being informed about the performance of persons who hold, or may in the future hold, *elected positions of responsibility in other public institutions*. That is particularly so where the institution in question is responsible for managing, and/or developing policy in respect of assets or activities that are *publicly owned or funded*. The public has a right to be informed when a person who has been, or may be, elected to such a position has acted in a manner that may *call into question his or her suitability to hold that position*.[159]

Notably, far more so than 'logic', of fundamental importance in *Dooley* was Justice Lang's theoretical sensitivity to political accountability and the checking function

[154] *Dooley* (n 144) [157].
[155] *Dooley* (n 144) [155].
[156] *Dooley* (n 144) [155] (emphasis added).
[157] *Dooley* (n 144) [170] (emphasis added).
[158] 388 US 130, 163–64 (1967).
[159] *Dooley* (n 144) [171] (emphasis added).

of the press. He observed generally that 'DWC is undoubtedly an institution that has an extremely important role to play in the future economic wellbeing of the entire West Coast region'.[160] Justice Lang also emphasised that 'DWC is [...] a form of *representative* and *responsible government*. Its governance is provided, in part at least, by trustees who are elected from different West Coast communities. They therefore hold elected public office'.[161] Justice Lang accordingly concluded:

> The communities of the West Coast therefore have a very real interest in ensuring that those who are elected (or for that matter appointed) as trustees of DWC have the necessary personal attributes to hold that position. For the same reason, those communities have a *vital interest in the integrity of the processes by which trustees are both elected and appointed*. [...] All of these factors suggest that *the defence may extend to statements made about persons who are elected or appointed as trustees of DWC*.[162]

Dooley therefore demonstrates that the *Lange* defence can be 'reasonably' expanded provided that free expression rationales—particularly the checking function of the press—are properly articulated and applied. Unfortunately, the Court of Appeal recently ignored Justice Lang's reasoning in *Dooley*, missing another opportunity to remedy its jurisprudential failings and further intensifying lower court confusion.[163] As a result, New Zealand's public libel jurisprudence awaits definitive and comprehensive articulation of the checking function and free expression justifications more generally.

D. Conclusion

The New Zealand Court of Appeal has expanded qualified privilege to protect defamatory publications on matters of political expression. Yet, despite liberalising its media defamation laws, serious concerns remain about their theoretical foundations. While New Zealand courts now evaluate media privilege claims in wider social and constitutional contexts, they have not consistently referenced free expression rationales. As in Britain, New Zealand courts have disregarded the checking function in paradigmatic cases involving official misconduct. This oversight has compromised New Zealand's public libel principles, ultimately underprotecting press interests through an artificially narrow view of

[160] *Dooley* (n 144) [174].

[161] *Dooley* (n 144) [175] (emphasis added).

[162] *Dooley* (n 144) [176] (emphasis added).

[163] See *Smith v Dooley* [2013] NZCA 428 [74], where the appeal turned on the absence of 'defamatory meaning', rendering Justice Lang's dicta redundant. For the most recent example of the confusion *Lange* has engendered, see *Durie v Gardiner* [2017] NZHC 377, where in dismissing the plaintiffs' motion to strike, the High Court both refused to extend the *Lange* defence to accusations of corruption concerning the co-chair of an elected, statutory body, but accepted as 'tenable' at law, the adoption of a 'public interest' defence similar to *Reynolds* and *Grant*.

'political expression', and by overlooking the functional equivalence of holding to account elected politicians, public servants, and certain 'public figures'. This undertheorising has ultimately weakened the Court of Appeal's otherwise more sophisticated comparative law framework for adapting public libel doctrine to distinct institutional settings.

V. Chapter Conclusion

Chapter four has examined two important developments contributing to the present-day undertheorising of public libel doctrine. Besides disregarding a credible and principled foundation for political libels advanced by the Strasbourg Court, Britain's highest courts have repeatedly overlooked the checking function in paradigmatic public libel cases involving investigative reporting of official misconduct by politicians and public officials. Likewise, the New Zealand Court of Appeal has disregarded strong domestic articulations of the checking function due to outmoded authorities evidencing substantial bias against the institutional press.

In our next and final section of Part B, chapter five concludes our comparative doctrinal analysis by examining the treatment of Meiklejohnian theory and the checking function rationale by UK and Canadian authorities. Both jurisdictions provide illustrative examples of the dangers of conflating these two democratic models when attempting to 'optimally' balance freedom of expression against reputational interests.

5

Conflating Meiklejohnian Theory and the Checking Function of the Press

I. Overview

Besides denying the checking function's limited foothold in public libel doctrine, an equally concerning (and related) manifestation of undertheorising is the conflation of the checking function with Meiklejohnian theory. As discussed in chapter two, despite their distinct emphases and assumptions, judges, legislators, and legal scholars have routinely construed these models as synonymous, showing little regard for their potentially sweeping implications for public libel doctrine and reform. Although this confusion is prevalent amongst all of our comparators, it is most instructively exhibited by UK authorities and the Supreme Court of Canada.

II. United Kingdom

British judges and legislators have struggled to describe the *Reynolds*[1] defence from its inception. Even after replacing *Reynolds* with a defence of 'Publication on Matter of Public Interest' under the Defamation Act 2013,[2] confusion persists regarding Britain's new approach. Based on structural similarities between the 'reciprocity obligations' of qualified privilege and the informational dynamics of Meiklejohn's 'self-governance' rationale, difficulties distinguishing the checking function from broader notions of democratic theory have most recently compromised parliamentary debates guiding the UK's latest defamation law reforms. As with the House of Lords in *Reynolds*, this undertheorising has led the UK Parliament to confuse doctrinal differences between American and English libel laws and to understate its commitment to freedom of expression.

[1] *Reynolds v Times Newspapers Ltd* [2001] 2 AC 127 (HL).
[2] Defamation Act 2013 (UK) c 26, s 4.

A. Reciprocity Obligations and Meiklejohnian Theory

A significant contributor to the checking function's undertheorising is the integration of Meiklejohnian theory into Britain's public libel doctrine. Since *Reynolds*, this feature of Britain's approach to enhancing libel protection for media defendants has further obscured independent recognition of accountability concerns and the checking function rationale.

The influence of Meiklejohn's democratic 'self-governance' rationale was apparent from the outset in *Reynolds*. Rejecting a generic qualified privilege for political expression, Lord Nicholls first characterised the relationship between freedom of expression and democracy in highly abstract terms reflecting Meiklejohn's prioritisation of deliberative processes, stating:

> The high importance of *freedom to impart and receive information and ideas* has been stated so often and so eloquently that this point calls for no elaboration in this case. At a pragmatic level, freedom to disseminate and receive information on political matters is *essential to the proper functioning of the system of parliamentary democracy* cherished in this country.[3]

Besides Lord Nicholls' reliance on this free speech justification, Lord Steyn's opinion in *Reynolds* also failed to differentiate Meiklejohnian theory from the checking function. Attempting to identify the 'foundational principle' of qualified privilege for *political expression*, Lord Steyn suitably nominated the '[…] "vital public watchdog role of the press" […]', underlining its 'essential role in a democratic society'.[4] However, instead of prioritising the checking of political and official misconduct, it was promptly conflated with distinctive 'self-governance' concerns. Stressing the press' role as 'information purveyor' for purposes of democratic deliberation, Lord Steyn reasoned:

> In *De Haes and Gijsels v Belgium* […] the European Court of Human Rights again emphasised that the press plays an essential role in a democratic society. The court trenchantly observed […]: 'It is incumbent on the press to impart information and ideas of public interest. Not only does the press have the task of imparting such information and ideas: the public also has a right to receive them.' *This principle must be the foundation of our law on qualified privilege of political speech.*[5]

The English Court of Appeal confirmed this understanding in *Loutchansky v Times Newspapers Ltd (Nos 2–5)*.[6] Providing groundwork for his judgment in *Flood v Times Newspapers Ltd*,[7] Lord Phillips MR, for a unanimous Court of Appeal in *Loutchansky*, confirmed that the *Reynolds* privilege was '[…] a *different*

[3] *Reynolds* (n 1) 200 (emphasis added).
[4] *Reynolds* (n 1) 214 (citation omitted).
[5] *Reynolds* (n 1) 214–15 (citations omitted) (emphasis added).
[6] [2002] QB 783 (CA).
[7] [2012] UKSC 11.

jurisprudential creature from the traditional form of privilege from which it sprang',[8] consisting of 'a single composite test' with a unique understanding of interest and duty. Plainly emphasising the informational dynamics of Meiklejohnian theory, Lord Phillips MR instructed:

> The interest is that of the public in a modern democracy in free expression and, more particularly, in the promotion of a *free and vigorous press to keep the public informed.* [...] The *corresponding duty* on the journalist (and equally his editor) is to play his proper role in discharging that function. His task is to behave as a responsible journalist.[9]

The *Reynolds* defence was placed into sharper relief in *Jameel v Wall Street Journal Europe*.[10] Although the House of Lords split on its proper classification, both Lord Hoffmann and Lady Hale reiterated that '[the] "*Reynolds* privilege" is "a different jurisprudential creature from the traditional form of privilege [...]"',[11] describing it as a 'defence of publication in the public interest'.[12] Lord Hoffmann signalled the *Reynolds* defence's controlling rationale by first contrasting it with qualified privilege, skilfully observing:

> Although Lord Nicholls uses the word 'privilege', it is clearly not being used in the old sense. It is the *material* which is privileged, *not the occasion* on which it is published. There is no question of the privilege being defeated by proof of malice because *the propriety of the conduct of the defendant is built into the conditions under which the material is privileged.*[13]

Lord Hoffmann then revealed the rationale for the House of Lords' approach, effectively identifying Meiklejohnian theory as embedded in the *Reynolds* defence:

> The *Reynolds* defence was developed from the traditional form of privilege by a *generalisation* that in *matters of public interest,* there can be said to be a professional duty on the part of journalists to impart the information and an interest in the public in receiving it. The House having made this generalisation, it should in my opinion be regarded as a *proposition of law* and not decided each time as a question of fact. If the publication is in the public interest, *the duty and interest are taken to exist.*[14]

Once past the 'public interest' test, Lord Hoffmann added that '[...] the inquiry then shifts to whether the steps taken to gather and publish the information were responsible and fair'.[15] Insisting that this conduct be assessed in a 'practical and

[8] *Loutchansky* (n 6) [35] (emphasis added).

[9] *Loutchansky* (n 6) [36] (emphasis added). See also *Bonnick v Morris* [2003] 1 AC 300 (PC) [23], where Lord Nicholls presumptively advised: '[r]esponsible journalism is the point at which a *fair balance* is held between freedom of expression on matters of public concern and the reputations of individuals' (emphasis added).

[10] [2007] 1 AC 359 (HL).

[11] ibid [46], quoting *Loutchansky* (n 6) [35].

[12] ibid [146].

[13] ibid [46] (emphasis added).

[14] ibid [50] (emphasis added).

[15] ibid [53].

flexible manner',[16] he maintained that Lord Nicholls' ten factors '[...] are *not* tests which the publication has to pass'.[17] Although Lord Bingham, Lord Hope, and Lord Scott supported the traditional duty-interest test of qualified privilege, Lady Hale agreed with Lord Hoffmann, stating '[w]e need more such serious journalism in this country and our defamation law should encourage rather than discourage it'.[18] Regrettably, as the free expression rationale most conducive to 'serious journalism', the checking function remained methodologically obscured in the House of Lords' doctrinal reflections.

Flood also demonstrates that democratic 'self-governance' remains the controlling rationale. Despite reluctance to confirm its foundational principles, Lord Phillips P tellingly quoted Lady Hale's dictum on reciprocal obligations, reaffirming that 'the *Reynolds* defence sprang from "the general obligation of the press, media and other publishers to communicate important information upon matters of general public interest and the general right of the public to receive such information"'.[19] He similarly endorsed Lady Hale's statement that 'there must be some real public interest in having this information in the public domain'.[20] Importantly, by describing the *Reynolds* defence without noting that the plaintiff in *Jameel* was *not* a public official, *Flood* demonstrates the subtle influence of Meiklejohnian theory on curtailing recognition of the checking function in England's public libel doctrine.

B. Undertheorising in the UK Parliament

While the UK Supreme Court has been reluctant to identify the principles underlying *Reynolds*,[21] the British Parliament has countered by enacting the Defamation Act 2013.[22] Section 4 abolishes the *Reynolds* defence, replacing it with a statutory defence intended to be more protective of freedom of expression and the press. However, in selecting an approach between the 'actual malice' rule and *Reynolds*, parliamentary debates regarding the Act reveal an all-too-familiar undertheorising of free expression justifications. As in England's highest courts, the most significant manifestation in Hansard is the conflation of the checking function with Meiklejohnian theory.

[16] ibid [56], quoting Lord Nicholls in *Bonnick* (n 9) [24].
[17] ibid (emphasis added).
[18] ibid [150].
[19] *Flood* (n 7) [42], quoting *Jameel* (n 10) [146].
[20] *Flood* (n 7) [42].
[21] Lord Phillips P remarked in *Flood* (n 7) that '[...] I do not consider that this Court should lay down any general principle as to the approach to be adopted by an appellate court to an issue of *Reynolds* privilege' (at [106]). Lord Mance agreed (at [182]), as did Lord Clarke (at [186]), and Lord Dyson (at [203]).
[22] Defamation Act 2013 (n 2).

i. Doctrinal and Theoretical Disjunctions

Recognising the close relationship between defamation law and democracy, present-day UK libel reform has sought to 'optimally balance' free expression and reputation, a point emphasised by the Joint Committee on the Draft Defamation Bill prior to parliamentary debates.[23] Although an approach similar to the 'actual malice' rule was considered,[24] the Joint Committee promptly rejected this option. It reasoned (curiously) that it would 'offer insufficient protection to people whose reputation is harmed by untruths and *overly focus* on the *mind of the publisher* [...]'.[25] The Joint Committee set the tone for parliamentary debate by providing no discernible rationale or justification for its doctrinal preferences.

ii. House of Lords

Compared to the sterile treatment of the proposed defence in the House of Commons,[26] the House of Lords favoured significant reforms. Whatever theoretical basis existed was provided most authoritatively by Lord Lester, who had represented the defendants in *Reynolds*. In contrast to the casual references to the checking function in both Houses of Parliament,[27] Lord Lester defended the proposed defence in familiar Meiklejohnian terms, advising that

> [i]t is not a privilege because the newspaper or whatever should have a special right. It is a privilege because the public, through the eyes and ears on [*sic*] the media, are *entitled* to have information provided to them on matters of public interest.[28]

Lord Lester also provided a surprising account of comparative differences between the 'actual malice' rule and Britain's proposed new defence. Staunchly defending the latter, he engaged in a deeply flawed instance of comparative legal analysis, reasoning:

> What came out of *Reynolds* was a compromise on the American position. The reason why the American position does not make much sense—with respect to the great court that decided *New York Times v Sullivan*—is that *it focuses on the identity of the publisher and not the content of the publication*. It asks: is the publisher a public figure? That is the wrong question. It *does not matter whether the publisher is a public figure*. What matters is *whether it is in the public interest* to publish what is in the publication.[29]

[23] Joint Committee on the Draft Defamation Bill, *Session 2010–12: Report, together with formal minutes* (HC 930–I, 19 October 2011) 15.

[24] ibid 27–28.

[25] ibid 28 (emphasis added).

[26] See HC Deb 12 September 2012 col 370, where Labour Party MP Sadiq Khan lamented: '[t]he Bill has reached Third Reading without any major improvements or changes since it was first published back in May'. The Bill passed to 'the other place' essentially unchanged.

[27] House of Commons, see ibid cols 372 (Morris MP), 378 (Hughes MP), and 380 (Russell MP). House of Lords, see HL Deb 9 October 2012 col 933 (Lord McNally).

[28] HL Deb 19 December 2012 col GC538 (emphasis added).

[29] ibid (emphasis added). See also *New York Times v Sullivan* 376 US 254 (1964).

What is particularly interesting about this passage is not that Lord Lester's analysis is incorrect, but in trying to understand it at all. The inaccuracy in Lord Lester's argument is, of course, that the US Supreme Court focussed on 'the identity of the publisher' in *New York Times v Sullivan*.[30] As exemplified in post-*Sullivan* jurisprudence, the Court's primary focus in tailoring doctrinal approaches was overwhelmingly the identity of the *target* of the defamatory remarks. Respectfully, Lord Lester appears to have gotten matters upturned. We can better understand this muddle by comparing how both jurisdictions have theorised the checking function of the press. These subtle but significant differences have important implications for public libel doctrine.

Beginning with *Reynolds*, Britain's preferred method has been an ad hoc, balancing approach, anchored in privileging defamatory statements on matters of public interest subject to a 'responsible journalism' test. The dominant theoretical rationale employed through *Reynolds*, *Jameel*, and *Flood*—to the extent it is discernible—has been Meiklejohn's democratic 'self-governance' rationale. This largely unspoken justification has supported doctrinal approaches more consistent with facilitating democratic deliberation and electoral decision-making, rather than alternatives more closely tied to ensuring adequate measures of democratic accountability.[31]

By comparison, America has endorsed a generic qualified privilege for public officials, public servants, and certain public figures. The overriding concern has *not* been the publisher's identity, but the identity of the *plaintiff*. Methodologically, although *Sullivan* predominately engaged Meiklejohnian notions, focussing on the identity of the plaintiff highlights concerns more resonant with the checking function's goals of holding power to account and reporting information about what government and influential individuals are up to. While the US Supreme Court has certainly not always relied on the checking function explicitly or even consistently,[32] shifting the focus of doctrinal and legislative attention from published content to the target of the defamatory statements engages deeper reflection on accountability mechanisms more resonant with the checking function than Meiklejohnian theory, particularly in cases involving political officials and public servants. In short, the level of abstraction at which we engage democratic theory matters greatly. Lord Lester's miscalculation of doctrinal differences between UK and US libel laws is perhaps best explained by misapprehending

[30] ibid.

[31] British scholars rarely discuss free expression theories. Nonetheless, examples supporting democratic 'self-governance' as public libel law's underlying rationale include, Ian Loveland, 'Defamation of "Government": Taking Lessons from America?' (1994) 14 *Legal Studies* 206; Ian Loveland, 'Reforming Libel Law: The Public Law Dimension' (1997) 46 *International and Comparative Law Quarterly* 561; Kyu Ho Youm, 'The Interaction Between American and Foreign Libel Law: US Courts Refuse to Enforce English Libel Judgments' (2000) 49 *International and Comparative Law Quarterly* 131; Ian Loveland, *Political Libels: A Comparative Study* (Oxford, Hart Publishing, 2000); Eric Barendt, 'Freedom of Speech in the Media' in Eric Barendt, *Freedom of Speech*, 2nd edn (Oxford, Oxford University Press, 2007).

[32] See Chapter three.

these concerns. Of course, he may also have simply raised an older procedural criticism regarding the 'actual malice' rule's alleged influence on the complications and costs of post-*Sullivan* libel litigation.[33] Still, it would seem that the UK Parliament's undertheorising of the checking function generally tracks the difficulties experienced by England's highest courts.

C. Conclusion

The UK's revised statutory defence lies somewhere between the 'actual malice' rule and the *Reynolds* defence. Although Parliament expects courts to consult *Reynolds*, *Jameel*, and *Flood* when interpreting this new defence,[34] it remains unclear whether English courts will embrace the legislation's broader intent to enhance freedom of expression and the press. Without a stronger lineage of jurisprudence carefully distinguishing accountability concerns and the checking function from Meiklejohnian theory, it is unrealistic that UK courts should achieve a clear and consistent view of these matters anytime soon.

III. Canada

Perhaps no legal body has confused the checking function with Meiklejohnian theory more revealingly than the Supreme Court of Canada. Historically, the Court recognised an implied right of 'public and political expression' that resonated strongly with the checking function rationale. Its post-Charter jurisprudence, on the other hand, demonstrates that this limited (but important) constitutional foothold quickly lost purchase, assured by its exclusion from the Supreme Court of Canada's official inventory of free expression rationales. In formulating its defence of 'Responsible Communication on Matters of Public Interest', the Supreme Court adopted a variation of *Reynolds* as an ostensible 'middle ground', without first considering the checking function, or its potential roots in the Court's pre-Charter jurisprudence. This methodological approach raises at least two serious concerns.

First, by disregarding the checking function as a 'core' value, the Court has unduly emphasised alternative free expression rationales to take up the analytical slack. Necessarily, this further intensifies the Court's predilection for conflating the checking function with Meiklejohnian theory. Second, by methodologically omitting the checking function from consideration, Canada's highest court has

[33] For a similar critique by the Supreme Court of Canada, see *Hill v Church of Scientology* [1995] 2 SCR 1130 [127]. See also Randall P Bezanson, 'Libel Law and the Realities of Litigation: Setting the Record Straight' (1985) 71 *Iowa Law Review* 226, 228–29; Richard A Epstein, 'Was *New York Times v. Sullivan* Wrong?' (1986) 53 *University of Chicago Law Review* 782.

[34] Explanatory Notes to the Defamation Act 2013 [29].

misleadingly reported that 'proper weight' was given to freedom of expression and press interests, and that it has justifiably 'tipped the balance' in support of stronger defamation defences for media defendants. Besides resulting in vague and unconvincing assessments of foreign doctrinal alternatives, above all, this undertheorising undermines the basis of the Supreme Court's current public libel regime.

A. A 'Quasi-Constitutional' Press: The Checking Function before the Charter

Prior to enacting the Charter, the Supreme Court of Canada recognised freedom of expression as fundamental to Canadian democracy. In *Reference re Alberta Legislation*,[35] the Court created a limited degree of constitutional protection for political expression, endorsing an implied right of free expression on 'public and political matters'. From inception, the Supreme Court characterised this right elegiacally as 'the breath of life for parliamentary institutions',[36] a phrase equally resonant with Meiklejohnian theory *or* the checking function rationale.

Alberta Legislation involved challenges to several bills passed by Alberta's legislative assembly, which aimed to substitute a novel credit structure for the prevailing financial system. Bill No 9, ironically titled An Act to Ensure the Publication of Accurate News and Information (Press Bill), contained the following restrictions aimed at owners, editors, publishers, and managers of newspaper organisations: (1) that newspapers publish (within 31 days) any statement directed by the Chairman of the Social Credit Board as a 'correction or amplification of any statement relating to any policy or activity of the government';[37] (2) that within 24 hours of a government request, newspapers reveal their journalistic sources and the identity of the writer of any disputed news item; (3) that publications made under authority of the Act be immune from defamation liability; and (4) that besides imposing penalties, the government may prohibit publication for fixed or indefinite periods, including prohibiting information from specific writers or sources.[38]

In view of this unprecedented array of prior restraints, subsequent punishment, and breaches of journalistic confidentiality, the Supreme Court justifiably

[35] [1938] SCR 100. For background on *Alberta Legislation*, see Robert Martin, *Essentials of Canadian Law: Media Law*, 2nd edn (Toronto, Irwin Law, 2003) 25ff.

[36] ibid [108] (Duff CJC). Despite resonating with the checking function, *Alberta Legislation* has been widely interpreted by Canadian scholars in Meiklejohnian terms. See Clare F Beckton, 'Freedom of Expression in Canada—How Free?' (1983) 13 *Manitoba Law Journal* 583, 588; Richard Moon, 'The Scope of Freedom of Expression' (1985) 23 *Osgoode Hall Law Journal* 331, 333–35; A Wayne MacKay, 'Freedom of Expression: Is It All Just Talk?' (1989) 68 *Canadian Bar Review* 713, 718–19; Keith Dubick, 'The Theoretical Foundation for Protecting Freedom of Expression' (2001) 13 *National Journal of Constitutional Law* 1, 2–6; Robin Elliot, 'The Supreme Court's Understanding of the Democratic Self-Government, Advancement of Truth and Knowledge and Individual Self-Realization Rationales for Protecting Freedom of Expression: Part I—Taking Stock' (2012) 59 *Supreme Court Law Review* 435 [56].

[37] *Alberta Legislation* (n 35) [136].

[38] *Alberta Legislation* (n 35) [136]–[140].

denounced the Press Bill, warning that it was '[...] attempting to revive the old theory of the crime of seditious libel [...]'.[39] Referencing important eighteenth-century libel reforms, Justice Cannon reminded Canadians that '[...] since the passing of Fox's Libel Act in 1792, [...] it is not criminal to point out errors in the Government of the country and to urge their removal by lawful means [...]'.[40]

The Supreme Court held that the Press Bill was ultra vires the Alberta legislature (due to exclusive federal jurisdiction over 'peace, order, and good government'). Both Justice Cannon and Chief Justice Duff stressed the importance to representative democracies of freedom of expression and the press. Specifically, Justice Cannon cautioned that the Press Bill unjustifiably restricted newspapers' ability to criticise government, observing:

> The bill does not regulate the relations of the newspapers' owners with private individual members of the public, but deals exclusively with expressions of opinion by the newspapers *concerning government policies and activities.* The pith and substance of the bill is to *regulate the press of Alberta from the viewpoint of public policy* by preventing the public from being misled or deceived as to any policy or activity of the Social Credit Government and by *reducing any opposition to silence or bring upon it ridicule and public contempt.*[41]

Chief Justice Duff also counselled that the Press Bill '[...] manifestly places in the hands of the Chairman of the Social Credit Commission *autocratic powers* [...]',[42] and that it disconcertingly '[...] effects such a curtailment of the exercise of the right of public discussion as substantially to interfere with the working of the parliamentary institutions of Canada [...]'.[43] The Chief Justice explained:

> The statute [*British North America Act*] contemplates a parliament working under the influence of public opinion and public discussion. There can be no controversy that such institutions derive their efficacy from the *free public discussion of affairs, from criticism and answer and counter-criticism, from attack upon policy and administration and defence and counter-attack;* from the freest and fullest analysis and examination from every point of view of political proposals.[44]

Implicating the press' 'information purveyor' and 'watchdog' roles, Justice Cannon likewise insisted that '[t]here must be an *untrammeled publication* of the news and political opinions of the political parties contending for ascendancy.[45]

Freedom of expression and press independence were also featured in three Québec cases from the 1950s. In *R v Boucher*,[46] a Jehovah's Witness was convicted

[39] *Alberta Legislation* (n 35) [147] (Cannon J).
[40] *Alberta Legislation* (n 35) [146].
[41] *Alberta Legislation* (n 35) [142] (Cannon J) (emphasis added).
[42] *Alberta Legislation* (n 35) [114] (Duff CJC) (emphasis added).
[43] *Alberta Legislation* (n 35) [111].
[44] *Alberta Legislation* (n 35) [106] (emphasis added).
[45] *Alberta Legislation* (n 35) [148] (Cannon J) (emphasis added).
[46] [1951] SCR 265.

of seditious libel for publishing a religious pamphlet criticising Québec courts. Describing seditious libel as '[…] contempt in words of political authority or the actions of authority', Justice Rand identified its underlying social assumption as the outmoded view of '[…] the governors of society *as superior beings*, exercising a divine mandate, by whom laws, institutions and administrations are given […] to be obeyed'.[47] Rejecting such notions as incompatible with Canadian democracy, a plurality of the Court overturned the conviction, protecting government criticism as a lawful form of expression and protest.

In *Saumur v Québec (City)*,[48] a Jehovah's Witness challenged a municipal by-law prohibiting unauthorised distribution of written material in city streets. Contravention was punishable by fine, with imprisonment in default of payment. Justices Rand, Kellock, and Locke quoted *Alberta Legislation* on safeguarding free public discussion of political affairs. Declaring the municipal by-law ultra vires the City of Québec, Justice Kellock analogised it to Alberta's Press Bill, quoting Chief Justice Duff's opinion in *Alberta Legislation* that legislative authority over newspapers ends when it '[…] effects such a curtailment of the exercise of the right of public discussion as substantially to interfere with the working of the parliamentary institutions of Canada […]'.[49]

Finally, the Supreme Court of Canada revisited these issues in *Switzman v Elbling*,[50] where the Court invalidated Québec's Act Respecting Communistic Propaganda, partly on considerations of freedom of expression and the press. Educing notions of democratic accountability and the checking function rationale, Justice Abbott reinforced Chief Justice Duff's reasoning in *Alberta Legislation*, concluding that '[t]he right of free expression of opinion and of criticism, upon matters of public policy and public administration, […] are essential to the working of a parliamentary democracy such as ours'.[51]

Overall, despite entanglement with Meiklejohnian theory, the Supreme Court's dicta on an implied right of political expression in *Alberta Legislation*—along with associated commentary in *Boucher*, *Saumur*, and *Switzman*—remain the clearest articulations of the checking function in Canadian constitutional law.

B. Post-Charter Methodological Errors

With the introduction of the Canadian Charter of Rights and Freedoms in 1982, Canada constitutionally entrenched human rights protection. As outlined in chapter one, the key free expression guarantees are found in subsection 2(*b*), which extends protection to the press and other media of communication.

47 ibid 285–86 (emphasis added).
48 [1953] 2 SCR 299.
49 ibid 354, quoting *Alberta Legislation* (n 35) [111].
50 [1957] SCR 285.
51 ibid 326.

Of decisive methodological importance to post-Charter public libel jurisprudence were *Ford v Québec (Attorney General)*[52] and *Irwin Toy Ltd v Québec (Attorney General)*.[53] In *Ford*, the Supreme Court considered Québec's Charter of the French Language, which required that public signs, posters, and commercial advertising read exclusively in French. Accepting that commercial expression, like political expression prior to the Charter, is '[...] one form of the great range of expression that is deserving of constitutional protection because it serves *individual and societal values* in a free and democratic society',[54] a unanimous Court took the exceptional step of *specifying* the 'societal values' underlying subsection 2(*b*). Crucially, the Supreme Court cited Professor Emerson's article 'Toward a General Theory of the First Amendment' which, as noted in chapter two, endorsed an incomplete array of free expression justifications.[55] Despite pedigree dating from *Alberta Legislation*, the checking function of the press was thereby overlooked.

The Court's methodology for litigating free expression claims was confirmed in *Irwin Toy*, which involved challenges to provisions in Québec's Consumer Protection Act prohibiting television advertising directed to persons younger than 13. Besides reciting the highly abstract statement from US Supreme Court Justice Benjamin Cardozo that free expression was 'the matrix, the indispensable condition of nearly every other form of freedom',[56] the Court also relied on Strasbourg jurisprudence. Quoting *Handyside v United Kingdom*,[57] Chief Justice Dickson endorsed government criticism, insisting that freedom of expression applies to information or ideas '[...] that *offend, shock or disturb the State* [...]'.[58] Remarkably, in striving for a '[...] *broad, inclusive approach* to the protected sphere of free expression', the Court's inventory of free expression justifications was restricted to: (1) truth-seeking; (2) democratic discourse; and (3) self-fulfilment.[59] Since Emerson's incomplete free speech model had been incorporated in *Ford*, the checking function was methodologically obscured.

Serious concerns with this partial inventory were underscored in *R v Keegstra*,[60] where McLachlin J instructed (in dissent):

> To make out a violation of s. 2(*b*) where the government infringement of expression is incidental to its pursuit of another goal, a complainant must show that one of the suggested values underlying the guarantee is infringed, *these being three.* [...] Thus a government action not aimed at suppressing free expression will constitute a violation *only if the complainant can show that one of these values is implicated in protecting his or her expression.*[61]

[52] [1988] 2 SCR 712.
[53] [1989] 1 SCR 927.
[54] *Ford* (n 52) [54] (emphasis added).
[55] *Ford* (n 52) [56]. See also Thomas I Emerson, 'Toward a General Theory of the First Amendment' (1962) 72 *Yale Law Journal* 877.
[56] *Irwin Toy* (n 53) [41], quoting *Palko v Connecticut* 302 US 319, 327 (1937).
[57] (1976) 1 EHRR 737.
[58] *Irwin Toy* (n 53) [41] (emphasis added).
[59] *Irwin Toy* (n 53) [43], [53] (emphasis added).
[60] [1990] 3 SCR 697.
[61] ibid [228] (citation omitted) (emphasis added).

The Supreme Court has confirmed that this methodology applies to newspaper organisations and broadcasters. In *Canadian Broadcasting Corp v Lessard*,[62] Justice McLachlin again confirmed (in dissent) that '[…] the values identified in *Irwin Toy* […] also underlie the guarantee of freedom of the press and media'.[63] She added, '[p]ress activities which are not related to the values fundamental to freedom of the press may *not* merit *Charter* protection […]'.[64] As a result, despite stock references in *Lessard* to the 'special position of the press',[65] its 'legitimate functions in our society',[66] and even its role '[…] as the agent of the public in monitoring and reporting on governmental, legal and social institutions',[67] it is of more significant juridical concern that press freedom was methodologically compromised by excluding the checking function from the Court's official inventory of free expression justifications.

The Supreme Court in *Keegstra* also confirmed (ironically) that free expression not only had increased importance under the Charter, but also warranted '[…] a more careful and generous study of *the values* informing the freedom'.[68] Instead, the Court's incomplete inventory has significantly compromised our understanding of freedom of expression and the press. Although it is tempting to explain this by appealing to the checking function's factual irrelevance in *Ford* and *Irwin Toy*, the Court's objective in these decisions was to liberally summarise the 'societal values' informing freedom of expression. The Supreme Court of Canada placed no restrictions on this vital task.

Whatever the explanation, these decisions have (at minimum) complicated theoretical inquiries into free expression rationales, and invited serious methodological concern by systematically downplaying the checking function and accountability concerns. In other words, since the checking function was not mentioned at the outset of Charter litigation, it remains undetected when political libel cases are brought before Canadian courts.

i. Hill v Church of Scientology

Most early Charter cases involving defamation actions were unsuccessful.[69] That the Charter had marginal impact on Canadian defamation law until recently was

[62] [1991] 3 SCR 421.

[63] ibid [65].

[64] ibid [68] (citation omitted) (emphasis added).

[65] ibid [61], [64].

[66] ibid [61].

[67] ibid [65].

[68] *Keegstra* (n 60) [26] (emphasis added). Justice McLachlin viewed pre-Charter cases such as *Alberta Legislation* as resonating most with the 'political process model' (ie self-government).

[69] See *Coates v The Citizen* (1988) 85 NSR (2d) 146 (SC TD); *BSOIW, Local 97 v Campbell* (1997) 40 BCLR (3d) 1 (SC) [47]; *Pressler v Lethbridge* (1997) 41 BCLR (3d) 350 (SC); *Goddard v Day* (2000) 282 AR 349 (QB); *Dhami v Canadian Broadcasting Corp* [2001] BCJ No 2773 (SC); *Clement v McGuinty* (2001) 143 OAC 328 (CA).

due primarily to the Supreme Court's controversial ruling in *Hill v Church of Scientology*.[70]

Scientology involved defamatory statements made during a press conference by a lawyer for the Church of Scientology, alleging that a Crown prosecutor had misled a judge and breached a sealing order. The prosecutor sued the Church of Scientology and its lawyer for defamation. The Church pleaded that the common law of defamation unjustifiably infringed the Charter right to free expression and argued boldly (at least on the facts) that the Court should strike the balance more in favour of freedom of expression by adopting the 'actual malice' rule.

Of particular importance to the Court's decision was Justice Cory's restricted application of free expression justifications. After citing *Alberta Legislation* and *Switzman*, he endorsed the following generic and well-rehearsed account of free expression's relationship to democracy:

> It is difficult to imagine a guaranteed right more important to a democratic society than freedom of expression. Indeed a democracy cannot exist without that freedom to express new ideas *and to put forward opinions about the functioning of public institutions*. The concept of free and uninhibited speech permeates all truly democratic societies and institutions. The vital importance of the concept cannot be over-emphasized.[71]

Despite implying concerns with accountability and the checking function rationale, Justice Cory considered and applied only those free expression values outlined in *Irwin Toy*. Demonstrating the deductive impact of this constitutional methodology, he concluded:

> *Certainly, defamatory statements are very tenuously related to the core values which underlie s. 2(b)*. They are inimical to the search for truth. False and injurious statements cannot enhance self-development. Nor can it ever be said that they lead to healthy participation in the affairs of the community. Indeed, they are detrimental to the advancement of these values and harmful to the interests of a free and democratic society.[72]

Justice Cory also reviewed *Sullivan* and rejected incorporating the 'actual malice' rule into Canadian jurisprudence. Without appreciating its roots in English law or the contribution of the checking function to Justice Brennan's majority opinion, he observed only that *Sullivan* had been 'severely criticized by American judges and academic writers', objecting that defamatory statements 'exact a major social cost by deprecating truth in public discourse'.[73] After reviewing *Sullivan*'s reception in England and Australia, Justice Cory concluded: 'I simply cannot see that the law of defamation is unduly restrictive or inhibiting. Surely it is not requiring too much of individuals that they ascertain the truth of the allegations they publish'.[74]

70 *Scientology* (n 33).
71 *Scientology* (n 33) [101], citing *Edmonton Journal v Alberta (Attorney General)* [1989] 2 SCR 1326, 1336 (emphasis added).
72 *Scientology* (n 33) [106] (emphasis added).
73 *Scientology* (n 33) [127]–[131].
74 *Scientology* (n 33) [137].

In the end, Justice Cory's judgment could have been improved by incorporating the checking function and accountability concerns into his Charter analysis. Ironically, rather than relying on its undertheorised and uneven expression in *Sullivan*, he need only have looked at his Court's own pre-Charter jurisprudence.

C. 'Rebalancing' Defamation Law without the Checking Function

As we have seen, appellate courts in England,[75] New Zealand,[76] and Australia[77] have recognised that defamation law fails to adequately protect press and media interests, at least involving publications on matters of public and political concern. Partially in response to these developments, the Supreme Court of Canada has finally recast Canadian defamation law in light of Charter values. Beginning with expanding fair comment in *WIC Radio Ltd v Simpson*,[78] the Supreme Court has shifted the balance decisively towards freedom of expression and the press.

i. Cusson v Quan

This broader shift arguably began with the Court of Appeal for Ontario's decision in *Cusson v Quan*.[79] Observing that '[i]n its traditional formulation, [...] defamation clearly favours the protection of reputation over freedom of expression',[80] Justice Sharpe (for a unanimous court) endorsed careful application of the Charter, remarking in broadly Meiklejohnian terms:

> Our task, it seems to me, is to interpret and apply the earlier decisions *in light of the Charter values at issue* and in light of the evolving body of jurisprudence that is plainly moving steadily towards broadening common law defamation defences to give appropriate weight to the *public interest in the free flow of information*.[81]

The facts in *Cusson* were as follows. Following 9/11, an Ontario police officer travelled to New York City without his employer's permission to assist at Ground Zero. A major Canadian newspaper reported that he misrepresented himself to New York authorities and possibly compromised rescue operations. The officer sued the newspaper, reporters, and his police supervisor for defamation. Due to its uncertain status in Canadian law, *Reynolds* was not pleaded. At trial, the

[75] *Reynolds* (n 1); *Jameel* (n 10); *Flood* (n 7).
[76] *Lange v Atkinson* (2000) 3 NZLR 385 (CA) (*Lange No 2*).
[77] *Theophanous v Herald & Weekly Times Ltd* (1994) 182 CLR 104 (HCA); *Lange v Australian Broadcasting Corporation* (1997) 189 CLR 520 (HCA).
[78] [2008] 2 SCR 420. Recall that *WIC Radio* expanded protection for defendants in cases involving defamatory statements of *opinion* by replacing the requirement that a defendant *actually* believe in the opinion expressed with an objective 'honest belief' test.
[79] (2007) 87 OR (3d) 241 (CA).
[80] ibid [37].
[81] ibid [133] (emphasis added).

defendants' qualified privilege claims were rejected. The jury decided certain factual assertions had not been proved, and awarded $125,000 damages.

Justice Sharpe began by describing Canadian defamation law as 'in a state of flux, evolution and, to some extent, confusion'.[82] Dutifully identifying free expression's 'core' values as 'self-fulfilment', the '*communal exchange of ideas*', and 'human dignity [...]',[83] the Court also implicitly recognised the checking function. Moving beyond Meiklejohnian notions (at least momentarily), Justice Sharpe stated parenthetically: '[d]emocracy depends on the free and open debate of public issues and the freedom to *criticize the rich, the powerful and those* [...] *who exercise power and authority in our society*'.[84]

After analysing foreign authorities, the Court held that on matters of public importance, Canada's defamation laws were too partial to reputation and inconsistent with Charter values. Keenly discerning the tension between democratic accountability and defamation law, Justice Sharpe reasoned:

> Under the traditional common law regime, *society makes a clear choice to forego a certain level of exposure, scrutiny and criticism on matters of public interest in the name of protecting individual reputation.* That choice sacrifices freedom of expression to the protection of reputation to a degree that today cannot be sustained as consistent with *Charter* values.[85]

Despite implicitly referencing the checking function, the Court simply incorporated *Reynolds* into Ontario law. Without offering any evaluative criteria—a criticism by no means limited to the Court of Appeal for Ontario—Justice Sharpe claimed presumptively that it 'gives *appropriate recognition and weight* to the *Charter* values of freedom of expression and freedom of the media without unduly minimising the value of protecting individual reputation'.[86]

On appeal to the Supreme Court of Canada,[87] the *Reynolds* defence was held to be available in principle.[88] However, in decisions released concurrently, the Court applied a new defence that originated in *Grant v Torstar Corp*,[89] namely, the defence of 'Responsible Communication on Matters of Public Interest'.[90] While clearly of 'public interest', the Supreme Court ordered a new trial in *Cusson* to decide whether the offending articles 'met the standard of responsibility articulated in *Grant*'.[91]

[82] ibid [131].
[83] ibid [125] (emphasis added), quoting *RWDSU v Pepsi-Cola* [2002] 1 SCR 156 [32].
[84] ibid (emphasis added).
[85] ibid [129] (emphasis added).
[86] ibid [140] (emphasis added).
[87] *Quan v Cusson* [2009] 3 SCR 712.
[88] ibid [35].
[89] [2009] 3 SCR 640.
[90] ibid [126].
[91] *Quan* (n 87) [32].

ii. Grant v Torstar Corp

Grant contains Canada's authoritative ruling on defamation law's compliance with Charter values and the availability of qualified privilege in public libel cases. But, even though it brought Canadian defamation law into line with international trends, *Grant* has reinforced the Supreme Court's incomplete inventory of free expression values by again conflating the checking function with Meiklejohnian theory.

The case involved a successful business owner in Northern Ontario, Peter Grant. Grant was a long-time supporter of the Ontario Progressive Conservative Party, and a personal friend of the Premier. His wealth and close government connections attracted attention. Grant brought a defamation action against a newspaper and reporter after a publication about a proposed private golf course on Grant's estate. The article contained criticisms of the development's environmental impact and suspicions that Grant was exercising improper political influence. The reporter conducted an independent enquiry, and attempted to verify the article's allegations. During his investigation, requests to interview Grant were repeatedly denied. When he informed Grant of the public's concerns and invited a response, Grant's lawyers threatened legal action.

The Supreme Court began by formulating the central issue on appeal at a very high level of abstraction, namely, whether defences for defamatory statements of fact published generally should be expanded 'in recognition of the importance of *freedom of expression in a free society*'.[92] Specific concerns with government and political misconduct were effectively marginalised. Even so, the Court's commitment to free expression was resolute. Recognising the inability of Canadian defamation laws to protect press and media interests, Chief Justice McLachlin correctly lamented that 'the defence of qualified privilege has seldom assisted media organizations'.[93] Instructing that 'the threshold for privilege remains high and the criteria for reciprocal duty and interest required to establish it unclear',[94] the Chief Justice concluded that '[i]t remains uncertain when, if ever, a media outlet can avail itself of the defence of qualified privilege'.[95] Supporting the prospect of libel reform, the Court insisted it '[…] will, from time to time, take a *fresh look* at the common law and re-evaluate its consistency with evolving societal expectations through the lens of *Charter* values'.[96]

Centrally important to this 'fresh look' was the Court's classification of free expression justifications. Citing *Irwin Toy*, Chief Justice McLachlin confirmed the usual suspects: (1) democratic discourse; (2) truth-finding; and (3) self-fulfilment.[97] Of these, the Court applied the first and second. The 'democratic discourse'

92 *Grant* (n 89) [32] (emphasis added).
93 *Grant* (n 89) [34].
94 *Grant* (n 89) [37].
95 *Grant* (n 89) [37].
96 *Grant* (n 89) [46] (emphasis added).
97 *Grant* (n 89) [47].

rationale was emphasised since 'freewheeling debate on matters of public interest is to be encouraged'.[98] It was also asserted in decidedly Meiklejohnian terms that '[p]roductive debate is dependent on the free flow of information'.[99] Further marginalising the checking function, the Chief Justice observed: '[t]he vital role of the communications media in providing *a vehicle for such debate* is explicitly recognized in the text of s. 2(*b*) itself'.[100]

Drawing a connection criticised earlier by Greenawalt when discussing Blasi's 'checking value' of the press, the Supreme Court also appealed to the 'truth-finding' rationale, noting awkwardly that '[f]ear of being sued for libel may prevent the publication of information about matters of public interest. The public may never learn the full truth on the matter at hand'.[101] Without acknowledging accountability concerns or the checking function's heightened importance on the facts, Chief Justice McLachlin summarised the Court's position by concluding:

> [i]t is simply beyond debate that the limited defences available to press-related defendants may have the effect of inhibiting political discourse and debate on matters of public importance, and impeding the cut and thrust of discussion necessary to discovery of the truth.[102]

Still, compared to *Scientology*,[103] the Court's understanding and use of free expression justifications was refreshingly probative.

The process of selecting a doctrinal option highlighted considerable methodological barriers. Specifically, the Supreme Court sought 'a *balanced approach* to libel law [that] *properly reflects* both the interest of the plaintiff and the defendant'.[104] Relying solely on the 'democratic discourse' and 'truth-finding' rationales, the Court held that 'the current law [...] *does not give adequate weight* to the constitutional value of free expression'.[105] In an instructively flawed passage, Chief Justice McLachlin strained commendably to correct this doctrinal imbalance, reasoning:

> The law of defamation currently accords no protection for statements on matters of public interest published to the world at large if they cannot, for whatever reason, be proven to be true. But such communications advance *both* free expression rationales mentioned above—*democratic discourse* and *truth-finding*—and *therefore require some protection* within the law of defamation. When *proper weight* is given to the constitutional value of free expression on matters of public interest, *the balance tips in favour of broadening the defences* available to those who communicate facts it is in the public's interest to know.[106]

98 *Grant* (n 89) [52].
99 *Grant* (n 89) [52].
100 *Grant* (n 89) [52] (emphasis added).
101 *Grant* (n 89) [54].
102 *Grant* (n 89) [57].
103 *Scientology* (n 33) [106].
104 *Grant* (n 89) [61] (emphasis added).
105 *Grant* (n 89) [65] (emphasis added).
106 *Grant* (n 89) [65] (emphasis added).

Besides confirming the impact of free expression theorising on selecting public libel doctrine, Justice McLaughlin's reasoning exposes the methodological vulnerabilities of ad hoc balancing. That is, selecting suitable doctrine is contingent upon both the comprehensiveness of free expression theorising,[107] and the application of a reliable 'selection theory'. Both requirements were missing in *Grant*. For instance, in determining how far the 'balance tips' towards freedom of expression and the press, the Court studied developments in England, the United States, Australia, New Zealand, and South Africa. Concluding only that each jurisdiction had given '*more weight* to the value of freedom of expression and robust public debate [...]',[108] the Court selected a doctrinal 'middle ground' allowing publishers '[...] to escape liability if they can establish that they acted responsibly in attempting to verify the information on a matter of public interest'.[109] Without applying the most relevant free expression justification, or any discernible criteria for assessing doctrinal alternatives, both the Court's methodology and results would appear to be highly questionable.

Yet based on these slight deliberations, the Court endorsed a new defence of 'Responsible Communication on Matters of Public Interest'.[110] Inspired by *Reynolds*, Chief Justice McLachlin insisted that it applies where the publication is on a matter of public interest, and the publisher was diligent in verifying the allegation, having regard to various factors.[111] Moreover, once a judge decides that a statement relates to a matter of public interest, the jury decides whether the defence is established.[112] Further reflecting Meiklejohnian theory's predominance, 'public interest' was not restricted to publications on *government* and *politics* as in Australia and New Zealand.[113] Rather, the Court required only that the subject matter 'must be shown to be one inviting public attention, or about which the public has some substantial concern because it affects the welfare of citizens, or one to which considerable public notoriety or controversy has attached'.[114]

Justice Abella's prescient dissent signalled substantial concerns with the majority's results and approach. Disagreeing on the respective roles of judge and jury,

[107] See Clare F Beckton, 'Freedom of Expression in Canada—How Free?' (1983) 13 *Manitoba Law Journal* 583, 584, where the author presciently noted: '[t]o minimize future inconsistencies the courts, when initially confronted with freedom of expression questions should attempt to articulate the values served by freedom of expression, for *it is only when a clear theory is created that subsequent decisions can be made in a rational manner which is consistently related to the theory*' (emphasis added).

[108] *Grant* (n 89) [66] (emphasis added).

[109] *Grant* (n 89) [85].

[110] *Grant* (n 89) [97]–[98].

[111] *Grant* (n 89) [126].

[112] *Grant* (n 89) [128].

[113] See, eg, *Theophanous* (n 77) 180–81; *Lange v Australian Broadcasting Corp* (n 77) 572; *Lange No 2* (n 76) [10], [41].

[114] *Grant* (n 89) [105], quoting Raymond E Brown, *The Law of Defamation in Canada*, 2nd edn (Toronto, Carswell, 1999) [loose-leaf] Vol 2, 15-137, 15-138.

Abella J also insisted upon careful identification and weighing of freedom of expression justifications, cautioning:

> By adopting the responsible communication defence, we are recognizing the sophistication and constitutional complexity of defamation cases involving communications on matters of public interest. *What is most important is protecting the integrity of the interests and values at stake in such cases*. This defence is a *highly complex legal determination* with constitutional dimensions. That takes it beyond the jury's jurisdiction and squarely into judicial territory.[115]

As indicated, Justice Abella appears to have understood the risks of mechanically applying legal principles based on incomplete or overly-simplistic understandings of constitutional interests. Without necessarily appreciating the Supreme Court's omission of the checking function and accountability concerns more broadly, she nonetheless observed more acutely than the majority that:

> The exercise as a whole involves balancing freedom of expression, freedom of the press, the protection of reputation, privacy concerns, and the public interest. Each of these is a complex value protected either directly or indirectly by the *Canadian Charter of Rights and Freedoms*.[116]

At last, Justice Abella's apprehensions were confirmed in *Grant*. By broadening protection for 'communications on matters of public importance' without appeal to the checking function in a case involving media defendants, allegations of government misconduct, and investigative journalism, Canada's highest court appears to be asking of juries that which it cannot ably mind itself.

D. Conclusion

The Supreme Court of Canada adopted its 'Responsible Communication on Matters of Public Interest' defence as an ostensible 'middle ground', without considering the checking function, or its roots in the Court's own pre-Charter jurisprudence. This methodological approach raises at least two concerns.

First, by disregarding the checking function as a 'core' value, the Court has placed undue emphasis on alternative rationales. Necessarily, this further intensifies the Court's propensity for conflating the checking function with Meiklejohnian theory. Second, by omitting the checking function from doctrinal selection, the Supreme Court of Canada has unjustifiably claimed that 'proper weight' was given

[115] *Grant* (n 89) [145] (emphasis added).
[116] *Grant* (n 89) [143] (citations omitted).

to freedom of expression and press interests, and that it has 'tipped the balance' in support of stronger defamation defences for media organisations. Under such limitations, it is hard to conceive how Canada's public libel regime is immune from serious critique.

IV. Chapter Conclusion

Part B confirmed that the primary concern in public libel doctrine is the widespread disregard of democratic accountability concerns and the checking function of the press. As we have seen, such undertheorising manifests in at least three distinct but interrelated forms.

First, both America and Australia have formulated distinctive doctrinal approaches militating against accurate recognition of the checking function rationale. After the US Supreme Court adopted the 'actual malice' rule in *Sullivan*, the High Court of Australia attempted to rationalise its innovative 'responsible journalism' defence by appealing to an indeterminate implied rights doctrine. Besides its flawed reliance on Canada's pre-Charter jurisprudence, Australia's implied rights methodology effectively rejects free expression theorising altogether, thereby precluding the tailoring of its public libel doctrine to its institutional milieu. Containing instances of all three forms of undertheorising, the peculiarities of Australian and American public libel doctrine highlight the methodological importance of identifying and considering all relevant freedom of expression justifications when regulating public libels.

Second, courts and legislatures have not paid sufficient attention to past references to the checking function. Both the UK Supreme Court and the New Zealand Court of Appeal have discounted or overlooked significant sources of domestic and international jurisprudence resonant with the checking function's premises and concerns. Where Britain's highest courts have overlooked significant advancements made by the European Court of Human Rights in fostering 'watchdog' journalism, New Zealand has been held back by an abiding distrust of its press.

Third, besides denying the checking function's limited jurisprudential base, courts, legislatures, and legal scholars have inappropriately conflated the checking function with Meiklejohnian theory. The widespread failure to differentiate between these models will inevitably impact public libel doctrine and reform. As we have seen, no legal body has exhibited this tendency more instructively than the Supreme Court of Canada. Due to confusion regarding the Court's pre-Charter 'implied right of political expression', the checking function has been effectively discounted as a separate free expression rationale. Specifically, Canada's highest court has entrenched an ambiguous understanding of democratic theory by omitting the checking function from its official inventory of free expression values. As a result, lower courts must either force accountability concerns into a Meiklejohnian framework and/or appeal to less relevant justifications.

But simply identifying the checking function as a missing rationale is not enough. Returning to our principal concern with misuse of democratic theory, the main difficulties in this respect are: (1) as revealed in Parts A and B, the relationship between freedom of expression and democracy is too often presented as a bald statement or unexamined assumption by courts, legislators, and legal commentators; (2) where more specific accounts are attempted, they resonate principally with *deliberative* and *electoral* concerns emblematic of Meiklejohnian theory. Democratic accountability concerns most relevant to adjudicating public libel cases are routinely and inexplicably ignored; and (3) even where a connection is sensed between variations in constitutional structure and the scope of protection for political speech, there has been scarce acknowledgement of accountability and its institutional repercussions. In sum, despite recurring references to democratic theory by leading authorities in Britain, the United States, Australia, Canada, and New Zealand, both its relationship to freedom of expression and its implications for public libel doctrine remain undeveloped and unclear.

Accordingly, in Part C we transition to a much needed process of 'system-building', where we consider new approaches for addressing the theoretical and comparative law errors described above, and for reintroducing the checking function back into public libel jurisprudence. Based on recent advances in public accountability scholarship—which endorse careful examination of the complex accountability networks in representative systems—this revised analytical framework is proffered as a workable 'selection theory' for the improved design and tailoring of public libel doctrine to our comparators' discrete institutional settings.

Part C

Reasserting Democratic Accountability

Overview of Part C

As confirmed in Part B, leading courts and legislatures have supported public libel doctrine through poorly reasoned appeals to democratic theory. Specifically, in balancing reputation against freedom of expression, our comparators have inexplicably preferred Meiklejohn's democratic 'self-governance' rationale to the checking function of the press. This is all the more perplexing given that, as between the two justifications, the checking function resonates more with exposing government corruption and enhancing democratic accountability. As we have seen, this collective undertheorising raises significant doubts as to the soundness of public libel doctrine in each of our comparators.

So where have things gone wrong? Why is Meiklejohnian theory so predominant in public libel jurisprudence? Why are there no serious articulations of the checking function of the press? On the whole, why the persistent legislative and judicial undertheorising and confusion of democratic models? Part C attempts to answer these questions by systematically reasserting the importance of democratic accountability for public libel doctrine. By exploring public accountability scholarship, neo-republicanism, and general systems theory, a special syntax and vocabulary is developed that progressively reveals the underlying functional problems behind public libel law's technical challenges.

Chapter six begins by sourcing these conceptual difficulties in the complex relationships between 'democracy', 'representation', and 'accountability'. At least since the publication of Pitkin's pivotal work on representation,[1] the role of accountability in representative institutions has called for greater scholarly attention.[2] Yet despite significant advancements in our understanding of these concepts,[3] political theorists, including those who have incorporated 'accountability' into

[1] See Hanna Fenichel Pitkin, *The Concept of Representation* (Berkeley, University of California Press, 1967).

[2] Commenting on the 'accountability view', Pitkin knew of no writer who had 'discussed it at length or developed it into a theoretical system' (ibid 55).

[3] See, eg, Bernard Manin, *The Principles of Representative Government* (Cambridge, Cambridge University Press, 1997); Philip Pettit, 'Varieties of Public Representation' in Ian Shapiro and others (eds), *Political Representation* (Cambridge, Cambridge University Press, 2010).

their definition of democracy, have provided remarkably little information about it.[4] Even established accountability scholars have advised that, unlike democracy and representation, the concept of accountability has not yet acquired its own tradition of academic analysis.[5] Given this acknowledged 'accountability crisis',[6] it would appear that judges and legislators responsible for shaping public libel doctrine are not alone in embracing incomplete articulations of the relationship between freedom of expression and democratic theory.

Fortunately, there has emerged in public accountability scholarship a 'minimal conceptual consensus',[7] which reflects widespread efforts to organise accountability research into a framework for systematic comparative analysis.[8] Besides clarifying the meaning of accountability as a 'virtue' and 'mechanism',[9] this conceptual stabilisation has also emphasised accountability's 'multidimensional' nature and overriding need for normative political criteria. As noted by a leading scholar, 'the assessment of accountability *cannot* be separated from the vision one has about what constitutes adequate democratic governance [...]'.[10]

Confirming the need for sound evaluative criteria, Chapter six examines the connections between accountability and 'neo-republicanism', a political theory leveraging to a remarkable degree the principal implications of public accountability's emergent analytical framework. Building on accountability theory's insights concerning the 'reality' and 'opacity' of political power,[11] neo-republicans insist that controlling political power through various 'accountability mechanisms' is a central feature of democratic institutional design.[12] As argued resourcefully by Professor Philip Pettit, rather than focus compulsively on democracy's core

[4] See, eg, Philippe C Schmitter and Terry Lynn Karl, 'What Democracy is ... and is Not' (1991) 2(3) *Journal of Democracy* 75; Philippe C Schmitter, 'The Ambiguous Virtues of Accountability' (2004) 15(4) *Journal of Democracy* 47.

[5] See Richard Mulgan, *Holding Power to Account: Accountability in Modern Democracies* (Basingstoke, Palgrave MacMillan, 2003) 6.

[6] See Michael W Dowdle, 'Public Accountability: Conceptual, Historical, and Epistemic Mappings' in Michael W Dowdle (ed), *Public Accountability: Designs, Dilemmas and Experiences* (Cambridge, Cambridge University Press, 2006) 1; Mark Bovens, 'Two Concepts of Accountability: Accountability as a Virtue and as a Mechanism' (2010) 33(5) *West European Politics* 946, 947.

[7] See Thomas Schillemans, 'Does Horizontal Accountability Work? Evaluating Potential Remedies for the Accountability Deficit of Agencies' (2011) 43(4) *Administration & Society* 387, 389; Thomas Schillemans, 'The Public Accountability Review: A Meta-Analysis of Public Accountability Research in Six Academic Disciplines' (2013) *University of Utrecht Working Paper*, 13 <www.researchgate.net/publication/48327755> (last accessed 17 January 2018).

[8] See Mark Bovens and others (eds), *The Oxford Handbook of Public Accountability* (Oxford, Oxford University Press, 2014).

[9] Bovens (n 6); *The Oxford Handbook* (n 8) 7–10.

[10] Mark Bovens, 'Analysing and Assessing Accountability: A Conceptual Framework' (2007) 13(4) *European Law Journal* 447, 467 (emphasis added).

[11] See Andreas Schedler, 'Conceptualizing Accountability' in Andreas Schedler and others (eds), *The Self-Restraining State: Power and Accountability in New Democracies* (Boulder, Lynne Rienner Publishers, 1999) 13; Richard Mulgan, '"Accountability": An Ever-Expanding Concept?' (2000) 78(3) *Public Administration* 555.

[12] See generally Philip Pettit, *Republicanism: A Theory of Freedom and Government* (Oxford, Oxford University Press, 1997); Philip Pettit, *On the People's Terms: A Republican Theory and Model of Democracy* (Cambridge, Cambridge University Press, 2012).

concepts, representative governments are in the end stabilised by political and constitutional arrangements that are no more beguiling than the provision of gas and water supply.[13]

The theoretical synergies here are considerable, if not entirely obvious. Alongside providing public accountability theory with a more complete metacriteria for assessing its various mechanisms and regimes, this 'gas-and-water-works' republicanism benefits from accountability scholarship's more rigorous analytical development and its implications for *actualising* democratic institutional designs. To be clear, our provisional emphasis on neo-republicanism is nothing more (or less) than part of a more general methodological reorientation from abstract theorising to concrete analysis of the functional pathways to effective democratic governance. It is a valuable pedagogical lens. After all, greater attention on institutional design benefits not only 'neo-republicans', but all democratic theorists intent on intelligently linking separation of powers and various governmental and non-governmental 'checks' on political power. Likewise, combining public accountability theory and neo-republicanism points us towards a method for evaluating the respective contributions of public libel law and the institutional press to interconnected webs of accountability in each of our comparators' unique contexts.

Chapter seven accordingly undertakes to formulate a revised analytical framework for public libel jurisprudence. Building on our opening accountability analysis, chapter seven looks deeper into the intricacies of accountability networks and their potential for dysfunction. These efforts at contextualising the checking function proceed in four stages. First, due to its multi-dimensional structure, 'accountability' is not an unqualified good to be maximised at all costs.[14] Although essential to democratic governance, it is challenging to build, and involves costs that must be weighed carefully against the problems that it proposes to address.[15] Second, this multi-layered structure often leads to dysfunctions that take the form of either accountability *deficits* or *overloads*, depending on whether accountability networks exhibit a shortage or overabundance of inputs and effects.[16] As we shall see, both concepts are essential for evaluating the accountability requirements of representative systems.

Third, alongside more conventional mechanisms of political accountability, the institutional press is positioned as perhaps the most critical in contemporary democracies.[17] Notionally, leading commentators have emphasised the vital contributions of 'watchdog' journalism and the institutional press to broader networks

[13] Pettit, *Republicanism*, ibid 239.
[14] Mulgan (n 5) 236.
[15] Mark E Warren, 'Accountability and Democracy' in *The Oxford Handbook* (n 8) 44.
[16] Bovens (n 10) 462.
[17] See Timothy Besley and others, 'Mass Media and Political Accountability' in Roumeen Islam and others (eds), *The Right to Tell: The Role of Mass Media in Economic Development* (Washington, World Bank, 2002) 45, 59; Sanghamitra Bandyopadhyay, 'Knowledge-Driven Economic Development' (University of Oxford, Department of Economics Discussion Paper No 267, June 2006) 4–5; Pippa Norris (ed), *Public Sentinel: News Media & Governance Reform* (Washington, World Bank, 2010) 131.

of government accountability to citizens.[18] Besides being the only accountability mechanism that applies to all public libel plaintiffs and branches of government, by providing the principal means by which information about government actions is reported to the broader public, the institutional press is fundamental to any system of democratic accountability. Moreover, a growing body of empirical evidence confirms the effects of a free and adversarial press on enhancing political governance, especially curbing government corruption.[19] This evidence is not only broadly consistent with the press' 'information conduit' and 'watchdog' roles, but supports adoption of a 'systems' approach for assessing accountability networks generally. Given this multi-dimensional understanding of 'accountability', the concept of an accountability dysfunction must broaden 'to allow for *all* the different possible dimensions where accountability may be found to be lacking',[20] including the effects of public libel doctrine on regulating the checking function of the press.

Lastly, chapter seven concludes by mapping our inventory of accountability mechanisms into a coherent analytical framework. A revised framework for public libel jurisprudence can be formulated by combining the effects of two sets of accountability mechanisms. The *primary* set represents a jurisdiction's 'basic architecture', or relatively fixed elements of constitutional design (ie elections, parliamentary/presidential structure, federal/unitary structure, legislative scrutiny, and judicial review). By contrast, the *secondary* set represents those relatively dynamic mechanisms that supplement a nation's basic accountability structure (ie government auditors, independent regulators, and direct public access mechanisms). Combining these two sets of accountability mechanisms provides the relevant background against which public libel doctrine must be matched. That is, from among the continuum of alternatives revealed by our comparative doctrinal analysis, the extent of legal regulation on the press' checking function will need to be more or less restrictive depending on this contextual background.

Importantly, while this analytical framework cannot determine whether outcomes in any particular system are categorically 'negative' or 'positive', it does provide a more sophisticated methodology by which accountability mechanisms may be examined, and for prescribing advice 'as to how strategic interventions, through shifting of balances, might be made in order to correct a system which is malfunctioning [...]'.[21] As stressed by neo-republicans and public accountability theorists alike, conflict and tension are inevitable within complex webs of accountability. The institutional design objective for representative democracies then should not be to iron out this conflict and tension, but to identify its many sources and to arrange it ideally so as to '[...] hold regimes in *appropriate tension*'.[22]

[18] Norris, ibid 115.
[19] Pippa Norris, 'Watchdog Journalism' in *The Oxford Handbook* (n 8) 538.
[20] Richard Mulgan, 'Accountability Deficits' in *The Oxford Handbook* (n 8) 552 (emphasis added).
[21] Colin Scott, 'Accountability in the Regulatory State' (2000) 27(1) *Journal of Law and Society* 38, 55.
[22] ibid 57 (emphasis added).

6

Distinguishing the Checking Function from Meiklejohnian Theory: Lessons from Public Accountability and Neo-Republicanism

I. Confronting a Conceptual Stalemate: 'Representation' and 'Accountability'

Any considered explanation of the undertheorising of democratic free speech justifications in public libel law must begin by examining the complex connections between 'democracy', 'representation', and 'accountability'. Particularly since the publication of Professor Hanna Pitkin's essential work on representation, the role of accountability in representative institutions has called for increased clarity and explication. In *The Concept of Representation*,[23] Pitkin considered two 'formalistic' interpretations of representation that she dismissed as 'partial and distorting'—the 'accountability view' and the 'authorization view'. Notably, shortly after introducing the 'accountability view', Pitkin concluded that '[i]t is *not* an important strand in the literature of representation; so far as I know, no writer has discussed it at length or developed it into a theoretical system'.[24] Observing that the link between representation and accountability 'crops up here and there, often articulated without much attention or thought', Pitkin nonetheless resolved that, despite its nascent status, 'it has a certain tempting rightness all the same'.[25]

This 'tempting rightness' is due to its capturing an important part of what 'representation' means.[26] Contrasted with Pitkin's description of the 'authorization view', which was developed in the context of Thomas Hobbes' absolutist political

[23] Pitkin (n 1).
[24] Pitkin (n 1) 55 (emphasis added).
[25] Pitkin (n 1) 55.
[26] Pitkin noted that 'both the concept and the practice of representation have had little to do with democracy or liberty. [...] Initially, neither the concept nor the institutions to which it was applied were linked with elections or democracy, nor was representation considered a matter of right' (Pitkin (n 1) 2–3).

philosophy, the accountability theorist 'defines representation in terms *not* of authority but of *accountability*'.[27] Describing in broad contours the differences between these two meanings, Pitkin instructed:

> In a sense, then, [it] is diametrically opposed to that of the authorization theorist. For the latter, being a representative means being freed from the usual responsibility for one's actions; for the accountability theorist, being a representative means precisely having new and special obligations. Whereas authorization theorists see the representative as free, the represented as bound, accountability theorists see *precisely the converse*.[28]

Pitkin also discerned that where the authorisation theorist defines representative democracy by equating elections 'with a grant of authority', the accountability theorist equates elections with 'a holding to account'.[29] Whereas the authorisation view places *no* obligations or controls on the representative authority, 'accountability theorists assert that, quite the contrary, genuine representation exists only where there are such controls [...]; indeed it is *identical with such controls*'.[30] In any case, Pitkin rejects both views as 'incomplete' and 'distorted' because they tell us nothing 'about what goes on *during* representation, how a representative ought to act or what he is expected to do, [or even] how to tell whether he has represented well or badly'.[31] At its simplest, the authorisation theorist sees representation '*initiated* in a certain way', while the accountability theorist sees it '*terminated* in a certain way'.[32] For Pitkin, this is all that can be said for the relationship between the two concepts.

As a result, while providing a valuable comparison of two preliminary views on representation, Pitkin does not have much to say about what accountability means. Although she identifies 'free elections', 'free communications', and a 'real choice of candidates' as important checks or 'controls' in representative systems,[33] no attempt is made to explore these mechanisms in detail. Moreover, even in Pitkin's ensuing attempt to 'penetrate beyond the formalities of representation to its substantive content',[34] the resulting analysis provides little else on accountability's broader significance or institutional implications. For example, her final word on representative government is that it 'is not defined by particular actions at a particular moment, but by *long-term systematic arrangements*—by *institutions* and the way in which they function'.[35] What is required is 'functioning institutions that are designed to, and really do, secure a government *responsive* to public interest and opinion'.[36] Nonetheless, for this vital business of governance, Pitkin endorses

[27] Pitkin (n 1) 55 (emphasis added).
[28] Pitkin (n 1) 55 (citations omitted) (emphasis added).
[29] Pitkin (n 1) 56.
[30] Pitkin (n 1) 57 (emphasis added).
[31] Pitkin (n 1) 58 (emphasis in original).
[32] Pitkin (n 1) 58 (emphasis added).
[33] Pitkin (n 1) 58.
[34] Pitkin (n 1) 59.
[35] Pitkin (n 1) 234 (emphasis added).
[36] Pitkin (n 1) 234 (emphasis added).

scarcely two institutional prerequisites—regular elections, and 'some sort of collegiate representative body'.[37] She thus leaves it to others to determine the properties and range of institutional accountability requirements for representative governments.

Other efforts to clarify this multifaceted relationship have improved our understanding of these foundational concepts. For example, Professor Bernard Manin has distinguished 'representative government' from earlier democratic systems by scrutinising their central institution of elections.[38] After classifying four principles of representative governance,[39] Manin insists that '[w]hat makes a system *representative* is not the fact that a few govern in the place of the people, but that they are selected by election *only*'.[40] Distinguishing the more widespread and democratic use of 'lot' and 'rotation in office' in Athens, Rome, and Italian city-republics, Manin argues convincingly that, in relying solely upon elections, it was clear that representative governments (at least in America) 'would not be based on resemblance and proximity between representatives and represented'.[41] Nor would they accept imperative mandates or discretionary revocability of representatives (voter recall).[42] Furthermore, endorsing what he terms the 'principle of distinction', Manin argues that '[r]epresentative government was instituted in full awareness that elected representatives would and should be *distinguished citizens*, socially different from those who elected them'.[43] What was intended was a government of elected social elites.

Interestingly, Manin moves a significant step beyond Pitkin's analysis by implying that the basic structure of representative governments influences their overall accountability requirements. In particular, as a 'check' on the inegalitarian and aristocratic effects of general elections and representatives' independence in office, Manin emphasises the vital importance of 'public access to political information', observing that '[s]ince the end of the eighteenth century, representation has been accompanied by the freedom of the governed at all times to form and express political opinions outside the control of the government'.[44] Characterising freedom of expression as an institutional imperative for all public decisions undergoing their requisite 'trial by debate', Manin reasons:

> Freedom of opinion, understood in its *political dimension*, thus appears as a *counterpart* to the absence of the right of instruction. *Freedom of public opinion* is a *democratic* feature

[37] Pitkin (n 1) 235.

[38] See Manin (n 3).

[39] These four 'principles of representative government' are: (1) Those who govern are appointed by election at regular intervals; (2) The decision-making of those who govern retains a degree of independence from the wishes of the electorate; (3) Those who are governed may give expression to their opinions and political wishes without these being subject to the control of those who govern; and (4) Public decisions undergo the trial of debate (Manin (n 3) 6).

[40] Manin (n 3) 41 (emphasis added).

[41] Manin (n 3) 129.

[42] Manin (n 3) 163.

[43] Manin (n 3) 94 (emphasis added).

[44] Manin (n 3) 167.

> of representative systems, in that it provides a means whereby the voice of the people can reach those who govern, whereas the *independence of the representatives* is clearly a *non-democratic* feature of representative systems. Representatives are not required to act on the wishes of the people, but neither can they ignore them: freedom of public opinion ensures that such wishes can be expressed and be brought to the attention of those who govern.[45]

While paralleling Pitkin's analysis of the difficulties associated with representative democracy's 'mandate-independence' controversy,[46] Manin succeeds in identifying the necessity for *other* accountability mechanisms to supplement representative democracy's basic institutional structure of elections and 'collective representative bodies'. However, despite grounding free expression and press liberty in representational dynamics, Manin (like Pitkin earlier) does not develop this insight into a broader theory of accountability through the press—or, of any sort of accountability at all. Also, by referring to freedom of expression as a 'democratic feature' in such vague and abstract terms, Manin invites similar confusion to that experienced when courts and legislatures arbitrarily apply Meiklejohn's and Blasi's democratic free expression justifications. At the end of the day, despite describing freedom of expression perceptively as 'a democratic *counterweight* to the undemocratic independence of representatives',[47] political theorists such as Pitkin and Manin only take us so far. While depicting in broad intellectual contours the thorny relationship between representation and accountability, little is gained about the meaning of accountability itself.

Political theorists proposing to incorporate 'accountability' into their definition of democracy have offered similarly little insight into the concept. For instance, in 1991 Schmitter and Karl hit upon 'accountability' as the key to the 'broadest and most widely applicable' definition of modern political democracy.[48] The authors defined democracy as 'a system of governance in which rulers are *held accountable* for their actions in the public realm by citizens, acting indirectly through the competition and cooperation of their elected representatives'.[49] Yet despite distinguishing 'democratic' from 'non-democratic' rulers by 'the norms that condition how the former come to power and *the practices* that hold them accountable [...]',[50] Schmitter and Karl offered few indications as to what an acceptable system of accountability might look like. Even their critique of 'electoralism' failed to explore

[45] Manin (n 3) 170 (emphasis added).

[46] See Pitkin (n 1) Ch 7. Pitkin noted that any answer to the question of mandates or instructions from the people admits of only a 'consistent position about a representative's duties [...], within which there remains room for a wide range of views on how a political representative should act or what distinguishes good from bad representing' (Pitkin (n 1) 146).

[47] Manin (n 3) 237 (emphasis added).

[48] Schmitter and Karl (n 4).

[49] Schmitter and Karl (n 4) 76 (emphasis added). Schmitter later clarified that they would have replaced 'governance' with 'government' (to avoid association with less-than-democratic practices), and deleted 'elected' since their concept of representation 'was and is far broader than the kind that is putatively secured through elections'. See Schmitter (n 4) 59, fn 1.

[50] Schmitter and Karl (n 4) 76 (emphasis added).

the limitations of elections as accountability mechanisms, the authors stressing only that '[h]owever central to democracy, elections occur intermittently and only allow citizens to choose between the highly aggregated alternatives offered by political parties [...]'.[51] No mention was made of whether and how general elections fit into broader networks of accountability in democratic regimes.

Even political theorists who argue that '[a] theory of accountability is *necessarily* a theory of representation'[52] bring us no closer to unravelling the riddle of accountability. For example, in setting out his thought-provoking theory of political representation, Ciarán O'Kelly argues that:

> Accountability is the *institutional vocabulary* through which ideas of representation, legitimacy, and authorization are presented. That is not to say that we ought simply to conclude that *accountability mechanisms* are the same as representativeness. Rather, the politics of accountability, the invocation and circumvention of rules, is the struggle to achieve and maintain control over an organization for one person or other.[53]

But once again we confront difficulties. Not only does O'Kelly fail to define an 'accountability mechanism', but the meaning of 'accountability' is once more obscured. Citing a slim and unrepresentative sample of accountability scholarship,[54] O'Kelly refers loosely to accountability mechanisms as 'rituals' surrounding the execution of 'political, bureaucratic, legal, or professional authority', which ultimately 'make up the vocabulary through which [an] organization's specific character of representation is negotiated and defined'.[55] Rejecting earlier uninfluential definitions of 'accountability',[56] O'Kelly posits that '[p]art of the clarification for what accountability might mean is that we must see it in the context of *struggles over representation*'.[57] Still, we remain no closer to distinguishing accountability's meaning or institutional importance.

In the end, despite recent (and authoritative) assurances that accountability is '*intrinsic* to democratic representation', and '[...] *inherent* in the representation cycle',[58] insufficient light has been shone on the 'black box' of accountability and its relationship to democratic governance. It is no wonder that leading common law courts and legislatures struggle with identifying and applying democratic free speech justifications in public libel jurisprudence.

[51] Schmitter and Karl (n 4) 78.

[52] Ciarán O'Kelly, 'Accountability and a Theory of Representation' in Melvin J Dubnick and H George Frederickson (eds), *Accountable Governance: Problems and Promises* (London, Routledge, 2011) 255 (emphasis added).

[53] ibid 256 (emphasis added).

[54] O'Kelly's primary source on accountability is the seminal but outdated article by Barbara S Romzek and Melvin J Dubnick, 'Accountability in the Public Sector: Lessons from the Challenger Tragedy' (1987) 47(3) *Public Administration Review* 227. Public accountability scholarship has progressed significantly in substance and methodology. See especially *The Oxford Handbook* (n 8).

[55] O'Kelly (n 52) 256.

[56] O'Kelly dismisses as unsatisfactory the overly-vague definition of accountability as 'a general strategic approach to the management of expectations' (O'Kelly (n 52) 265).

[57] O'Kelly (n 52) 265 (emphasis added).

[58] See Warren (n 15) 41 (emphasis added).

II. Public Accountability Scholarship

A. Preliminary Observations

The most significant developments in advancing these matters have taken place in the emergent field of public accountability scholarship.[59] The last 15–20 years have seen a rapid increase in public accountability research across multiple disciplines.[60] Perhaps reflecting the mixed results of political theorists before them, accountability scholars have noted that, unlike our understanding of democracy and representation, '"accountability" has not yet had time to acquire an established tradition of academic analysis [...]'.[61] Indeed, several of the discipline's pioneering scholars have described accountability as a 'fundamental but *underdeveloped* concept'.[62] Acknowledging many of the difficulties faced by Pitkin and Manin, Professor Andreas Schedler describes accountability most convincingly as 'an underexplored concept whose meaning remains evasive, whose boundaries are fuzzy, and whose internal structure is confusing'.[63] This assessment was confirmed recently by a comprehensive literature review of accountability scholarship, which revealed that nearly half of the 210 publications examined failed to define 'accountability' at all,[64] leading some to propose that such complications '[have] been a strong impediment to systematic comparative, scholarly analysis'.[65]

Despite unstable conceptual foundations, accountability scholarship has made welcome contributions to clarifying the relationship between 'accountability' and 'democracy'. For example, Romzek and Dubnick have from the outset insisted on strictly separating the two terms. Defining accountability as 'a *generic form of social relationship* found in a variety of contexts',[66] the authors advised:

> Accountability relationships in the public sector have distinct and empirically observable phenomena associated with them. In many instances accountability is associated with democratic administration, but in reality it is as relevant to *nondemocratic regimes* as it is to those tied to popular rule. [...] Thus, accountability does not necessarily imply the

[59] The editors of *The Oxford Handbook* (n 8) define public accountability simply as 'accountability in, and about, the public domain' (at 7).

[60] See generally *The Oxford Handbook* (n 8).

[61] Mulgan (n 5) 6.

[62] Romzek and Dubnick (n 54) 228 (emphasis added). See also Amanda Sinclair, 'The Chameleon of Accountability: Forms and Discourses' (1995) 20(2/3) *Accounting Organizations and Society* 219, who describes accountability as a cherished but 'elusive' concept (ibid 220); and Richard L Sklar, 'Democracy and Constitutionalism' in *The Self-Restraining State* (n 11) 53 (describing accountability as an 'elusive conception').

[63] Schedler (n 11) 13.

[64] Schillemans, 'Public Accountability Review' (n 7) 7, 13.

[65] Bovens (n 6) 946.

[66] See Barbara S Romzek and Melvin J Dubnick, 'Accountability' in Jay M Shafritz (ed), *International Encyclopedia of Public Policy and Administration* (Boulder, Westview Press, 1998) Vol 1, 6 (emphasis added).

existence of democracy; rather it suggests *any form of governance conducted through some delegation of authority*.[67]

Developing this point further, accountability scholars have maintained that while accountability does not necessarily imply democracy, '[a]ll representative democracies *entail* delegation and accountability'.[68] As explained by Professor Mark Warren in *The Oxford Handbook of Public Accountability*, a democratic government is also necessarily a 'system of accountabilities':

> There are many forms of accountability that have nothing to do with democracy, but democracy could not be conceived, let alone practiced, without *vast and complex webs of accountabilities* between peoples and those who govern on their behalf and in their name. Indeed, *accountability is so central to democracy* that much of the literature on democracy could be recast in these terms.[69]

Accountability scholars have also offered considered diagnoses of society's need for accountability, basing it in both the uncertain nature of political representation, and a demonstrably poor track record of representatives acting in their self-interest. For instance, addressing whether representatives can be trusted to act in the public interest without external scrutiny, Professor Richard Mulgan prudently cautioned:

> We do not live in such a world. The need for extensive mechanisms of accountability is largely a consequence of the *natural human propensity to place self-interest above the public interest*. People with power have a well-documented tendency to use it for their own ends unless they are subjected to scrutiny and threatened with possible sanctions if they transgress.[70]

Warren explains more specifically that 'the need for accountability arises from the intersection of *social co-dependence* and *interest divergence*'.[71] Emphasising the potential for abuse resulting from the independence associated with political representation, accountability assumes critical importance for Warren precisely because 'social co-ordination risks *exploitation*, *oppression*, or *other harms* to the interests of those affected'.[72] Building on earlier insights from Pitkin and Manin, he advised:

> [...] in a democracy the most basic problem to which accountability is the solution is that even though government is 'owned' by the people, the powers of collective decision and action are held by elites, to which the people are vulnerable, both negatively (the possibilities for harms) and positively (the opportunities for collective action).[73]

[67] ibid (emphasis added).

[68] Kaare Strøm, 'Delegation and Accountability in Parliamentary Democracies' (2000) 37 *European Journal of Political Research* 261, 267 (emphasis added).

[69] Warren (n 15) 39 (emphasis added).

[70] Mulgan (n 5) 14 (emphasis added). To be fair, Mulgan later acknowledged the importance of 'balancing' accountability and trust relationships in designing appropriate governmental structures. Still, the underlying concern is clear enough.

[71] Warren (n 15) 40 (emphasis in original).

[72] Warren (n 15) 40 (emphasis added).

[73] Warren (n 15) 40–41, citing Mulgan (n 5) 12.

As a necessary counterweight or corrective to these political concerns, leading scholars have insisted that, as an 'ever-expanding concept', accountability is best understood as 'a general term for *any* mechanism that makes powerful institutions responsive to their particular publics'.[74] Accountability, then, is 'a method of *keeping the public informed* and the *powerful in check*'.[75] The twin pillars of Meiklejohnian theory and the checking function are again raised for consideration.

But these admittedly important advances leave many core matters unsettled. For example, what is meant by 'accountability'? What is an 'accountability mechanism'? What are the different accountability mechanisms or 'devices' in representative governments? And how are broader accountability arrangements to be mapped and assessed? Answers to these questions not only assist in more convincingly differentiating the checking function from Meiklejohnian theory, but also in determining our prospects for formulating a suitable framework for public libel jurisprudence.

B. Accountability's 'Minimal Conceptual Consensus'

Despite its undertheorised past, a 'minimal conceptual consensus' has emerged in public accountability scholarship,[76] which reflects widespread efforts to organise accountability research into an appropriate framework for analysis.[77] As a foremost commentator on this conceptual stabilisation, Professor Thomas Schillemans urges the discipline's main contributors not to overstate the appearance of conceptual confusion, advising:

> After reading about accountability for a decade or so, I am sometimes haunted by the nagging feeling that we, social scientists, may be generally overstating the level of complexity and diversity of the concepts with which we work and, simultaneously, underestimate the extent to which we actually agree about them. By failing to see the extent to which we do indeed agree on important concepts, we also miss out on important opportunities to *build on each other's' [sic] work and insights*.[78]

This 'conceptual agreement' noted by Schillemans is comprised of three analytical stages. First, the opening phase involves the provision of relevant *information*. That is, accountability is first and foremost about 'answerability towards others with a legitimate claim to demand an account'.[79] Second, besides requiring the rendering of an account, accountability requires a forum in which an actor has an obligation to explain and justify their conduct. This *debating* phase must also

[74] Mulgan (n 5) 8 (emphasis added).
[75] Mulgan (n 5) 1 (emphasis added).
[76] Schillemans, 'Public Accountability Review' (n 7) 25.
[77] See generally *The Oxford Handbook* (n 8).
[78] Schillemans, 'Public Accountability Review' (n 7) 4 (emphasis added).
[79] *The Oxford Handbook* (n 8) 6.

allow the forum to pose questions and make further inquiries of the actor. Lastly, to speak of accountability is to emphasise its association with a forum's right to form a *judgment* and levy *sanctions* in connection with the actor's behaviour.[80]

Schillemans identified this 'minimal conceptual consensus' based on earlier accounts supplied by two of the discipline's most prolific scholars.[81] For instance, Mulgan insists on an 'inner core' of accountability consisting of the following three stages: 'initial reporting and investigating (*information*), justification and critical debate (*discussion*), and the imposition of remedies and sanctions (*rectification*)'.[82] Similarly, Professor Mark Bovens defines accountability as 'a relationship between an actor and a forum, in which the actor has an obligation to explain and to justify his or her conduct, the forum can pose questions and pass judgement, and the actor may face consequences'.[83] Endorsing this distinctly *functional* definition, Schillemans suggests that 'scholars accept to work with [this] (necessarily less than perfect) minimal definitional consensus, [so that] it will be possible to study accountability within a common conceptual framework [...]'.[84]

C. Accountability Mechanisms, Arrangements, and Regimes

i. A Multi-ordinal Term

Before specifying more technical aspects of *political* accountability, our analysis may benefit from a quick epistemic note on 'accountability' itself. As we have seen, prior to identifying its minimal conceptual consensus, accountability was labelled as 'elusive', 'underdeveloped', 'fuzzy', and 'confusing'.[85] Yet despite overstating conceptual confusion and underreporting the lexis shared amongst accountability scholars, such terminology did contain an important element of truth. For instance, while describing accountability vaguely as 'chameleon-like'—a term endorsed by other leading scholars[86]—Amanda Sinclair discovered an important insight into accountability's meaning that has not been fully explored. Specifically, Sinclair's research reported that accountability 'exists in *many forms* and is sustained and given extra dimensions of meaning by its *context*'.[87] Her interviews with 15 chief executive officers of Australian government agencies revealed five

80 *The Oxford Handbook* (n 8) 6.

81 See Bovens (n 6); Bovens (n 10); Mulgan (n 5).

82 Mulgan (n 5) 30 (emphasis in original).

83 Bovens (n 10) 450 (emphasis removed). See also Mark Bovens, 'Public Accountability' in Ewan Ferlie and others (eds), *The Oxford Handbook of Public Management* (Oxford, Oxford University Press, 2005).

84 Schillemans, 'Public Accountability Review' (n 7) 25.

85 See authorities at n 62.

86 See Sinclair (n 62) 219–20; Mulgan (n 11) 555, referencing accountability as a 'complex and chameleon-like term'.

87 Sinclair (n 62) 219 (emphasis added).

forms of accountability (political, public, managerial, professional, and personal), and two discourses (structural and personal).[88] Building on her research subjects' mutual experiences of multiple and conflicting accountabilities, Sinclair argued for a 'new conception' of accountability and 'new approaches' to its institutionalisation. But despite rejecting 'one-size-fits-all' approaches, Sinclair did not specify the particulars of this new conception or approach, resolving only that '[a]ccountability will be enhanced by recognising the multiple ways in which accountability is *experienced*, rather than by attempting to override this chameleon quality'.[89] However, besides acknowledging accountability's subjective experiences, Sinclair failed to consider whether unlocking this 'new conception and approach' might also require distinguishing the multiple ways in which accountability is *objectively* manifested and institutionally bound.

Professor Sinclair's research outcomes on the changeable nature and meaning of accountability resonate strongly with Alfred Korzybski's theory of '*multiordinal terms*'.[90] In *Science and Sanity*, Korzybski identified a special group of terms that 'may have different uses or meanings if applied to different orders of abstraction'.[91] The principal characteristic of these terms is that 'they are *ambiguous*, or ∞-valued [infinite-valued], in general, and that each has a definite meaning, or one value, *only and exclusively in a given context* […]'.[92] According to Korzybski, multi-ordinal terms are unavoidable and are at base 'a part and parcel of the structure of "human knowledge" and of our language',[93] explaining:

> The reader should be warned from the beginning of a very fundamental semantic innovation; namely, of the discovery of the *multiordinality* of the most important terms we have. […] Terms like 'yes', 'no', 'true', 'false', 'fact', 'reality', 'cause', 'effect', […] etc., are such that if they can be applied to a statement they can also be applied to a statement about the first statement, and so, ultimately, to all statements, no matter what their order of abstraction is. […] The main characteristic of these terms consists of the fact that on different levels of orders of abstractions they may have different meanings, with the result that they have *no general meaning*; for their meanings are determined *solely by the given context* […].[94]

In the context of public accountability scholarship, rather than describe accountability obliquely and fatalistically as 'elusive', 'fuzzy', 'confusing', or 'chameleon-like', we would be much farther ahead by simply recognising its multi-ordinal nature. As contemporary research increasingly shows, accountability has a multitude of

88 Sinclair (n 62) 223–24.

89 Sinclair (n 62) 219 (emphasis added).

90 See Alfred Korzybski, *Science and Sanity: An Introduction to Non-Aristotelian Systems and General Semantics*, 5th edn (Brooklyn, Institute of General Semantics, 1994) 433ff.

91 ibid 433.

92 ibid (emphasis added).

93 ibid 434.

94 ibid 14 (emphasis added).

meanings depending on the level of abstraction being studied. For example, the scholarly literature has so far identified many 'types' or 'forms' of accountability, such as 'political', 'professional', 'social', 'personal', 'administrative', 'legal', etc.[95] Rather than perpetuate the false impression of terminological confusion and overall scholarly befuddlement, the benefits of recognising the multi-ordinality of terms like 'accountability' are (at least) sevenfold:

> (1) we gain an enormous economy of 'time' and effort, as we stop [hunting] for a one-valued general definition of a *m.o.* [multi-ordinal] term [...]; (2) we acquire great versatility in expression, as our most important vocabulary consists of *m.o.* terms, which can be extended indefinitely by assigning many different orders and, therefore, meanings; (3) we recognize that a definition of a *m.o.* term must, by necessity, represent not a proposition but a propositional function involving variables; (4) we [...] may use the term freely, realizing that its unique, in principle, meaning in a given context is *structurally indicated by the context*; (5) under such structural conditions, the freedom of the writer or speaker becomes very much accentuated [...]; (6) [...] a reader who understands that ∞-valued mechanism will never be confused as to the meaning intended; and (7) the whole linguistic process becomes extremely flexible, yet it preserves its essential extensional one-valued character, *in a given case*.[96]

As discussed below, interpreting accountability as a 'multi-ordinal term' not only assists with developing more precise understandings of the various types and forms of accountability, but also with bridging the interdisciplinary gap between public accountability scholarship and 'neo-republican' theory.

ii. Accountability as a 'Virtue' and 'Mechanism'

Public accountability scholarship has been most fundamentally influenced by two different usages of accountability. While both are important for studying democratic governance, they ultimately address 'different sorts of issues and imply very different sorts of standards and analytical dimensions'.[97]

The first usage of accountability is as a normative concept—accountability as a *virtue*—described as 'a set of standards for the behaviour of actors, or as a desirable state of affairs'.[98] Recalling Pitkin's deliberations on 'accountability theorists' and 'descriptive representation',[99] this interpretation of accountability 'comes close to "responsiveness" and "a sense of responsibility", a willingness to act in a

[95] See Bovens (n 10) 455–57.

[96] Korzybski (n 90) 436–37 (emphasis added). Schillemans has argued along the same lines by making a 'plea for hyphenation' when referencing 'accountability' in academic discourse. See Schillemans, 'Public Accountability Review' (n 7) 13–14.

[97] Mark Bovens and others, 'Does Public Accountability Work? An Assessment Tool' (2008) 86(1) *Public Administration* 225, 227.

[98] Bovens (n 6) 949.

[99] Pitkin (n 1) chs 3, 4.

transparent, fair, and equitable way'.[100] Yet despite its appeal in America, articulating a single definition or standard is difficult, if not impossible. Bovens explains:

> Accountability in this active sense of virtuous behaviour is easily used, but very hard to define substantively. Accountability as a virtue is an essentially contested and contestable concept [...] *par excellence*, because there is no general consensus about the standards for accountable behaviour, and because these standards differ, *depending on role, institutional context, era, and political perspective.*[101]

The focus of this distinctly American approach to accountability is 'the evaluation of the *conduct of actors* and an analysis of the factors that induce accountable behavior'.[102] According to this model, accountability is treated by researchers as a *dependent* variable, '[...] the *outcome* of a series of interactions between various factors, actors, and variables'.[103] As far as potential malfunctions go, the focus is primarily on 'accountability deficits', which '[...] manifest themselves as inappropriate behavior, or "bad" governance—unresponsive, opaque, irresponsible, and ineffective'.[104] The main levels of abstraction being studied then are personal and organisational patterns and behaviours.

By contrast, the predominant usage (and meaning) of accountability in Britain, Australia, and continental Europe is more descriptive and technical—as a 'social, political, or administrative *mechanism*'.[105] As with the 'minimal conceptual consensus' noted by Schillemans, accountability is conceptualised as an 'institutional relation or arrangement' in which an agent can be held to account by an individual or organisation.[106] According to this view, objects of study are not fixed at the level of abstraction of individual public agents, but include more highly abstract and interdependent events concerning how institutional structures affect their behaviour. That is, 'the focus of accountability studies in this mode is not whether agents have acted in an accountable way, but rather whether and how they are or can be held to account ex post facto by accountability forums'.[107] For political scientists especially, such studies are essentially about *political* and *social control*, where 'accountability is the *independent* variable',[108] which may or may not *affect* the behaviour of particular agents or actors. Compared to accountability as a 'virtue', accountability deficits manifest not as 'inappropriate behaviour', but as figurative 'loopholes in the web of control mechanisms'.[109]

[100] Bovens (n 6) 949.
[101] Bovens (n 6) 949 (citations omitted) (emphasis added).
[102] Mark Bovens and others, 'Public Accountability' in *The Oxford Handbook* (n 8) 8 (emphasis in original).
[103] ibid (emphasis in original).
[104] ibid.
[105] ibid (emphasis added).
[106] ibid.
[107] ibid 8–9.
[108] ibid (emphasis in original).
[109] Bovens (n 6) 957.

The distinctive features of these two concepts of accountability may be summarised in the following table:

Table 2: Accountability as a Virtue and Mechanism[110]

Accountability as a	***Virtue***	***Mechanism***
Locus	Behaviour of actor	Relation actor-forum
Focus	Evaluative/prescriptive Substantive standards	Analytical/descriptive Effect of arrangements
Field of study	Good governance	Political and social control
Research design	Dependent variable	Independent variable
Importance	Legitimacy	Various goals
Deficit	Inappropriate behaviour	Absent or malfunctioning mechanisms

Three observations bear mention. First, both concepts are 'closely related and mutually reinforcing'.[111] As explained by Bovens, '[b]oth have to do with transparency, openness, responsiveness, and responsibility. In the former case, these are properties of the *actor*; in the latter, these are properties of the *mechanisms*, or *desirable outcomes* of these mechanisms'.[112] Second, as implied from the above, '[a]ccountability mechanisms are meaningless without a sense of virtue and, vice versa, there is no virtue without mechanisms'.[113]

Third, and most importantly, as the approach most relevant to interpreting the institutional press and public libel jurisprudence as instruments of political and social control, the narrower, more technical meaning of accountability as a *mechanism* will be adopted as an integral part of our 'system-building' in Parts C and D.

iii. 'Vertical' and 'Horizontal' Accountability

Accountability has also been routinely categorised as 'horizontal' or 'vertical'.[114] For instance, it is usually assumed that '[t]raditional accountability mechanisms are

[110] Bovens (n 6) 962.
[111] Bovens (n 6) 962.
[112] Bovens (n 6) 962 (emphasis added).
[113] Bovens (n 6) 962.
[114] See Bovens (n 10) 460ff; Schillemans, 'Does Horizontal Accountability Work?' (n 7) 389–92; Guillermo O'Donnell, 'Horizontal Accountability in New Democracies' in *The Self-Restraining State* (n 11) 29; Philippe C Schmitter, 'The Limits of Horizontal Accountability' in *The Self-Restraining State* (n 11) 59; Erik Hans Klijn and Joop FM Koppenjan, 'Accountable Networks' in *The Oxford Handbook* (n 8) 243.

very often *vertical* forms of accountability, [...] where a superior usually demands accountability from a subordinate'.[115] As observed by Mulgan, vertical accountability is based on the 'principle of ownership', which requires representative governments to 'answer to their ultimate owners, the people [...]'.[116] This concept is implicit in most 'principal-agent' relationships and is typically linked to accountability arrangements in parliamentary democracies.[117] Notable examples of vertical accountability therefore include voters, Parliament, ministers, departments, and agencies.

By contrast, *horizontal* accountability refers to relationships 'where the accountee is not hierarchically superior to the accountor'.[118] In other words, it may be understood as 'a form of accountability to *third parties*'.[119] Besides lacking a hierarchical relationship between actor and forum, there is no formal obligation for the actor to render an account. Noteworthy examples of horizontal accountability include semi-autonomous agencies, independent evaluators, boards of stakeholders or commissioners, interest groups, clients, and a free and adversarial press.[120]

Regardless of the importance of differentiating 'vertical' and 'horizontal' lines of accountability, their operations and effects must not be seen separately 'but as a *system* which is woven into the fabric of political and social life *as a whole*'.[121] As Day and Klein keenly observed:

> What matters [...] is that the *system should be seen as a whole* in recognition of the *interdependence* of the *different forms of accountability*, and the *linkages* between them. The challenge of modern accountability is all about responding to the complexity by repairing linkages which have snapped or frayed and inventing new ones where they do not exist, and *creating a framework which brings together politics and techniques in a new dialogue*.[122]

As indicated above, even when accountability mechanisms are correctly identified and accurately mapped, some form of evaluative criteria is required for assessing their overall effectiveness in particular domains. Given recent admissions that public accountability literature is 'remarkably light on assessment tools and methods',[123] this leaves much ground to be covered.

[115] Schillemans, 'Does Horizontal Accountability Work?' (n 7) 390 (emphasis in original) (citations omitted).

[116] Mulgan (n 5) 12.

[117] See generally Strøm (n 68).

[118] Schillemans, 'Does Horizontal Accountability Work?' (n 7) 390.

[119] Schillemans, 'Does Horizontal Accountability Work?' (n 7) 390 (emphasis added).

[120] Schillemans, 'Does Horizontal Accountability Work?' (n 7) 390.

[121] Patricia Day and Rudolf Klein, *Accountabilities: Five Public Services* (London, Tavistock Publications, 1987) 249 (emphasis added).

[122] ibid (emphasis added).

[123] Bovens and others (n 97) 230.

D. Assessing Accountability

Accountability has not only been characterised as a 'vertical' or 'horizontal' mechanism of control—it has also become identified with control itself.[124] According to this view, if democracy's central problem is controlling government so that it periodically complies with the people's preferences, 'then the *entire complex edifice* of a modern democratic political system becomes in effect a system for securing government accountability'.[125] Significantly expanding our previous inventory and understanding of accountability mechanisms, Professor Mulgan instructs:

> From this perspective, *institutions of accountability* include all institutions that are aimed at controlling or constraining government power, for instance legislatures, statutory authorities, and courts. *Devices of accountability* then include the separation of powers, federalism, constitutionalism, judicial review, the rule of law, public service codes of conduct and so on, *all of which have an effect on the control of public power*. Also to be added are the key *extra-governmental institutions* of a democratically effective civil society which help to constrain governments, for instance competitive markets, interest groups and *the mass media* [...].[126]

As this expanded view of accountability highlights, behind any mapping of accountability arrangements 'ultimately lies a *theory*, often implicit, about what constitutes sufficient democratic control, or adequate checks and balances, or satisfactory reflexivity'.[127] That is to say, 'the assessment of accountability *cannot* be separated from the vision one has about what constitutes adequate democratic governance [...]'.[128]

Professor Bovens has recommended three investigational models for evaluating accountability arrangements: a *democratic* perspective, a *constitutional* perspective, and a *learning* perspective. The 'democratic' perspective is concerned primarily with 'whether the accountability arrangement adds to the possibilities open to voter, parliament or other representative bodies to control the executive power'.[129] The central evaluative criteria under this perspective is '[t]he degree to which an accountability arrangement or regime enables democratically legitimised bodies to monitor and evaluate executive behaviour and to induce executive actors to modify that behaviour in accordance with their preferences'.[130] Therefore, as epitomised by ministerial responsibility in parliamentary democracies, the

124 Mulgan (n 11) 563.
125 Mulgan (n 11) 563, citing Day and Klein (n 121) Ch 1 (emphasis added).
126 Mulgan (n 11) 563 (citation omitted) (emphasis added).
127 Bovens (n 10) 467 (emphasis added).
128 Bovens (n 10) 467 (emphasis added).
129 Bovens (n 10) 465.
130 Bovens (n 10) 465.

quality of accountability arrangements depends upon their ability to consolidate the 'democratic chain of delegation'.[131]

The principal focus of Bovens' 'constitutional' perspective is 'preventing the tyranny of absolute rulers, overly presumptuous, elected leaders or of an expansive and "privatised" executive power'.[132] According to this view, the remedy against imperious, improper or corrupt governments is 'the organisation of "checks and balances", of institutional countervailing powers' directed towards achieving a 'dynamic equilibrium between the various powers of the state'.[133] The principal evaluative criteria is therefore whether 'an accountability arrangement curtails the abuse of executive power and privilege'.[134]

Lastly, the central concern of the 'learning' perspective is that accountability provides political representatives and agencies with 'feedback-based inducements to increase their effectiveness and efficiency'.[135] According to Bovens, '[t]he crucial questions from this perspective are whether the accountability arrangements offer sufficient feedback, but also the right incentives, to officials and agencies to reflect upon their policies and procedures and to improve upon them'.[136]

Although these three perspectives provide a useful overview of why accountability should matter to us, they fall short in several respects. Besides significant normative tension—particularly between the constitutional and learning perspectives—there exists a familiar and undesirable splitting in democratic theorising involving Bovens' 'democratic' and 'constitutional' models. While each perspective corresponds roughly with Meiklejohnian theory (democratic perspective) or Blasi's checking function (constitutional perspective), neither perspective specifically analyses the institutional press as an accountability mechanism of any sort. This is highly problematic. Without such an examination, the press cannot be assessed amongst broader networks of accountability in representative systems. Also, Professor Bovens' constitutional perspective, while closest in spirit (if not substance) to the checking function rationale, is focused explicitly on curtailing abuses of *executive* power, a much narrower field of governmental scrutiny than is commonly associated with the checking function *of the press*.

Therefore, if public libel jurisprudence is to benefit fully from our 'reassertion of democratic accountability' in Part C, there is need for a more comprehensive theory that can incorporate the effects of all relevant mechanisms of accountability, including and especially public libel law's regulation of the institutional press.

[131] Bovens and others (n 97) 231.
[132] Bovens (n 10) 463.
[133] Bovens (n 10) 463.
[134] Bovens (n 10) 466.
[135] Bovens (n 10) 466.
[136] Bovens (n 10) 466.

III. Neo-Republicanism: A Return to Institutional Design

Political theorist Philip Pettit has developed a model of republican governance contrasting sharply with established views. Singling out Professor Manin for account, Pettit stresses that rather than being conceptualised as democratic alternatives, differing systems of representative government essentially '[...] embody an *institutional framework*—or rather a *family of frameworks*—for realizing the democratic ideal of giving *kratos* to the *demos*, power to the people'.[137] Pettit therefore insists that '[t]he distinction between a participatory and a representative system is not one between democracy proper and some faint approximation but a distinction between rival proposals for the implementation of democracy'.[138] Rather than concentrating disproportionately on abstract political theory, Pettit distinctively directs us to the commonly overlooked necessity and rigours of democratic institutional design.

A. Liberty as 'Non-Domination'

The foundation to Pettit's republican theory is a distinct view of political power, and its implications for political liberty. Distinguished from the 'positive' and 'negative' conceptions of liberty found in classical liberal thought, Pettit argues that there exists '[...] a third, *radically different* way of understanding freedom and [its] institutional requirements [...]'.[139] Designated the ideal of 'freedom as non-domination', this conception of liberty essentially requires that 'no one is able to interfere on an arbitrary basis—at their pleasure—in the choices of [a] free person'.[140] Basing this concern about avoiding domination in the vagaries of the master-servant relationship, Pettit relates:

> Domination, as I understand it here, is exemplified by the relationship of master to slave or master to servant. Such a relationship means, at the limit, that the dominating party can interfere on an arbitrary basis with the choices of the dominated: can interfere, in particular, on the basis of an interest or an opinion that need not be shared by the person affected. The dominating party can practise interference, then, at will and with impunity: *they do not have to seek anyone's leave and they do not have to incur any scrutiny or penalty*.[141]

[137] Pettit (n 3) 61 (emphasis added).
[138] Pettit (n 3) 61.
[139] See Philip Pettit, *Republicanism: A Theory of Freedom and Government* (Oxford, Oxford University Press, 1997) 19 (emphasis added).
[140] ibid 271.
[141] ibid 22 (emphasis added).

'Non-domination' for Pettit then involves the absence of domination in the presence of others. More precisely, 'it is a social ideal which requires that, although there are other people who might have been able to interfere with the person on an arbitrary basis, they are *blocked from doing so*'.[142] Pettit advises that this ideal of non-domination may be attained in two ways: it can be secured either 'through people coming to have equal powers *or* through a legal regime stopping people from dominating one another without itself dominating anyone in turn'.[143]

Pettit's preferred route to securing liberty as non-domination is embedded in the directives of Britain's 'commonwealthmen' tradition and the American Federalists. As we have seen, eighteenth century theorists such as Cato, Wilkes, Father of Candour, Junius, and others routinely expressed the dangers of unchecked ambition and political tyranny in distinctive 'liberty-servitude' terminology. According to Pettit, 'it did not matter to the commonwealthman that the government he attacked was Whig; power was *always* dangerous and power *always* needed to be watched'.[144] Therefore, due to republicans' enduring concern with the corruptibility of political representatives and human nature, the social ideal of freedom as non-domination could not safely be left to 'the people' to secure it individually. Rather for Pettit, 'all signs are that it is best pursued for each under the centralized, political action of all: it is best pursued *via the state*'.[145]

B. 'Gas-and-Water-Works' Institutional Design

Accepting the necessity for state involvement, republican theorists have obsessed over the importance of designing 'stabilizers' and incorporating 'checking devices' in their pursuit of safe and reliable institutional structures. Instead of focussing with 'breathless, often witless devotion' on democracy's core concepts, Pettit contends that representative governments come to be stabilised 'only via arrangements that are no more intellectually beguiling than the infrastructure of gas and water supply'.[146] Pettit instructs:

> Political theorists have long neglected such questions in favour of more metaphysical or foundational matters. They have preferred to spend more of their time reflecting on the meaning of consent, or the nature of justice, or the basis of political obligation, than they have on *mundane issues of institutional design*. They have chosen to do ideal theory, in John Rawls's phrase, rather than the sort of theory that would tell us *how best to advance our goals in the actual, imperfect world*. Such detachment from institutional analysis may be consistent with certain political philosophies but it would mean the death of any serious concern for freedom as non-domination.[147]

[142] ibid 272 (emphasis added).
[143] ibid 273 (emphasis added).
[144] ibid 33 (emphasis added).
[145] ibid 274 (emphasis added).
[146] ibid 239.
[147] ibid 240 (emphasis added).

Embracing Pettit's republican vision for our purposes means simply that the pressing questions for investigation relate primarily to 'the shaping and reshaping of institutions'.[148] They are questions about how best to design institutions to ensure that they not only serve the republican ideal of 'freedom as non-domination', but the accountability requirements of representative systems more generally.

But similar to political theorists before him, Pettit has precious little to say about the specific mechanisms and 'institutional arrangements' required for his political ideals. For example, Pettit maintains that the institutional resources available for guarding against corruptibility boil down to two possibilities: *sanctioning* and *screening*. That is, the 'possibilities of punishing or rewarding what people do and possibilities of screening for the presence of suitable agents and options'.[149] Yet regardless of whether one adopts what he calls a more 'deviant-centred' versus a 'complier-centred' regulatory approach,[150] Pettit's political philosophy overlooks details as to what mechanisms or arrangements one requires, and their optimal structure in a given domain. The closest Pettit gets to depicting a suitable institutional arrangement is his endorsement of a combination of deviant- and complier-centred strategies used to achieve his idealised republican model. He instructs:

> The project of designing *stabilizers* for our ideal republic, then, need not involve a radical break with the project of identifying the forms—the constitutionalist and democratic forms—that a republican state has to assume if it is to reduce the presence of arbitrary will. Articulating the shape that a republic has to assume if it is not to be a dominating presence means articulating a shape under which there are *plentiful devices* available for *policing public officials*. In particular, of course, it means putting many independently motivated devices in place—usually independently motivated *sanctions*—so that there is no problem of the sort that arises with deviant-centred regulation.[151]

Along with maximising screening efforts for selecting appropriate 'agents and actions', Pettit insists that 'we should also consider how to arrange for the *escalation of sanctions* that may prove necessary in order to cope with the true knave [...]'.[152] Nonetheless, however laudable these general strategies may be, they are utterly lacking in operational detail that alone might fulfill Pettit's hope for a 'gas-and-water-works' republicanism that instructs 'how best to advance our goals in the *actual, imperfect world*'.[153]

i. Public Accountability Theory and Institutional Design

These theoretical gaps are eased considerably by public accountability scholarship's insights into political power, and achieving sound institutional design

[148] ibid.
[149] ibid 279.
[150] ibid.
[151] ibid 233 (emphasis added).
[152] ibid 238 (emphasis added).
[153] ibid 240 (emphasis added).

through comprehensive accountability structures. Accountability scholars have in fact strengthened and particularised Pettit's neo-republican project in three ways. First, at its most abstract, Professor Michael Dowdle warns that, when designing accountability systems for representative governments, we must use 'another kind of epistemic logic'.[154] Dowdle recommends conceptualising power in terms of *hydraulics* and as 'the product of institutional mechanics'.[155] According to this view, accountability is secured through 'using and channeling (rather than binding and restraining) these hydraulics via effective, *a priori* design of institutional architectures'.[156]

Second, building on Dowdle's 'hydraulics' image, Schedler advises that '[t]he guiding idea of political accountability is to *control* political power, not to eliminate it'.[157] Since accountability presupposes power and imperfect information, establishing effective accountability systems is ultimately a modest project fraught with difficulties. Much like Pettit, Schedler insists that accountability arrangements must 'strive to keep power from running wild; they strive to bound, to discipline, to restrain it. Their mission is to make power predictable by limiting its arbitrariness and to prevent or redress the abuse of power [...]'.[158] But power cannot be fully controlled, and 'should not be confused with narrow notions of regulation, control, or steering'.[159] Schedler wisely cautions:

> Holding power accountable does not imply determining the way it is exercised; neither does it aim at eliminating discretion through stringent bureaucratic regulation. It is a *more modest project* that admits that politics is a human enterprise whose elements of agency, freedom, indeterminacy, and uncertainty are ineradicable; that *power cannot be subject to full control* in the strict, technical sense of the word; and that even in a hypothetical world of perfect accountability, *political power would continue to produce harm, waste, and any other kind of irreversible 'public bads'* that even ideal agents of accountability could only ascertain, expose, and punish but neither repair nor undo.[160]

Lastly, in addressing the institutional significance of 'separation of powers', neo-republican sympathiser John Braithwaite insists that one should embrace 'such *plural* separations of disparate modalities of private *and* public power as will maximize freedom as non-domination'.[161] Instead of restricting a separation of powers analysis to checking only public power, Braithwaite argues that '[r]epublican theory of the sort Philip Pettit and I endorse requires *detailed empirical investigation* of the different ways of organizing independence and interdependence so

[154] Dowdle (n 6) 13.
[155] Dowdle (n 6) 13.
[156] Dowdle (n 6) 13 (emphasis in original).
[157] Schedler (n 11) 18 (emphasis added).
[158] Schedler (n 11) 19.
[159] Schedler (n 11) 19.
[160] Schedler (n 11) 19–20 (emphasis added).
[161] John Braithwaite, 'On Speaking Softly and Carrying Big Sticks: Neglected Dimensions of a Republican Separation of Powers' (1997) 47 *University of Toronto Law Journal* 305, 313 (emphasis added).

as to discover a set of institutional arrangements most likely to maximize freedom as non-domination'.[162] Braithwaite decries that '[a]fter 200 years of ugly tyranny in nations with beautiful constitutions, it is no longer persuasive to suggest that a separation of state powers will ensure that the government "will be controlled by itself"'.[163] For neo-republicans like Braithwaite and Pettit, the checking of power between various government branches is simply not good enough.

In its place, Braithwaite insists that we 'should want a world where different branches of business, public, and civil society are all checking each other'.[164] More precisely, '[...] the more plural the separations of powers (a) the more overdetermined is the capacity to prevent abuse; and (b) the more cases there are of disjuncture between an interest in the abuse and a capacity to prevent it'.[165] A neo-republican conception of 'good governance' arises then from achieving a *dynamic equilibrium* between the public and private powers in any institutional setting.[166] All in all, few if any restrictions on the origins and nature of these various 'checking powers' were contemplated by Professor Braithwaite.

Public accountability scholars therefore have much to recommend to Pettit's rudimentary sketch of 'republican' checking mechanisms. Dowdle, Schedler, and Braithwaite invite deeper understanding of the *specific components* of republican institutional design by adopting a 'systems-oriented' approach to accountability. As explored in chapter seven, whether comprised of public *or* private sources, vertical *or* horizontal mechanisms,

> [t]he various accountability networks which operate uniquely within each policy domain have the character of a *complex system of checks and balances* in which particular forms of behaviour are inhibited or encouraged by the overall balance in the system at any particular time.[167]

But that is not all. Chapter seven establishes that Professor Pettit's neo-republican programme benefits most dramatically from using a 'systems approach' to organise and assess accountability theory's extensive inventory of mechanisms and arrangements. As revealed by our revised analytical framework, a combination of public accountability theory and neo-republicanism is vital for optimising the effects of the institutional press on reducing government corruption. This is achieved by adjusting public libel doctrine in response to our revised framework's comprehensive 'collibration' approach to evaluating accountability networks in representative systems.

162 ibid 344 (emphasis added).
163 ibid.
164 ibid.
165 ibid 342.
166 See Elizabeth Fisher, 'The European Union in the Age of Accountability' (2004) 24(3) *Oxford Journal of Legal Studies* 495, 506–07.
167 Scott (n 21) 55 (emphasis added).

IV. Chapter Conclusion

We began by sourcing public libel doctrine's undertheorising in the complex relationships between democracy, representation, and accountability. Whether considering Pitkin's seminal work on representation, or more contemporary analyses of democracy and representative government, the precise role of 'accountability' in representative systems requires further explanation. Despite establishing the necessity for accountability in representational dynamics, political theorists have contributed relatively little to discerning accountability's meaning or specific institutional requirements.

Fortunately, there has emerged in public accountability scholarship a 'minimal conceptual consensus' reflecting efforts to organise accountability research into an appropriate framework for analysis. Besides clarifying accountability's core meaning, this conceptual stabilisation has also emphasised accountability's multifaceted nature and need for external political criteria. Interestingly, public accountability scholarship's 'minimal conceptual consensus' and detailed inventory of accountability mechanisms demonstrates that it would be as ill-advised to subsume 'accountability' into 'representation' as it would be to conflate the checking function with Meiklejohnian theory. In both cases, each model has its own discrete areas of emphasis, analytical methods, and unique institutional implications. It would appear that they capture two distinct but interrelated aspects of democratic governance.

Finally, we reviewed in chapter six the various complications of mapping and assessing accountability, and the benefits from 'bridging the gap' between accountability scholarship and neo-republican theory. Alongside providing public accountability theory with yet another criterion (other than Bovens' three investigatory models) for assessing its various mechanisms and arrangements, Pettit's 'gas-and-water-works' republicanism benefits from public accountability scholarship's more rigorous analytical development and its clearer implications for democratic institutional design. As a result, we may be left with the impression that there are almost limitless accountability mechanisms and arrangements that can be used in designing accountability systems. As argued in chapter seven, this simply cannot be the case. As it turns out, you can have too much of a good thing—even the checking function of the press.

Therefore, as part of Part C's 'system-building' and overall objective to 'reassert democratic accountability', we next examine accountability networks and their various dysfunctions. In particular, chapter seven undertakes the four remaining tasks of: (1) evaluating the necessity for adopting a 'systems approach' to accountability; (2) examining the associated concepts of accountability deficits and overloads; (3) determining the precise nature of the institutional press as a 'horizontal' accountability mechanism, including reviewing empirical evidence on the checking function of the press; and (4) translating our overall understanding of accountability networks and legal regulation of the checking function into a revised analytical framework for public libel jurisprudence.

7

A Revised Analytical Framework: Accountability Dysfunctions, Public Libel Doctrine, and the Institutional Press

I. Overview

Building on our introduction to accountability and our efforts distinguishing it from representation and democracy, chapter seven emphasises four additional concerns for placing the checking function in proper context. First, in order to understand the vast multitude of accountability mechanisms (including the checking function of the press) identified in chapter six, adopting a broader 'systems approach' to accountability is essential. This model eschews overly-simplistic, linear models of public accountability in favour of mapping and assessing more complex *networks* or *webs* of accountability mechanisms in specific settings. Second, since accountability mechanisms can interrelate and affect one another across multiple levels of abstraction, an expanded notion of dysfunctions must allow for both accountability 'deficits' *and* 'overloads'. While rarely acknowledged, it is possible to have too much accountability.

Third, despite its multi-faceted relationship with other accountability mechanisms, a convincing blend of theory and empirical evidence supports ascribing to the institutional press a special role in representative democracies. As examined in chapter seven, a revised framework for public libel jurisprudence is only possible when proper effect is given to the impact of regulatory restrictions on the press' vital 'watchdog' and 'information conduit' functions. Lastly, this revised analytical framework can be formulated by combining two sets of political accountability mechanisms. The aggregate effect of these mechanisms provides the relevant background against which public libel doctrine must be coordinated. In essence, a more or less restrictive legal regulation on the press' checking function will be required as changes occur across the several dimensions of our expanded accountability framework.

II. Accountability Dysfunctions

A. A 'Systems Approach' to Accountability

Accountability is essential to democracy. As we have seen, even if it does not *infer* the existence of democratic governance,[1] '[...] democracy could not be conceived, let alone practiced, without vast and complex *webs of accountabilities*' between populations and their elected representatives.[2] Mapping these 'webs of accountability' requires not only grasping 'if and how particular accountability relations have been institutionalized into *arrangements* but also to carefully check how various types of arrangements combine into overall accountability *regimes*'.[3] When we add the numerous 'types' of accountability into the mix (ie professional, political, legal, administrative, personal, etc), labelling accountability as a 'mechanism' has distinct implications for how it must be represented and assessed. In particular, a more expansive, 'systems-oriented' approach for tracking the operations and dysfunctions of complex accountability networks is required.

When compared to Professor Bovens' three perspectives for assessing accountability networks (ie democratic, constitutional, and learning), 'systems accountability' approaches the issue of assessment quite differently. Public accountability scholar Frank Vibert instructs that instead of focussing 'on the individual institutional arrangements [...], or on the "regime," where a complex of arrangements may be involved',[4] a 'systems approach' looks to broader *interrelationships* between various systems and subsystems of socio-political coordination. Vibert explains:

> [...] a systems approach looks at accountability in terms of how *powers are exercised* through a system or subsystem of social coordination. A systems approach looks at the social system as the *totality of different systems and subsystems* of social coordination—including politics, *the law*, and the market. From this viewpoint it is important to know how *power and authority* is being exercised within a particular system, to monitor whether or not the system is operating as envisaged, and to look at system *inter-relationships* and for *adjustments* to be made if the system is not working as intended.[5]

Furthermore, instead of diagnosing accountability's dysfunctions as either 'absent or malfunctioning mechanisms', or 'inappropriate behaviour', a systems approach

[1] Barbara S Romzek and Melvin J Dubnick, 'Accountability' in Jay M Shafritz (ed), *International Encyclopedia of Public Policy and Administration* (Boulder, Westview Press 1998) Vol 1, 6.

[2] Mark E Warren, 'Accountability and Democracy' in Mark Bovens and others (eds), *The Oxford Handbook of Public Accountability* (Oxford, Oxford University Press, 2014) 39 (emphasis added).

[3] Mark Bovens and others (eds), *The Real World of EU Accountability: What Deficit?* (Oxford, Oxford University Press, 2010) 40 (emphasis added).

[4] Frank Vibert, 'The Need for a Systemic Approach' in *The Oxford Handbook* (n 2) 657–58 (emphasis added).

[5] ibid 658 (emphasis added) (fnn omitted).

inquires about the overall health or capability of the system or sub-systems under examination.[6] Vibert relates:

> Accountability from this perspective is not about informing ourselves about a particular institution or decision with possible 'consequences' for *that institution*. It is about informing ourselves about the *performance of the system* to which the institution belongs and that information leading to 'consequences' for the way *that system* is organised. It involves an '*integrity*' approach rather than a 'compliance' approach.[7]

Professor Mulgan has also adopted an 'expansive approach' to accountability. But besides endorsing a 'macro' perspective, he has exploited a more technical understanding of accountability mechanisms to anticipate the implications of many of the more highly abstract points made by systems theorists. For instance, although public accountability must be viewed as 'a complex *network* or *web* of different accountability mechanisms',[8] reliably assessing *dysfunctions* calls for a more sophisticated analysis along the following lines.

First, recognising that 'political accountability' is supplemented by a wide range of mechanisms at multiple levels of abstraction—legal, administrative, professional, etc—Mulgan insists that, at least provisionally, 'the concept of an accountability deficit must be widened to allow for *all* the different possible dimensions where accountability may be found to be lacking'.[9] Second, due to this 'multi-faceted' nature of accountability mechanisms, Mulgan contends that to avoid confusion and enhance diagnostic and prescriptive efficacy, any alleged defect 'must be *clearly specified* and *contextualised*'.[10] Expressing evaluatory concerns shared with many systems theorists (including Korzybski's theory of multi-ordinality), Mulgan instructs:

> Talk of a single, unqualified accountability deficit assumes a single variable which is somehow in the red (as a budget deficit implies a negative financial result in the government's total revenue and expenditure). Public accountability, however, is *not a simple quantum in this way*. It consists of *countless relationships*, between different accountees and account-holders over different issues, not reducible to a single measure or variable.[11]

As a result, while it is important to understand that accountability mechanisms can potentially interrelate and affect one another across multiple levels of abstraction, the assessment of accountability networks is entirely dependent upon accurately identifying which accountability mechanisms are relevant in *any given context*, and whether and how they impact the specific area of performance or concern being studied.

[6] ibid.

[7] ibid (emphasis added) (citations omitted).

[8] See Richard Mulgan, 'Accountability Deficits' in *The Oxford Handbook* (n 2) 545, 552 (emphasis added).

[9] ibid 547, 552 (emphasis added).

[10] ibid 553 (emphasis added).

[11] ibid (emphasis added).

B. Accountability Deficits

Dysfunctions in accountability networks thus can take either of two forms: (1) accountability *deficits*, inferring a deficiency of accountability mechanisms, arrangements, and regimes; or (2) accountability *overloads*, indicating a dysfunctional accumulation or over-abundance of accountability dynamics. Interestingly, far more attention has been devoted to investigating alleged accountability deficits.[12] In a recent literature review of public accountability scholarship, Schillemans reported that 'accountability papers [...] are generally forms of accountability-deficit research',[13] observing that '[n]early two thirds of the papers focus on situations where the agent or actor has somehow been decoupled from the person or institution authorized to hold him accountable'.[14]

An 'accountability deficit' is both broadly familiar and of lasting historical significance, with generations of political theorists and reformers striving for greater empowerment and answerability to 'the people'. In public accountability scholarship, an accountability deficit refers more specifically to conditions 'where [representatives] are not sufficiently hemmed in by requirements to explain their conduct publicly—to legal, professional, administrative, social or political forums who have some sort of power to sanction them'.[15] Condemning the over-abundance of 'accountability-deficit' research reported by Schillemans, Mulgan warns that '[t]he concentration on gaps in political accountability, found in most of the deficit literature, provides a *distorted view* of possible accountability deficits'.[16] More precisely, '[e]ach of the commonly distinguished types of accountability such as legal/judicial, administrative/managerial, peer professional, media, etc., can also be subject to significant gaps or deficits'.[17] This potential proliferation of accountability deficits, and their interactions in complex networks of accountability mechanisms, supports Mulgan's insistence that any alleged deficit must be clearly *specified* and *contextualised*.

Another important feature of accountability deficits is that 'judgments [...] need to be made against an *explicit normative view* of why the deficit is regrettable and why it should, if possible, be mitigated or removed altogether'.[18] As shown by

[12] See, eg, Bovens and others (n 3); Thomas Schillemans, 'Does Horizontal Accountability Work? Evaluating Potential Remedies for the Accountability Deficit of Agencies' (2011) 43(4) *Administration & Society* 387.

[13] Thomas Schillemans, 'The Public Accountability Review: A Meta-Analysis of Public Accountability Research in Six Academic Disciplines' (2013) University of Utrecht Working Paper, 12 www.researchgate.net/publication/ 48327755 (last accessed 23 January 2018).

[14] ibid 12–13.

[15] See Mark Bovens and others, 'Does Public Accountability Work? An Assessment Tool' (2008) 86(1) *Public Administration* 225, 229. Note that this definition does not identify the institutional press as a horizontal accountability mechanism.

[16] Mulgan (n 8) 552 (emphasis added).

[17] Mulgan (n 8) 552.

[18] Mulgan (n 8) 554 (emphasis added).

Bovens, the political goals of accountability are multiple and potentially conflicting. Therefore, whether an accountability gap is 'regrettable' must be a matter of normative judgment. Endorsing the assessment of accountability deficits against Bovens' three normative perspectives (or some functionally similar criteria), Mulgan explains:

> The concept of an accountability deficit is, to some extent at least, in the eye of the beholder. It depends on the *political values* adopted, including the *preferred model of democracy* as well the approach taken to other *principles of government*, such as constitutionalism, the rule of law, and good governance. The best recent analyses of accountability deficits [...] sensibly embrace a form of *normative pluralism*. They not only carefully specify the different empirical dimensions of accountability but also assess them for possible deficits in terms of a range of different value perspectives.[19]

To date, studies of accountability deficits have focussed on two developments. The first has been the formidable growth in powers, numbers of employees, and organisational complexity of the executive branch of government as compared with the legislature.[20] The second involves newly emergent international theatres of networked governance such as the European Union.[21] Both have eclipsed studies of other political accountability deficits, including that present-day courts and legislatures have disregarded the press' role in holding society's powerful to account.

C. Accountability Overloads

A major difficulty with 'expanded views' of accountability is that the concept of an 'accountability deficit' must be correspondingly broadened. Even so, accountability is not an unqualified good to be maximised at all costs; it 'must always be subject to reasonable limits in the light of other conflicting values [...]'.[22] Accountability is challenging to construct, and comes with costs that must be weighed against the (often substantial) harms that it addresses.[23] While it is surely beneficial for maximising institutional design options to combine 'horizontal' and 'vertical' accountability mechanisms, special care must be taken in their assembly as efforts meant to assure accountability can ultimately have direct and indirect consequences that undermine it.

This prospect of an accountability *overload* has received minor scholarly attention. As it happens, an overload of accountability mechanisms may cause various

[19] Mulgan (n 8) 556 (citations omitted) (emphasis added).

[20] Patricia Day and Rudolf Klein, *Accountabilities: Five Public Services* (London, Tavistock Publications, 1987) 33–34.

[21] See Elizabeth Fisher, 'The European Union in the Age of Accountability' (2004) 24(3) *Oxford Journal of Legal Studies* 495.

[22] Richard Mulgan, *Holding Power to Account: Accountability in Modern Democracies* (Basingstoke, Palgrave MacMillan, 2003) 236.

[23] ibid. See also Warren (n 2) 44.

'organisational pathologies', such as unintentional, but systematic undermining of 'productivity, responsiveness, and service quality'.[24] According to Professor Arie Halachmi, '[a]n organizational pathology is likely to develop whenever demonstrated accountability becomes the paramount consideration in evaluating organizational performance—making efficiency and effectiveness secondary in importance'.[25] An accountability overload thus develops when accountability arrangements such as 'political, legal, professional, social, bureaucratic, or environmental, become *dysfunctional*—when good intentions end up undermining the effectiveness and efficiency of the organization [...]; when it reduces responsiveness and flexibility or discourages innovations'.[26]

According to Halachmi, important examples of accountability overloads include:

— Large opportunity and transaction costs.
— The audit society: a society devoting too much attention to the 'rituals of verification'.
— Discouraging innovation: fixed accountability standards may thwart and discourage innovation.
— Awakenings syndrome: dwelling on short-term success, while disregarding future goals.
— Gaming: actors exploiting the indicators and mechanisms for accountability.
— Blame games: the accountability process results in fault-finding only, not in remedial action.
— Multiple accountability: the demands for accountability from different relevant stakeholders invoke confusing expectations.
— Multiple Accountabilities Disorder: conflicting demands for accountability may paralyse agents.[27]

Recognising these dangers, Professors Bovens and Schillemans have recommended that 'it would make sense, both in accountability studies and in practice, to focus more on the *quality* of accountability, on tackling and effectively redressing accountability overloads'.[28] Their well-reasoned approach to achieving 'meaningful accountability' essentially requires

> a more careful look at the *design* of accountability mechanisms [...] and signals a shift in focus from demands for more (or less) accountability to questions about what *types* of accountability are relevant and the *conditions* and *contexts* in which they are effective.[29]

[24] Arie Halachmi, 'Accountability Overloads' in *The Oxford Handbook* (n 2) 560.
[25] ibid.
[26] ibid 560–61.
[27] ibid 561 (citations omitted).
[28] Mark Bovens and Thomas Schillemans, 'Meaningful Accountability' in *The Oxford Handbook* (n 2) 674 (emphasis in original).
[29] ibid (emphasis in original).

Given our adoption of an 'accountability mechanism' as the basic unit of analysis, these are precisely the concerns that must direct our formulation of a revised framework for public libel jurisprudence.

With these methodological fundamentals in hand, we are now positioned to survey the press' vital role as a 'horizontal' accountability mechanism in democratic governance. As discussed below, support for the institutional press as the 'fourth estate' of representative democracy is comprised of a powerful combination of theory and empirical evidence.

III. The Institutional Press as a Horizontal Accountability Mechanism

A. Preliminary Observations

Despite the pervasiveness of Meiklejohnian theory in public libel jurisprudence, public accountability scholarship provides important theoretical and empirical support for the press' role in democratic governance.

First, among the inventory of accountability mechanisms accessible for institutional design, a 'free and independent press' has been acknowledged as 'perhaps *the most important*' by leading accountability scholars.[30] In particular, Professor Pippa Norris insists that '[t]he checks and balances inherent in the representative system [...] legitimize journalistic inquiry as part of a broader framework of government accountability to citizens'.[31] This journalistic influence involves 'dual functions'. Namely, the institutional press performs both 'a direct *primary* role, when investigating the behavior of the powerful and instigating reports about alleged malfeasance', along with 'a more diffuse and weaker *secondary* role, when disseminating general information about public affairs which was previously hidden from public attention [...]'.[32] While fulfilling these roles, journalists are expected to 'question the accuracy of information, interrogate officials, and investigate whether actual conduct reflects high standards of public life'.[33] Curiously, the contrast between public accountability scholars and common law judges and legislators on these issues is stark. Where accountability scholars plainly recognise the 'checking function' as the press' principal role, in public libel jurisprudence the checking function is either ignored or subsumed in Meiklejohnian theory.

[30] Pippa Norris (ed), *Public Sentinel: News Media & Governance Reform* (Washington, World Bank, 2010) 131 (emphasis added). Recall that the press is the only accountability mechanism that applies to all libel plaintiffs and branches of government, engaging in a form of 'full spectrum' accountability.

[31] ibid 115.

[32] Pippa Norris, 'Watchdog Journalism' in *The Oxford Handbook* (n 2) 525–26.

[33] ibid 526.

Second, public accountability scholars have also documented a growing body of empirical evidence confirming that a free and adversarial press enhances political governance, especially by curbing governmental corruption.[34] Describing a 'somewhat mysterious relationship' between democracy and corruption, researchers have learned that 'free and fair elections' alone are not enough to curb malfeasance. Rather, it is the 'interacting effect' of free and fair elections with a *free press* that gives the necessary kick.[35] This evidence is consistent with a theory of political accountability that sees the informational environment as crucial to facilitating effective accountability and electoral control. Even so, as discussed further below, this does not bode well for established democracies currently undergoing a well-documented 'crisis of journalism'.[36]

Lastly, expanding marginally on Professor Blasi's original formulations, these theoretical and empirical sources confirm that the 'institutional press' must refer essentially to those print, broadcast, and digital news organisations and individuals—comprising well-organised, well-financed, professional critics—that are *independent*, *adversarial*, and *powerful* enough to serve as a worthy counter-force to government and influential private actors.

B. Watchdog or Guard Dog?

Alongside Blasi's influential work on the 'checking value', public accountability scholars have observed that 'watchdog journalism' has long been advocated as a mechanism for strengthening accountability in representative democracies. For instance, Norris reminds us that '[t]he watchdog ideal reflects the long-established liberal conception of the news media as the *fourth estate*, an independent guardian located in civil society and counterbalancing the power of executive, legislative, and judiciary branches in government'.[37] Notably, this 'fourth estate' conception embraces a much larger scope of checking function than is implied by Professor Bovens' 'constitutional' perspective. That is, instead of checking executive power only, 'watchdog' journalism endeavours to monitor *any* and *all* levels of governmental and non-governmental activity. Consistent with this claim, the

[34] ibid 538.

[35] See Catharina Lindstedt and Daniel Naurin, 'Transparency and Corruption: The Conditional Significance of a Free Press' (2005) Göteborg University Quality of Government Institute Working Paper <www.qog.pol.gu.se/digitalAssets/1350/1350633_2005_5-lindstedt_naurin.pdf> (last accessed 23 January 2018).

[36] For well-documented accounts of the crisis of journalism, see n 99. Although some digital media may function as accountability mechanisms (eg WikiLeaks, Guido Fawkes' blog, etc), I am emphasising the industry-wide economic displacement of journalism's traditional business model and its restrictive effects on society's largest conventional source of investigative journalism and 'accountability news' production. See Alex S Jones, *Losing the News: The Future of the News that Feeds Democracy* (Oxford, Oxford University Press, 2009) Ch 1.

[37] Norris (n 32) 525 (emphasis added).

'fourth estate' describes its primary role broadly as 'investigating the behavior of *the powerful* and instigating reports about alleged malfeasance'.[38]

When describing the press' 'watchdog' function, public accountability scholars also acknowledge the press' 'weaker and secondary' role in disseminating information. As the Nieman Foundation relates:

> The premise of watchdog journalism is that the press is a *surrogate for the public*, asking probing, penetrating, questions at every level from the town council to the state house to the White House, as well as in corporate and professional offices, in union halls, on university campuses and in religious organizations that seek to influence governmental actions. The goal of watchdog journalism is to see that people in power *provide information the public should have*.[39]

Media and accountability scholars have recognised that these twin functions of 'watchdog' journalism embrace the same fundamental distinctions captured by Professor Blasi's 'checking value' and Meiklejohnian theory. For instance, the press' primary role is described as a 'checking function' by Cammaerts and Carpentier.[40] British media scholar James Curran likewise distinguishes the press' 'watchdog' and 'information conduit' functions.[41] Besides recognising a 'liberal watchdog argument' of the media as a 'check on the state',[42] Curran acknowledges in a more Meiklejohnian vein that 'the media can also be viewed in a more expansive way […] as an *agency of information and debate* that facilitates the functioning of democracy'.[43] Lastly, as summarised deftly by Professor Norris, '[l]iberal theories claim therefore that news coverage can inform the public and official bodies, catalyze electoral, managerial, or legal sanctions against transgressors, and thus provide incentives for better performance'.[44]

Still, the watchdog concept is not without its detractors. Professor George Donohue has argued that instead of performing like a 'watchdog', the institutional press has in fact performed as a sentry 'not for the community as a whole, but for groups having sufficient power and influence to create and control their own security systems'.[45] The press therefore, performs essentially as a 'guard dog'. According to Donohue, the 'fourth estate' model is premised on the following idealised claims: (1) substantial media autonomy; (2) their representation of popular

[38] Norris (n 32) 525–26 (emphasis added).

[39] Norris (n 32) 525–26 (emphasis added), quoting Nieman Foundation, *The Nieman Watchdog Journalism Project* (Harvard, 2010) <www.niemanwatchdog.org/index.cfm?fuseaction=about.Mission_Statement> (last accessed 23 January 2018).

[40] Bart Cammaerts and Nico Carpentier (eds), *Reclaiming the Media: Communication Rights and Democratic Media Roles* (Bristol, Intellect, 2007) xii.

[41] James Curran, 'Mediations of Democracy' in James Curran and Michael Gurevitch (eds), *Mass Media and Society*, 4th edn (London, Hodder Arnold, 2005) 122, 129.

[42] ibid 122–23.

[43] ibid 129 (emphasis added).

[44] Norris (n 32) 527.

[45] George A Donohue and others, 'A Guard Dog Perspective on the Role of the Media' (1995) 45(2) *Journal of Communication* 115.

interests rather than dominant groups; and (3) their independent power to directly and independently challenge those dominant groups.[46]

The 'guard dog' model contests these claims in full. Professor Donohue explains:

> This perspective [...] suggests that the fourth estate watchdog role, as traditionally defined, is not only *unachieved* but is *fundamentally unrealistic*. There is rarely a single public interest, but a configuration of organized interests that vary greatly in power. Media emphasis is upon maintenance of power relationships, that is, power structures. *Power structure* refers to a configuration of roles and groups that has the capacity to make decisions on a community, regional or societal level.[47]

The 'guard dog' perspective, therefore, does not regard the press as equal co-actors, but as dependent on dominant powers.[48] In other words, '[i]n supporting the structure, guard dog media display a tendency to concentrate on individuals while accepting the structure'.[49]

Curran also instructively criticises over-simplification of the press' 'watchdog' role. Arguing colourfully that 'the literature on media and democracy is in need of a removal van to carry away lumber accumulated over two centuries',[50] he insists that the watchdog concept is 'timeworn' in at least two ways. First, contrary to its idealised 'fourth estate' conception, the news media does not in fact allocate a sufficient proportion of its published content to 'disclosure of official wrongdoing' such that this one issue should dictate media policy.[51] Second, Curran criticises the watchdog concept as 'timeworn' in that liberal theory mistakenly holds that 'government' continues to be 'the sole object of press scrutiny'.[52] Stemming from the outmoded view that government is invariably the 'seat' of power, he argues that 'this fails to take account of *shareholder and other forms of authority*'.[53] Similar to neo-republicans like John Braithwaite, Curran insists that '[a] revised conception is needed in which the media are conceived as being a check on the abuse of all sources of power in both the public *and* private realms'.[54] Finally, Curran warns that, whereas '[e]laborate checks and balances have been established in old liberal democracies to shield public media from the state, [...] equivalent checks have not yet been developed to shield private media from corporate abuse'.[55]

Notwithstanding the thoughtful contributions of Professors Donohue and Curran, their critiques of 'watchdog' journalism would appear to be overstated. Indeed, recent empirical evidence casts serious doubts on their claims. Besides establishing a statistically robust correlation between increased press freedom

[46] ibid 118.
[47] ibid 119 (emphasis added).
[48] ibid 121.
[49] ibid 123.
[50] Curran (n 41) 122.
[51] Curran (n 41) 124.
[52] Curran (n 41) 124.
[53] Curran (n 41) 124 (emphasis added).
[54] Curran (n 41) 124(emphasis added).
[55] Curran (n 41) 128.

and reduced corruption, the weight of empirical evidence ultimately supports our endorsement of a 'systems approach' to accountability, concluding at its most dramatic that *anything* restricting the institutional press potentially compromises effective democratic accountability.

C. Empirical Evidence

Whatever theoretical discrepancies remain concerning the institutional press and its characterisation as an 'accountability mechanism',[56] a growing body of empirical evidence derived from experimental research, econometric cross-national analysis, and specific case studies confirms the benefit of a free press on the quality of political governance, especially on controlling corruption.[57] This evidence not only demonstrates that democracy and press freedom have significant impacts on reducing corruption, but confirms that 'watchdog journalism' is widely endorsed among contemporary liberal democracies.

In fact, as such empirical studies amass, it is perhaps ironic that there 'is now a strong need for *improved theory* and *sharper measurements* of a wider range of characteristics' of the institutional press and other relevant accountability mechanisms.[58] Although we 'need to dig deeper' by evaluating *interrelationships* between press structures, legal contexts, and political environments,[59] the weight of empirical evidence is nonetheless substantial, with powerful implications for upholding the checking function by carefully scrutinising proposed legal regulations or threats to its performance.

i. Inaugural Econometric Studies

Empirical research on the relationship between press freedom and corruption has matured significantly over the last two decades. In an early study on investigative journalism and political accountability,[60] Silvio Waisbord observed that, in our attempts to discern the most effective foundations for political accountability, '[...] we still lack a persuasive argument about why one model of journalism is better equipped than its alternatives to make government more transparent in different societies'.[61] Implicitly recognising the 'twin functions' of the institutional

[56] See Cammaerts and Carpentier (n 40), where the authors correctly note that '[w]hatever perspective on the democratic roles of media organizations is taken, all perspectives are in agreement when it comes to the vital role media play in contemporary democracies' (at xv).

[57] Norris (n 32) 538.

[58] See Henrik Oscarsson, 'Media and Quality of Government: A Research Overview' (2008) University of Göthenberg QoG Working Paper Series 2008:12, 1 (emphasis added).

[59] Norris (n 32) 535.

[60] Silvio R Waisbord, 'Investigative Journalism and Political Accountability in South American Democracies' (1996) 13 *Critical Studies in Mass Communication* 343.

[61] ibid 358.

press, Waisbord concluded that '[w]e still do not know whether one type of journalism is better than the next to check the powerful, to provide a forum for public discussion, to build a more robust democracy, and to empower and reconnect citizens'.[62]

The primary concern of Waisbord and others since has been understanding the press' vital role in curbing governmental corruption. At its most rudimentary, 'corruption' has been defined as 'the abuse of public power for personal gain or for the benefit of a group to which one owes allegiance'.[63] Citing Klitgaard's model of corruption dynamics, Rick Stapenhurst has emphasised that corruption depends ultimately on the amount of monopoly power and discretion that a government official exercises: ie, C (Corruption) = M (Monopoly Power) + D (Discretion) $-A$ (Accountability).[64] Stapenhurst explains:

> Successful strategies to curb corruption will have to simultaneously seek to reduce an official's monopoly power (e.g. by market-oriented reforms), his/her discretionary power (e.g. by administrative reforms) and enhance his/her accountability (e.g. through *watchdog agencies*). Such strategies comprise a *system of checks and balances*, designed to manage conflicts of interest in the public sector and limit situations in which conflicts of interest arise or have a negative impact on the common good.[65]

Seeking to identify the 'actual means' by which the press limits corruption, Stapenhurst endorsed the following possibilities:

1. Investigating and exposing corrupt officials and office-holders;
2. Prompting investigations by official bodies;
3. Reinforcing the work and legitimacy of the state's anti-corruption bodies;
4. Helping to shape public opinion hostile to public malfeasance;
5. Pressuring for legal and regulatory change;
6. Deterring through adverse media publicity; and
7. Through such *intangible effects* as 'checks' related to enhanced political pluralism, enlivened public debate, and a heightened sense of accountability among politicians, public bodies, and institutions that are the by-product of hard-hitting independent news media.[66]

Regardless of means, early micro level studies report that a nation's control of corruption sharply accelerates in democracies rated 'above-average' for press freedom. For example, using Freedom House's 'Freedom of the Press' index, Brunetti

[62] ibid.

[63] Rick Stapenhurst, 'The Media's Role in Curbing Corruption' (2000) World Bank Institute Working Paper 1 <http://siteresources.worldbank.org/INTWBIGOVANTCOR/Resources/media.pdf> (last accessed 23 January 2018).

[64] ibid, citing Robert Klitgaard, 'Bolivia: Healing Sick Institutions in La Paz' in Patrick Meagher (ed), *Governance and the Economy in Africa: Tools for Analysis and Reform of Corruption* (University of Maryland IRIS Center, 1996).

[65] ibid (emphasis added).

[66] ibid 2–10.

and Weder reported a strong association between press freedom and corruption across countries, suggesting that an independent press 'may represent an important check against corruption'.[67] Similarly, although conceding that 'the empirical literature is [still] in its infancy', an early study led by Timothy Besley concluded that 'a free and independent media should not be viewed as a luxury that only rich countries can afford. Instead, our analysis suggests that it should be viewed as a *requisite and integral part* of representative democracy'.[68]

Relationships between democracy, press freedom, and reduced corruption were also investigated by Shyamal Chowdhury.[69] Without identifying particular causal mechanisms, Chowdhury nonetheless reported that both democracy and press freedom evolve jointly. That is, 'countries that stand high in democracy and low in corruption are the countries that are high in press freedom and low in corruption'.[70] Chowdhury's study is particularly significant for acknowledging the effects of undertheorising alternative accountability mechanisms. For instance, as between the two components being examined (ie elections and press freedom), it was suggested incorrectly (as it turned out) that 'it is the voters' participation that seems more robust'.[71] Nonetheless, Chowdhury did acknowledge that 'the findings of this paper should be taken with cautions since the indices employed in our empirical analysis may be endogenous and the observed relations may be due to mere *correlations* rather than *actual causation*'.[72]

ii. Examining the Press in Institutional Context

More recent empirical analyses have moved beyond 'elections' as the primary connecting factor, proposing instead an 'interacting' or conditional effect.[73] For example, Lindstedt and Naurin maintain that '[o]ne reason for this somewhat

[67] Aymo Brunetti and Beatrice Weder, 'A Free Press is Bad News for Corruption' (2003) 87 *Journal of Public Economics* 1801, 1820. The 'Freedom of the Press' index is an annual survey conducted by the American-based, non-partisan non-governmental organisation Freedom House, which assesses global print, broadcast, and internet freedom. See generally <https://freedomhouse.org> (last accessed 23 January 2018).

[68] Timothy Besley and others, 'Mass Media and Political Accountability' in Roumeen Islam and others (eds), *The Right to Tell: The Role of Mass Media in Economic Development* (Washington, World Bank, 2002) 15 (emphasis added).

[69] Shyamal K Chowdhury, 'The Effect of Democracy and Press Freedom on Corruption: An Empirical Test' (2004) 85 *Economics Letters* 93.

[70] ibid 99.

[71] ibid 100.

[72] ibid (emphasis added). Interestingly, Bandyopadhyay makes the same point when reporting that both mass media and information and communications technologies are negatively associated with corruption, warning that '[t]he empirics derived in this paper are still associations and causality remains difficult to identify'. See Sanghamitra Bandyopadhyay, 'Knowledge-Driven Economic Development' (University of Oxford, Department of Economics Discussion Paper No 267, June 2006) 15.

[73] Catharina Lindstedt and Daniel Naurin, 'Transparency and Corruption: The Conditional Significance of a Free Press' (2005) Göteborg University Quality of Government Institute Working Paper <www.qog.pol.gu.se/digitalAssets/1350/1350633_2005_5-lindstedt_naurin.pdf> (last accessed 23 January 2018).

mysterious relationship between democracy and corruption […] is that free and fair elections is not enough to increase the risk of accountability'.[74] Rather, the authors reported that 'a *high risk of publicity* is also necessary in order for the elections to be an effective instrument against corruption and other forms of misconduct'.[75] Differentiating 'transparency' and 'publicity', Lindstedt and Naurin argued that the institutional press will usually promote both, linking transparency to the press' investigatory 'digging function', and the latter to its more common 'publishing function'.[76] While the authors' multivariate analyses confirmed earlier results of 'a strong negative effect of freedom of the press on corruption',[77] they concluded that this effect was 'not produced by the correlation between press freedom and electoral democracy […]'.[78]

Instead, Lindstedt and Naurin endorsed the following three observations and conclusions. First, the authors observed that the negative indication reported by previous studies even holds when controlling for electoral democracy. Harkening back to De Lolme's central claims, they resolved, '[i]t really seems as if having nosey journalists around can make political actors more nervous about corrupting themselves'.[79] Second, the study results indicated that transparency is simply not enough. That is, '[i]n order to get to the corrupt activities increasing transparency *must affect* the probability of publicity, which in turn should *raise the risks* for policy-makers of being held accountable'.[80] Unlike previous econometric studies, the authors insisted that one cannot presuppose that transparent information about the agent (ie the political actor) will always reach the principal (ie the public). Lastly, Lindstedt and Naurin insisted that '[c]orruption researchers must acknowledge that democracy is not just a question of elections'.[81] Rather, 'it is the interacting effect of having free and fair elections and a free press (or civil liberties more broadly) which gives the necessary kick'.[82] Their ultimate take-away was that it is only with a lively public sphere of educated people, where the risk for media scrutiny is omnipresent, will elections start to reduce corruption.

[74] ibid 10.

[75] ibid (emphasis added).

[76] ibid 15.

[77] ibid 18. The authors specified that '[p]ress freedom has indeed a significant negative effect on corruption, controlling for electoral democracy, economic development and rule of law. The effect is also relatively large—almost the size of rule of law' (ibid 17).

[78] ibid 18–19. This conclusion squares with the views of Mark N Franklin, who argues that '[e]lectoral accountability may be a central component of representative democracy, but it can often be both unclear and ineffective'. See Mark N Franklin and others, 'Elections' in *The Oxford Handbook* (n 2) 390. Incidentally, Franklin accepts the necessity of an 'interacting role' between elections and press freedom, insisting that 'the mass media play an important role' in that '[u]nless voters have information […], electoral accountability is impossible' (ibid 399).

[79] Lindstedt and Naurin (n 73) 26.

[80] Lindstedt and Naurin (n 73) 26 (emphasis added).

[81] Lindstedt and Naurin (n 73) 26.

[82] Lindstedt and Naurin (n 73) 26 (emphasis in original).

Another sophisticated empirical study led by Sebastian Freille has come to less certain but no less intriguing results.[83] Confirming that examining the subcomponents of press freedom indices (eg Freedom House) is a profitable enterprise in pushing corruption research forward, the Freille study nevertheless reported unexpected results. Interestingly, despite supporting the theoretical view that restrictions on press freedom lead to higher corruption levels, it reported that the subcomponent 'laws and regulations' of the Freedom House index failed to qualify as robust, while two other subcomponents—political and economic pressures—proved to be robust to changes in model specification.[84] In other words, the study results suggested that it was the *political* and *economic* environment (in that order), and *not* 'laws and regulations', that was driving the strong statistical relationship between press freedom and corruption.

The obvious inconsistency on the face of the results was not lost on the authors. Responding to this perplexing result, the authors reported that 'examination of which *Z*-variables leads to insignificance of the laws and regulations index yields little that is obvious in terms of providing an explanation of this finding'.[85] Acknowledging the potential for methodological complications from using 'inclusive press freedom indices', the Freille study ultimately speculated that 'it may be that many effects of improving the laws and regulations are passed onto corruption through economic development'.[86] Either way, rather than obsess over problems of data and estimation (as with early econometric studies), the authors at least engaged in some theoretical discussion about potential causal mechanisms to account for their disconcerting results.

Further empirical research has also made a statistically convincing case for the far-reaching role of *political institutions* (as accountability mechanisms) on reducing corruption. For instance, Daniel Lederman headed a cross-country panel positing that political institutions affect corruption through two channels: political accountability and the structure of the provision of public goods.[87] As the authors explained, '[t]he main contribution of this paper is its search for the *ultimate determinants of corruption*, in the form of the political institutions that determine specific policies as well as political outcomes'.[88] The results were significant. The study reported that '[…] political institutions really matter because they

[83] Sebastian Freille and others, 'A Contribution to the Empirics of Press Freedom and Corruption' (2007) 23 *European Journal of Political Economy* 838.

[84] ibid 840, 848. The level of press freedom reported in Freedom House's 'Freedom of the Press' index is evaluated by ranking answers to 23 methodology questions divided into three broad categories: (1) the legal environment; (2) the political environment; and (3) the economic environment. See <https://freedomhouse.org/report/freedom-press-2016-methodology> (last accessed 23 January 2018).

[85] ibid 848–49.

[86] ibid 854.

[87] Daniel Lederman and others, 'Accountability and Corruption: Political Institutions Matter' (2001) World Bank Policy Research Working Paper No 2708 <https://openknowledge.worldbank.org/handle/10986/19420> (last accessed 23 January 2018).

[88] ibid 11 (emphasis added).

establish the monitoring and accountability mechanisms, which in turn reduce the incentives for corruption by public servants'.[89] Arguing that '[f]rom a policy viewpoint, this study should raise the attention given to accountability mechanisms more generally',[90] the authors reported specifically that '[t]he empirical analysis using panel data based on the [International Country Risk Guide] corruption index indicates that corruption tends to *decrease systematically* with democracy, parliamentary systems, political stability, and freedom of the press'.[91] Concluding in a manner reflecting a 'systems approach' to accountability, the authors advised:

> Political institutions, by determining this environment, are extremely important in determining the incidence of corruption. Ultimately, the *political macrostructure*—related to *the political system, balance of powers, electoral competitiveness, and so on*—determines the incentives for those in office to be honest, and to police and punish misbehavior of others, such that the effects are propagated throughout the system to the lower levels of government.[92]

iii. Primacy of the Informational Environment

Despite the undertheorising of accountability mechanisms displayed in most, if not all, empirical studies exploring press freedom and corruption, the weight of empirical evidence is at least consistent with a theory of political accountability that sees the *informational environment* as crucial to holding power to account. In a recent empirical study led by Eric Chang,[93] the authors examined the 'unique empirical setting' of post-war Italy, which eventually saw voters turn on an entire class of corrupt members of the Italian lower house of Parliament and eject them from office.

Interpreting this unprecedented act of democratic accountability, the Chang study identified 'the time series of press reports' as the variable explaining the dramatic change in voter behaviour. More precisely,

> [o]nly when the press began reporting on political corruption on a *daily basis* did the issue become sufficiently salient to voters that they altered their habitual electoral behavior and refused to reelect incumbents who were likely to be involved in wrongdoing.[94]

Although criminal charges against members of Italy's Chamber of Deputies were levied in each of the first 11 post-war legislatures, 'it was only in the early 1990s

89 ibid 32 (emphasis added).
90 ibid.
91 ibid 31–32 (emphasis added).
92 ibid 31 (emphasis added). Interestingly, another empirical study reports that the effect of openness on corruption is conditioned by domestic institutions. The analysis showed that 'socio-political openness has little to no impact on corruption in the absence of press freedom'. See Nicholas Charron, 'The Impact of Socio-Political Integration and Press Freedom on Corruption' (2009) 45(9) *Journal of Development Studies* 1472, 1488.
93 Eric CC Chang and others, 'Legislative Malfeasance and Political Accountability' (2010) 62(2) *World Politics* 177.
94 ibid 214 (emphasis added).

that press coverage of corruption rose dramatically—just one year before the electorate voted out the corrupt legislative elite'.[95] Therefore, the study revealed that '[w]hen major national newspapers repeatedly and insistently covered corruption as a major and ongoing story, the voters added corruption charges to their voting calculus'.[96]

Significantly, while commenting on the 'external validity' of their empirical study, the authors confirmed the press' essential role as a political accountability mechanism, observing:

> All of the cases of major changes in the informational environment of which we are aware document subsequent reductions in corruption and improved political accountability. Indeed, our results help explain why it is so difficult to alter situations of widespread and entrenched political corruption. Doing so requires a *massive and thorough change in the political information available to the public*. Even if the public does not approve of illegal behavior by elected officials and even if the judiciary is zealous in investigating and indicting, it *requires* an *aggressive free press* for corruption to become sufficiently salient to enough voters for them to achieve electoral retribution.[97]

Major changes in public opinion thus arise only when the informational environment undergoes sufficient improvement due to aggressive investigating and reporting by the institutional press. So convinced were the authors of upholding this 'checking function' of the press that they insisted that '*anything* that compromises the press potentially compromises democratic accountability'.[98]

For example, as much as the Chang study is a triumph for Blasi's checking function rationale, it is equally noteworthy for questioning our prospects of achieving effective accountability. Identifying the current 'crisis of journalism' as a significant threat to democratic accountability, the study authors warned:

> If our interpretation is correct, it does not bode well for political accountability in established democracies. The informational environment is currently undergoing a *rapid and dramatic change* as the ability and willingness of the companies that own much of the television and print media to pay for investigative reporting declines with the shift of information to the Internet. Investigative reporting lacks a business model to support it in the current trajectory toward online content. A *free and aggressive press* is likely to be *critical* to protecting the public from a creeping degeneration of the political elite toward greater corruption.[99]

[95] ibid 213.

[96] ibid 212.

[97] ibid 215–16 (emphasis added) (fn omitted).

[98] ibid 216 (emphasis added).

[99] ibid (emphasis added). See also Robert W McChesney and John Nichols, *The Death and Life of American Journalism: The Media Revolution That Will Begin the World Again* (Philadelphia, Nation Books, 2010). See also Jones (n 36); Lee C Bollinger, *Uninhibited, Robust, and Wide-Open: A Free Press for a New Century* (Oxford, Oxford University Press, 2010) Ch 3; Robert W McChesney and Victor Pickard (eds), *Will the Last Reporter Please Turn out the Lights: The Collapse of Journalism and What can be Done to Fix It* (New York, New Press, 2011). For an excellent discussion of media ownership concentration, see C Edwin Baker, *Media Concentration and Democracy: Why Ownership Matters* (Cambridge, Cambridge University Press, 2007).

D. Conclusion

At last, while it is true that most empirical studies on press freedom and corruption provide 'little or no theoretical discussion about what causal mechanisms are operational',[100] it is perhaps overstating matters to suggest that this literature '[…] has taken a *non-critical* view of the media's "watchdog" role'.[101] To the contrary, much can be learned from their results. Even in its most coarse statistical form, earlier studies by Brunetti and Weder, Besley, and Chowdhury provide evidence of a robust negative correlation between press freedom and corruption. This alone should solidify the checking function's status as an independent free expression justification.

In subsequent attempts to improve upon the over-simplified principal-agent model used earlier, Lindstedt and Naurin stressed that we cannot take for granted that transparent information about political actors will always reach the general public. Placing significant emphasis on the generation and reporting of 'accountability news',[102] the authors concluded that a high risk of publicity *and* accountability is required for transparency to reduce corruption. Similarly, recent attempts to reverse engineer the pre-packaged data in inclusive press freedom indices (eg Freedom House) have confirmed the relationship of press freedom to broader accountability mechanisms such as the political and economic environment. For instance, the Lederman study expressly concluded that the political macro-structure establishes the *monitoring* and *accountability capabilities* that operate alongside the press to control corruption. This is not only broadly consistent with the checking function rationale, but lends considerable support to employing a 'systems approach' for assessing accountability networks more generally.

Above all, there is now considerable evidence that a nation's 'informational environment' is crucial to facilitating democratic accountability. A powerful implication of the Chang study is that whether or not a jurisdiction requires a stronger commitment to investigative journalism and the 'watchdog' role of the press, it seems that a baseline requirement for representative democracies is supporting the institutional press' 'information conduit' function through appropriately designed legal regulations.

Therefore, much can and should be done with this information. As developed in our last section of Part C, there is room to improve our best developed theoretical and empirical approaches to studying the checking function in representative

[100] See Oscarsson (n 58) 1.

[101] Samarth Vaidya, 'Corruption in the Media's Gaze' (2005) 21 *European Journal of Political Economy* 667, 667–68 (emphasis added).

[102] The term 'accountability news' is used by Harvard professor Alex S Jones to describe the generation and reporting of fact-based news whose purpose is to hold government and those in power accountable. See Jones (n 36) Ch 1.

democracies. As will become evident shortly, a revised framework for public libel jurisprudence will only work if proper effect is given to the institutional press and the impact of legal and regulatory restrictions on its 'watchdog' and 'information conduit' functions. In other words, given the special importance and potency of press freedom to the overall accountability balance, public libel doctrine must ideally be chosen on the basis of whether a more liberal or restrictive approach is needed in the context of each jurisdiction's distinct accountability profile.

IV. Public Libel Doctrine: Balancing Reputation and Freedom of Expression in Contemporary Democracies

A. Moving Toward a Revised Analytical Framework

Before proposing a revised framework for public libel jurisprudence, we must identify the fundamental 'primary' and 'secondary' accountability mechanisms comprising the complex structure of representative governments.[103] Restricting the focus of our analysis to *political* accountability, the accountability arrangements in any representative system can be usefully divided into *two* sets of relevant mechanisms. The *primary* set represents a jurisdiction's 'basic architecture', or relatively fixed elements of constitutional design. It comprises the underpinning of institutional relationships responsible for '[setting] limits to the type of accountability mechanisms that can be applied to them',[104] and determining a jurisdiction's fundamental accountability requirements and vulnerabilities.

By contrast, the *secondary* set represents those dynamic mechanisms supplementing a state's basic accountability structure. The aggregate effects of both sets of accountability mechanisms provide the relevant background against which public libel doctrine must be matched. That is, from among the continuum of doctrinal options revealed by our comparative analysis of public libel jurisprudence, a more or less restrictive legal regulation on the press' checking function will be necessary. To be clear, while this framework cannot determine whether outcomes in any particular representative system are categorically 'negative' or 'positive', adopting a comparative approach to this 'calculus' of accountability mechanisms can help identify doctrinal outliers so we can better evaluate their significance when invoked by leading courts and legislatures.

103 Mulgan (n 22) 40.
104 Mulgan (n 22) 190.

B. Primary Mechanisms: Constitutional Structure

Public accountability scholarship confirms that 'accountability' is highly dependent on constitutional structure.[105] Even so, 'to talk of a "structure" or "system" of accountability may be to exaggerate the extent of overall cohesion in a somewhat haphazard set of relationships'.[106] Precise analysis of political accountability then requires 'a survey of the various institutional mechanisms through which governments are held accountable and an *assessment* of their respective contributions to [political] accountability'.[107] This requires examining *five* principal accountability mechanisms comprising a state's 'basic architecture' of separation of powers and institutional features determining its overall accountability effects and requirements. These five primary mechanisms are: (1) general elections; (2) parliamentary/presidential structure; (3) federal/unitary structure; (4) legislative scrutiny; and (5) judicial review.

C. Secondary Mechanisms: Dynamic Variables

Alongside these more fixed, primary accountability mechanisms are the following three secondary accountability mechanisms supplementing a nation's principal accountability network: (1) governmental auditors; (2) independent regulators; and (3) direct public access mechanisms. At any point in time, a combination of these two sets of accountability mechanisms provides the relevant background against which public libel doctrine must be ideally tailored to employ the checking function in a stronger or weaker role as appropriate. Our next section on 'collibration' theory explains these dynamics in greater detail.

D. Collibration

As we have seen, all political accountability systems are pluralistic, consisting of 'a complex set of accountability relationships which apply differently to different sections of the executive and to different types of issue'.[108] As accountability scholars have acknowledged, the immense variety of potential relationships and perspectives tends to negate any chance of constructing a comprehensive structure of political accountability, one that could be reduced to a 'two-dimensional flow chart of accountability and control'.[109]

[105] Mulgan (n 22) 108.
[106] Mulgan (n 22) 40.
[107] Mulgan (n 22) 40 (emphasis added).
[108] Mulgan (n 22) 111.
[109] Mulgan (n 22) 227.

Nevertheless, there exists an approach to measuring and assessing accountability systems that fulfils our 'gas-and-water-works' approach to institutional design. In particular, Professor Colin Scott emphasises that the various accountability mechanisms and arrangements operating uniquely in each jurisdiction have the character of 'a *complex system of checks and balances* in which particular forms of behaviour are inhibited or encouraged by the overall balance in the system at any particular time'.[110] This model of 'extended accountability' is consistent with a 'systems approach' in that it does not look to determine whether outcomes in any particular system are decidedly 'negative' or 'positive'. Rather, it provides a more sophisticated method for examining accountability mechanisms, and for prescribing advice 'as to how strategic interventions, through *shifting of balances*, might be made in order to correct a system which is malfunctioning [...]'.[111]

Consistent with our efforts to formulate a revised framework for coordinating public libel doctrine with our comparators' distinct accountability networks, Scott astutely observes that '[t]he challenge for public lawyers is to know when, where, and how to make appropriate strategic interventions in complex accountability networks to secure appropriate normative structures and outcomes'.[112] In response, Scott has adapted Andrew Dunsire's theory of 'collibration' for evaluating accountability networks,[113] describing collibration as 'a *stratagem* common to a wide variety of processes by which balances are shifted to change the nature of the way that control systems (such as accountability mechanisms) work'.[114]

Focussing on how legal regulation can impact 'guidance, control and evaluation in government', Scott emphasises that the value of such changes may not lie in their effects on a single accountability mechanism, 'but rather in the effects on the overall balance within the regime'.[115] As understood profoundly by neo-republicans and public accountability theorists,

> [t]he logic of the argument presented here is that conflict and tension are inevitable within the complex accountability webs within any particular domain, and that the objective should not be to iron out conflict, but to *exploit* it to hold regimes in appropriate tension.[116]

This 'systems-inspired' approach to assessing accountability captures to a remarkable degree both the theoretical aspirations and concrete workings of neo-republicanism's 'gas-and-water-works' approach to democratic institutional design.

[110] Colin Scott, 'Accountability in the Regulatory State' (2000) 27(1) *Journal of Law and Society* 38, 55 (emphasis added).
[111] ibid (emphasis added).
[112] ibid 57.
[113] Andrew Dunsire, 'Tipping the Balance: Autopoiesis and Governance' (1996) 28(3) *Administration & Society* 299, 318ff.
[114] Scott (n 110) 57 (emphasis added) (fn omitted).
[115] Scott (n 110) 57.
[116] Scott (n 110) 57 (emphasis added).

Above all, while accountability scholars have long advocated for thoughtful 'readjustments' to the 'balance of public accountability' in representative democracies,[117] only recently have researchers like John Braithwaite been advocating to include private actors (such as the media) in the overall calculus. Indeed, Professor Scott maintains that chief among the accountability mechanisms requiring further research is the role of '*the media* in rendering public and quasi-public bodies accountable'.[118] Having consolidated the empirical evidence establishing the press' vital role in curbing governmental corruption, it is high time to add to the mix legal regulation in the form of public libel doctrine.

E. Public Libel Doctrine: Legal Restrictions on the Press

Introduced in chapter one, public libel doctrine can be charted on a continuum depicting degrees of support for reputational interests or freedom of expression and the press.

Table 3: Continuum of Doctrinal Solutions (Condensed)

Protected Value	Doctrinal Solution	Scope	Jurisdiction/Decision
Freedom of Expression	Absolute Privilege	No distinction (at its most absolute; otherwise limited to official conduct)	United States (*Sullivan; Garrison*) (Justices Black, Douglas, Goldberg)
	'Actual Malice' Rule	Public Officials Public Figures	United States (*Sullivan*) (Justice Brennan, for majority) United States (*Curtis*) (Chief Justice Warren, for majority)
▲	Qualified Privilege	Matters of public concern about former, current, or aspiring *parliamentary officials* published to world at large	New Zealand (*Lange No 2*) *Per Curiam*

(*continued*)

[117] See E Leslie Normanton, 'Public Accountability and Audit: A Reconnaissance' in Bruce LR Smith and DC Hague (eds), *The Dilemma of Accountability in Modern Government: Independence versus Control* (New York, St Martin's Press, 1971) 313.

[118] Scott (n 110) 59 (emphasis added).

Table 3: (***Continued***)

Protected Value	Doctrinal Solution	Scope	Jurisdiction/Decision
	Gross Negligence	Public Figures	United States (*Curtis*) (Justice Harlan, plurality)
	Negligence	Private Individuals	United States (*Gertz*) (Justice Powell, for majority)
	Publication on Matter of Public Interest	Information of public interest or concern	United Kingdom Defamation Act 2013, s 4
▼	Responsible Journalism 2	Information of public interest or concern	United Kingdom (*Flood*) (Lord Phillips P et al) Canada (*Grant*) (Chief Justice McLachlin, for majority)
	Responsible Journalism 1	Information on 'governmental and political matters' published to world at large	Australia (*Lange*) *Per Curiam*
Reputational Interests	Qualified Privilege	Information on 'governmental and political matters' <u>not</u> published to world at large	Australia (*Lange*) *Per Curiam*

As Table 3 reveals, not only are there significant doctrinal alternatives for regulating public libels but, as illustrated in Part B, the reasons given by courts and legislatures for choosing their approach have been unconvincing. Specifically, leading common law authorities have repeatedly adopted public libel doctrine with surprisingly little rigour when it comes to supporting theory. This collective undertheorising raises significant doubts as to the soundness of public libel doctrine in each of our five comparators. Fortunately, our present analysis of public accountability scholarship in Part C provides the foundation for a revised analytical framework for public libel jurisprudence. The checking function of the press can therefore be reasserted and restored in each of our comparators by engaging in the public accountability 'calculus' depicted in Figure 1.

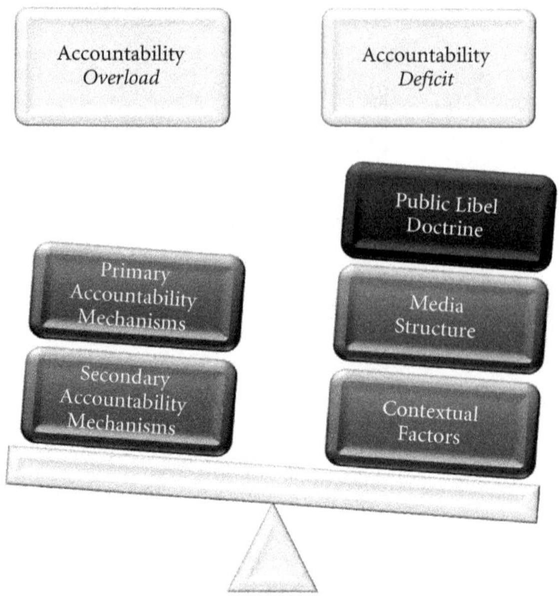

Figure 1: Accountability 'Calculus' for Public Libel Jurisprudence

Consistent with Dunsire's 'collibration' model and a 'systems approach' to public accountability, each jurisdiction's accountability measurement will ultimately be a unique combination of the five accountability elements depicted above.[119] As any one or more elements can fall *on either side of the register*, a nation's accountability calculation can result in one of three options: (1) accountability overload; (2) accountability deficit; or (3) 'balanced' or 'optimised' accountability. Given the special importance and potency of press freedom to the overall accountability balance, public libel doctrine must ideally be chosen on the basis of whether a more *liberal* or *restrictive* approach is needed in the context of each jurisdiction's overall accountability landscape. For instance, if a representative democracy finds itself in an accountability *deficit* relative to other comparators or as a result of a comprehensive measurement by legislative or judicial authorities, a more liberal public libel doctrine along the lines of the 'actual malice' rule may be preferable. In other words, greater allowance for press criticism of government may help tip the scale in favour of greater overall balance in accountability. By contrast, if a jurisdiction records an *overload* of political accountability mechanisms and arrangements, then a more conservative public libel doctrine may be in order.

[119] Analysis and application of the 'media structure' and 'contextual factors' are not within the scope of this work but provide opportunities for future study. Nevertheless, the results of coordinating public libel doctrine with a preliminary assessment of the primary and secondary accountability mechanisms described above provide an indicative and reliable representation of the expected outcomes of our revised framework.

At the very least, such a calculation can quickly identify gross mismanagement of public libel doctrine where, for instance, a jurisdiction that arguably suffers organisational pathologies due to accountability overloads insists upon an overly liberal approach to its balancing of reputational interests and freedom of expression. As demonstrated in Part B, attempts to support such questionable doctrinal positions through undertheorised appeals to Meiklejohnian theory would remain unconvincing.

As will be established in Part D, precise application of this revised framework provides workable 'selection criteria' for public libel jurisprudence. Its implications for law reform proposals are both wide-ranging and (in many respects) unexpected.

V. Chapter Conclusion

Chapter seven focussed on formulating a revised framework for public libel jurisprudence. Building on concepts introduced in chapter six, we have seen that 'meaningful accountability' must not be pursued at any price. Although essential to democracy, accountability is difficult to construct and involves significant costs relative to the problems it was intended to redress. Moreover, rather than focus disproportionately on accountability deficits, we have demonstrated the importance of accountability *overloads*, which signal a pathological accumulation of checking inputs and effects. Both are necessary for assessing accountability in representative systems.

Second, we have shown that the institutional press remains a critical accountability mechanism in modern democracies. By providing the primary means by which information about government activities is reported to the general public, the institutional press is integral to any properly designed system of democratic governance. This was confirmed by our examination of the empirical evidence for the checking function rationale, which not only demonstrated a robust negative correlation between press freedom and corruption, but confirmed that a nation's 'informational environment' is critical to facilitating electoral control over political representatives. Empirical studies also showed that each jurisdiction's political macrostructure establishes the broader monitoring and accountability capabilities that operate in conjunction with the institutional press to control political corruption.

Finally, a revised analytical framework for public libel jurisprudence was formulated by combining two sets of accountability mechanisms. Their aggregate accountability effects provide the pertinent background against which public libel doctrine must be matched. In the end, a 'dynamic equilibrium' must be sought by adjusting public libel doctrine to mitigate exposed accountability dysfunctions in each institutional context.

In our next and final section, Part D concludes our study by restoring democratic accountability in our most instructive comparator through context-specific proposals for public libel law reform.

Part D

Restoring Democratic Accountability

Overview of Part D

Part D explores the implications of our revised framework by applying it to Britain and its newly-updated public libel doctrine. Aside from restricting the scope of the project, the rationale for selecting our law reform candidate is described in chapter eight as follows.

First, the earliest formulation of public libel law emerged within the UK's unique political and constitutional experience. As we have seen, defamation's strict liability model and the 'actual malice' rule both originated in English law. The mere fact of these alternatives occurring in the same jurisdiction calls for careful review. A second and related reason for selecting Britain is that the First Amendment to the US Constitution was based partially on rudimentary comparative law arguments that demand reassessment in light of our revised framework. Third, since the Westminster systems of Canada, Australia, and New Zealand have inherited similar accountability characteristics as Britain's parliamentary government, starting at the beginning of our story makes considerable sense. The rich and extensive consideration of public libel law theory and doctrine by British authorities provides yet another reason to select the UK, particularly with the recent backdrop of popular interest in public libel law reform as demonstrated by the Leveson Inquiry and the Defamation Act 2013.

Finally, Britain's lack of a written constitution and bill of rights provides a fairly straightforward constitutional model for analysis. Understanding the accountability effects of more sophisticated constitutional structures is perhaps best approached by first obtaining a 'baseline' or reliable point of departure. Overall, due to its historical importance and comparative structural simplicity, the UK is an ideal candidate for our law reform purposes.

Chapter eight's investigation of Britain's primary and secondary accountability mechanisms reveals the following points of interest. Besides benefitting from alternative sources of political information generated by its mechanisms of legislative scrutiny, the UK is still beleaguered by transparency concerns associated with the overriding effects of its parliamentary-unitary structure and its delegation model of ministerial responsibility. Furthermore, this informational discrepancy between government and citizens is not fundamentally altered by Britain's independent auditors, regulators, or direct public access mechanisms. Due to a highly attenuated bandwidth of audit inputs and effectiveness, restrictions on citizen access to the Parliamentary Ombudsman, and an expansive exemption regime undermining access to information under British legislation, there remains a strong need for auxiliary accountability mechanisms to fill such aggregate shortfalls in government transparency.

Chapter nine contains our project's law reform recommendations. When judged against the undertheorised basis for its current public libel regime, the most appropriate doctrinal match for the UK's accountability profile requires, at a minimum, adopting a generic qualified privilege not unlike the 'actual malice' rule. What is more, an absolute privilege for political speech cannot be ruled out. This is deeply ironic since alongside discounting accountability concerns in leading cases, Britain's public libel doctrine exhibits both a firm reluctance to privilege political speech and deeply-rooted misconceptions about categorical defences. Alternatively, Britain's latest statutory defence could be adapted by introducing presumptions of 'public interest' and 'reasonable belief' rebuttable on 'clear and convincing' evidence to the contrary in cases involving plaintiff politicians, public officials, and influential public figures and corporations. Such plaintiff-centric amendments are vital for ensuring an effective foothold for the checking function and addressing accountability concerns in free speech litigation involving media defendants.

Despite their prescriptive force, these law reform recommendations raise significant concerns with institutional competence and the need for further research and methodological refinement. Although analysing public libel doctrine along the lines suggested benefits adjudication by placing the defamation inquiry on a more sophisticated theoretical foundation, the increased resources and enlarged scope of review characteristic of legislative bodies suggests that selecting Britain's public libel doctrine would best be reserved to some form of parliamentary inquiry. After all, the more granular and extensive the analysis of accountability effects, the more clearly and confidently public libel doctrine can be matched to *actual* institutional settings.

Similarly, although our revised framework can identify gross mismanagement of public libel doctrine and establish justifiable ranges of possible alternatives, the analysis proposed here is unavoidably *preliminary*. As indicated in chapter seven, a comprehensive accountability assessment must also consider a jurisdiction's media structure and any relevant contextual factors affecting its accountability profile and embodiments of the checking function rationale. Above all, an accountability assessment along such lines must still be balanced against a jurisdiction's commitment to protecting reputation. Such factors will invariably affect the most appropriate form of public libel doctrine in potentially drastic ways.

In the end, while much work remains to refine our methodology for formulating public libel doctrine, the theoretical repositioning required by our proposed framework provides a long overdue and promising foundation for undertaking this ongoing process of methodological refinement.

8

Assessing Britain's Political Accountability Profile

I. Selecting a Law Reform Candidate

As established in Part C, our revised framework for public libel jurisprudence combines two sets of accountability mechanisms. These interconnected features of a jurisdiction's accountability network provide the institutional backdrop against which public libel doctrine must be matched.

Part D therefore explores the implications of our revised framework by applying it to Britain and its newly-updated public libel doctrine. Aside from sensibly restricting the scope of this comparative project,[1] the justification for selecting the UK as our law reform candidate is based on the following six considerations.

First, as amongst our comparators, the earliest formulation of public libel law emerged within Britain's distinct political and constitutional experience. As introduced in chapter one, the original formulations of an 'optimal' relationship between freedom of expression and reputation were established by British judges, legislators, and commentators.[2] Emerging quickly as one of the common law's 'perennial problems',[3] very nearly the entire range of doctrinal alternatives—from defamation's 'strict liability' model to the mid-twentieth century transplantation of the 'actual malice' rule to America—originated in English law.[4] The mere fact

[1] It is neither necessary nor possible (at this stage) to analyse the implications of our revised framework for all of our comparators. While it was necessary to examine each to discover the nature of the concrete problems besetting public libel jurisprudence, establishing our framework's efficacy presents a more focussed and modest challenge. Chapter eight's case study is intended for illustrative purposes only.

[2] See, eg, *Tuchin's* case [1704] Holt KB 424, 90 ER 1133; William Blackstone, *Commentaries on the Laws of England* (Oxford 1765–1769) Vol 4, 150–53.

[3] John Burrows, 'Lange v Atkinson 2000: *Analysis*' (2000) *New Zealand Law Reports* 389, 398.

[4] On the latter point, see *Wason v Walter* (1868) LR 4 QB 73; *Briggs v Garrett* 111 Pa St 404 (1886); *Jackson v Pittsburgh Times* 152 Pa 406 (1893); *Klos v Zahorik* 113 Ia 161 (1901); *Coleman v MacLennan* 78 Kan 711 (1908). For relevant commentary, see George Chase, 'Criticism of Public Officers and Candidates for Office' (1889) 23 *American Law Review* 346; Van Vechten Veeder, 'Freedom of Public Discussion' (1910) 23 *Harvard Law Review* 413; John E Hallen, 'Fair Comment' (1929) 8 *Texas Law Review* 41. See also Ian Loveland, *Political Libels: A Comparative Study* (Oxford, Hart Publishing 2000).

of such diverse doctrinal approaches co-existing in one jurisdiction calls for close scrutiny of the reasons proffered by British authorities.

A second and related reason for selecting Britain is that America's First Amendment was based (at least partially) on rudimentary comparative law arguments that demand reconsideration in light of our revised framework. George Hay's *An Essay on the Liberty of the Press*[5] provides an instructive example. Stating boldly that 'freedom of the press' meant a '[...] *total exemption* from any law making any publication whatever criminal',[6] Hay justified enhanced press freedoms by comparing British and American constitutional features. Responding to supporters of the Sedition Act of 1798, who claimed that 'freedom of the press' meant only exemption from prior restraint, Hay rejected this as 'extreme fallacy', predicting that within one year, '[...] a press absolutely free, would [...] "humble in the dust and ashes," the "stupendous fabric," of the British government'.[7] In statements begging for more careful analysis, Hay reasoned that '[i]n Britain, a legislative control over the press, is, perhaps essential to the preservation of the "present order of things;" but it does not follow, that such control is essential here'.[8] Speculating on America's need for a 'total exemption of the press from any kind of legislative control',[9] Hay observed simply that in England '[...] the parliament is acknowledged to be omnipotent. [...] In Britain there is no constitution, no limitation of legislative power [...]'.[10]

Many questionable leaps pervade Hay's argument. Due to an excessively narrow institutional analysis, what escaped Hay's notice was that the British constitutional order might require a *more* independent, adversarial press precisely because of its relative absence of institutional checks and balances. Without a written constitution, the power of judicial review of legislative enactments, or a prescribed sharing of power amongst the branches of government, the role of the institutional press in checking elected representatives arguably assumes *greater* importance for ensuring adequate accountability measures within Britain's institutional structure. At the very least, this prospect cannot simply be sidestepped as Hay's analysis deftly ensures.

A remarkably similar comparative analysis was proffered by James Madison in his *Virginia Report of 1799–1800*.[11] Like Hay, Madison reflected upon broader constitutional differences between Britain and America to 'place this subject in the clearest light'.[12] Observing narrowly that in Britain 'the danger of encroachments

[5] George Hay, *An Essay on the Liberty of the Press* (Philadelphia, 1799).
[6] ibid 43 (emphasis added).
[7] ibid 48.
[8] ibid 49.
[9] ibid 50.
[10] ibid 49.
[11] See James Madison, *The Virginia Report of 1799–1800* in Gaillard Hunt (ed), *The Writings of James Madison*, 9 vols (New York, GP Putnam's Sons, 1900–1910) Vol 6, 341–406.
[12] ibid 386.

on the rights of the people is understood to be *confined to the executive magistrate*',[13] Madison insisted that '[t]he representatives of the people in the Legislature are not only exempt themselves from distrust, but are considered as sufficient guardians of the rights of their constituents against the danger from the Executive'.[14] Disregarding radical Whig ideas—not to mention the considerable body of evidence documenting history's most notorious political rogues—he concluded, '[u]nder such a government as this, an exemption of the press from previous restraint [...] is *all the freedom that can be secured to it*'.[15] Without apparent explanation, Madison then asserted that republican governments '[...] may well be supposed to require a greater freedom of animadversion than might be tolerated by the genius of such a government as that of Great Britain'.[16] All told, these analyses provide remarkably little insight or support on such far-reaching constitutional matters. Our revised framework promises significant advances for reinterpreting these claims and their implications for public libel doctrine in the UK, and elsewhere.

A third reason for selecting the United Kingdom is that the Westminster systems of Canada, Australia, and New Zealand have inherited sufficiently similar accountability characteristics. Despite their distinctive 'hybrid' structures, all three representative democracies owe their basic institutional framework and common law systems to the British constitutional order. Beginning with defamation law's doctrinal origins and earliest institutional context thus makes considerable sense.

The relatively profound consideration of public libel law theory and doctrine by British authorities provides a fourth reason for selecting the UK. Besides extensive judicial consideration in *Reynolds v Times Newspapers Ltd*,[17] *Jameel v Wall Street Journal Europe*,[18] and *Flood v Times Newspapers Ltd*,[19] British courts are also obliged to consider decisions of the European Court of Human Rights, including its comparatively strong references to the checking function of the press. The reluctance of Britain's highest courts to fully consider cases like *Handyside v United Kingdom*,[20] *Lingens v Austria*,[21] and *Castells v Spain*[22] provides valuable insights into the weaknesses of the theory-doctrine nexus in public libel jurisprudence.

Similarly, widespread interest in public libel law reform as evidenced by the Leveson Inquiry and the Defamation Act 2013 provides a fifth and related justification. As illustrated by Britain's newest defence of 'Publication on Matter of

[13] ibid (emphasis added).
[14] ibid.
[15] ibid (emphasis added).
[16] ibid 387–88.
[17] [2001] 2 AC 127 (HL).
[18] [2007] 1 AC 359 (HL).
[19] [2012] UKSC 11.
[20] (1976) 1 EHRR 737.
[21] (1986) 8 EHRR 407.
[22] App no 11798/85 (ECtHR, 23 April 1992).

Public Interest',[23] arguments for liberalising Britain's media defamation defences have been supported by undertheorised appeals to 'democratic' theory and deeply flawed descriptions of 'American' defamation doctrine. Besides providing no convincing rationale for pursuing more liberal alternatives, it is equally concerning that prominent MPs have provided surprisingly poor accounts of essential differences between the 'actual malice' rule and Britain's new statutory approach.

Lastly, Britain's lack of a written constitution and bill of rights provides a reasonably straightforward constitutional model for analysis. Understanding the accountability effects of more sophisticated structures is perhaps best facilitated by first obtaining a 'baseline' or reliable point of departure. Alongside the comparatively generous body of scholarship on the accountability effects of Britain's parliamentary government,[24] its more streamlined constitutional order augurs well for more direct, less confounded analyses of accountability effects and their implications for public libel reform. Combined, these reasons provide strong justification for selecting the UK as the focus of our law reform efforts.

Our first step is to assess the primary and secondary accountability mechanisms defining Britain's overall accountability profile.

II. Britain's *Primary* Accountability Mechanisms

The UK lacks a written constitution. Without a formal and enduring statement of its defining values, the British constitutional order can be understood as 'a body of rules, conventions and practices which describe, regulate or qualify the organisation, powers and operation of government and the relations between persons and public authorities'.[25] Even without a 'single constitutional theory',[26] Britain's constitution has been shaped by a few central ideas, the most fundamental being representative democracy, parliamentary sovereignty, separation of powers, and the rule of law.[27]

[23] Defamation Act 2013 (UK) c 26, s 4.

[24] See Bernard Manin and others, 'Elections and Representation' in Adam Przeworski and others (eds), *Democracy, Accountability, and Representation* (Cambridge, Cambridge University Press, 1999); Kaare Strøm, 'Delegation and Accountability in Parliamentary Democracies' (2000) 37 *European Journal of Political Research* 261; Kaare Strøm, 'Parliamentary Democracy and Delegation' in Kaare Strøm and others (eds), *Delegation and Accountability in Parliamentary Democracies* (Oxford, Oxford University Press, 2008); Mark N Franklin and others, 'Elections' in Mark Bovens and others (eds), *The Oxford Handbook of Public Accountability* (Oxford, Oxford University Press, 2014); Mark E Warren, 'Accountability and Democracy' in *The Oxford Handbook*, ibid; Paul L Posner and Asif Shahan, 'Audit Institutions' in *The Oxford Handbook*, ibid; Colin Scott, 'Accountability in the Regulatory State' (2000) 27(1) *Journal of Law and Society* 38; Albert Meijer, 'Transparency' in *The Oxford Handbook*, ibid.

[25] Colin Turpin and Adam Tomkins, *British Government and the Constitution*, 7th edn (Cambridge, Cambridge University Press, 2011) 4.

[26] ibid 48.

[27] ibid 48ff. See also Peter Leyland, *The Constitution of the United Kingdom: A Contextual Analysis* (Oxford, Hart Publishing, 2007) 35ff.

Additionally, despite its complex associations with representation and democracy, 'accountability' has also been recognised as a leading constitutional principle. Besides the more well-known accountability mechanisms of general elections, ministerial responsibility, and judicial review,[28] evaluating Britain's accountability profile under our revised framework also requires examining its parliamentary and unitary structure. Overall, this opening phase of analysis exposes significant transparency concerns relative to other constitutional structures, placing considerable pressures on secondary mechanisms of accountability and the institutional press.

A. Parliamentary/Presidential Structure

Britain's constitutional order is one of 'responsible government'. Although incorporating concerns with control and accountability shared by all democracies,[29] the British system is one in which government is responsible to Parliament. Parliamentary government can thus be defined as 'a system of government in which the prime minister and his or her cabinet are accountable to any majority of the members of parliament and can be voted out of office by the latter'.[30] Parliament is of course the governing body in which legislative power is vested in the UK, consisting of an elected House of Commons and a House of Lords comprised of hereditary and life peers, bishops, and Law Lords.[31] This system derives its political authority from upholding the confidence of the elected House, which retains power to dismiss administrations. This requirement to maintain parliamentary confidence imposes significant fetters on governments, compelling them periodically 'to explain, justify, bargain and concede' in response to popular sentiments and pressure.[32]

Among the most significant factors affecting a democracy's accountability profile is the structural differences between *parliamentary* and *presidential* systems. Although it is difficult to determine their relative superiority (at least in the abstract), political researcher Kaare Strøm advises that 'each regime type represents a trade-off among desirable (and less desirable) institutional properties'.[33] Employing different mechanisms for controlling agent behaviour and channeling political power,[34] four of their contrasting features are illustrated by the British example.

[28] Turpin and Tomkins (n 25) Part III.
[29] Turpin and Tomkins (n 25) 566–67.
[30] Strøm, 'Delegation and Accountability' (n 24) 265.
[31] Leyland (n 27) 81.
[32] Turpin and Tomkins (n 25) 569.
[33] Strøm, 'Delegation and Accountability' (n 24) 262.
[34] Strøm's objective is not 'to determine whether parliamentary government is inherently superior or inferior to presidentialism. Indeed, such a judgment cannot be made in general terms, since each regime type represents a particular trade-off among desirable (and less desirable) institutional properties' (Strøm, 'Delegation and Accountability' (n 24) 262).

First, parliamentary governments are characterised by more indirect delegation and accountability. Employing 'more stages of delegation from voters to ultimate policy makers',[35] the primary challenge for parliamentary governments like the UK is guaranteeing 'effective representation' and accountability across multiple stages of delegation.[36] Additionally, leading commentators advise of aggravating concerns with the 'great increase in the work of government departments in modern times, which has made it impossible for ministers to supervise directly or even know about the bulk of their departments' everyday business [...]'.[37]

A second contrasting feature is that parliamentarism depends less on competing governmental agents. The broader range of elected representatives in presidential systems commonly establish executive agencies with similar or overlapping jurisdictions.[38] British representation, by contrast, is defined by the 'singularity principle', which features 'a single chain of command, in which at each link a single principal delegates to one and only one agent (or several non-competing ones), and where each agent is accountable to one and only one principal'.[39] At risk of over-simplification, the 'delegation relationships under parliamentarism take the form of a *long and singular chain*, whereas under presidentialism they look like a *grid*'.[40] Relying on longer, more indirect chains of delegation, guaranteeing effective measures of political accountability is a serious challenge for the United Kingdom.[41]

A third contrasting feature is parliamentarism's lesser reliance on institutional checks and balances. As examined in *The Federalist Papers*,[42] some presidential systems have instituted a prescribed sharing of power amongst the three branches of government. Concerned to devise more effective barriers to the 'encroaching spirit of power',[43] American Federalists re-engineered the 'interior structure' of government by checking each branch against the others. Innovating on classical separation of powers theory, Madison insisted that Montesquieu '[...] did not mean that these departments ought to have no partial agency in, or no control over, the acts of each other', but only that '[...] where the whole power of one department is exercised by the same hands which possess the whole power of another department, the fundamental principles of a free constitution are subverted'.[44] Professor Strøm has since recognised parliamentarism's incompatibility with this

[35] Strøm, 'Delegation and Accountability' (n 24) 272.

[36] Strøm, 'Delegation and Accountability' (n 24) 273.

[37] Turpin and Tomkins (n 25) 576. See also ACL Davies, *Accountability: A Public Law Analysis of Government by Contract* (Oxford, Oxford University Press, 2001).

[38] Strøm, 'Delegation and Accountability' (n 24) 273.

[39] Strøm, 'Delegation and Accountability' (n 24) 269.

[40] Strøm, 'Delegation and Accountability' (n 24) 270 (emphasis added).

[41] Strøm, 'Delegation and Accountability' (n 24) 273.

[42] Alexander Hamilton and others, *The Federalist Papers* (edited by Lawrence Goldman) (Oxford, Oxford University Press, 2008) nos 10, 51.

[43] ibid 246.

[44] ibid 240–41.

arrangement, instructing that due to the 'singularity principle', '[…] ex post controls, particularly in the form of institutional checks, are less likely to be effective […]'.[45]

Finally, parliamentarism relies heavily on ex ante control mechanisms, especially 'prior screening',[46] which is particularly prevalent in selecting and recruiting cabinet ministers. Unlike America, which prohibits the simultaneous holding of cabinet and legislative positions, parliamentary governments like Britain 'require cabinet members to hold parliamentary office'.[47] Due to this significant personnel overlap, the British constitutional order 'greatly facilitates prior parliamentary screening of cabinet members compared to the American one'.[48] Parliamentarism also promotes prior screening due to the greater influence of political parties, which control the delegation process from voters all the way to the chief executive.[49] Party influence thus results in 'extensive screening of prospective parliamentarians as well as potential cabinet members'.[50]

i. Accountability Consequences of Parliamentary Government

At base, presidentialism and parliamentary government can each be understood as 'a particular way to organize the policy process, [or] as a delegation regime'.[51] Among their distinguishing properties, parliamentarism benefits from important advantages, including 'decisional efficiency and the inducements parliamentarism creates toward effort'.[52] At its best, it incentivises direct agent monitoring and compliance.[53]

But parliamentary governments do suffer familiar perils,[54] especially ineffective accountability and transparency limitations.[55] That is, parliamentarism's first weakness is an overall increase in agency loss, due to its more indirect delegation schemes and that it receives less benefit from constraint and competition.[56] A second and arguably more concerning weakness is that parliamentary systems generally score lower on measures of informational transparency.[57] As Strøm capably notes, 'the main problem is not that parliamentary systems lack the opportunity to sanction, but rather that *they do not have the monitoring capacity* necessary to determine when such sanctions might be appropriate'.[58] Contrastingly,

[45] Strøm, 'Delegation and Accountability' (n 24) 273.
[46] Strøm, 'Delegation and Accountability' (n 24) 273.
[47] Strøm, 'Delegation and Accountability' (n 24) 273.
[48] Strøm, 'Delegation and Accountability' (n 24) 273.
[49] Strøm, 'Delegation and Accountability' (n 24) 274.
[50] Strøm, 'Delegation and Accountability' (n 24) 274.
[51] Strøm, 'Delegation and Accountability' (n 24) 285.
[52] Strøm, 'Delegation and Accountability' (n 24) 285.
[53] Strøm, 'Delegation and Accountability' (n 24) 276.
[54] Strøm, 'Delegation and Accountability' (n 24) 277.
[55] Strøm, 'Delegation and Accountability' (n 24) 261.
[56] Strøm, 'Delegation and Accountability' (n 24) 277, 286.
[57] Strøm, 'Delegation and Accountability' (n 24) 281.
[58] Strøm, 'Delegation and Accountability' (n 24) 274 (emphasis added).

presidential systems '[…] are more likely to *generate transparency*, because they contain mechanisms by which agents are forced to share information and principals can learn'.[59] Such informational advantages are strengthened because more policy bargaining takes place in the public domain[60] through proposals and counter-proposals 'shuttled back and forth between different chambers or branches of government'.[61] Policy bargaining in parliamentary governments, by contrast, tends to take place out of sight.[62]

Parliamentary governments are therefore beset by transparency deficiencies and increased accountability concerns relative to their presidential counterparts. While neither alternative safeguards against dishonest or incompetent public servants,[63] their accountability effects represent distinct structural trade-offs. In the end, residual concerns with agency loss and informational transparency provide a credible prima facie case for strengthening the institutional press through more liberal approaches to public libel doctrine.

B. Federal/Unitary Structure

Another essential feature of a jurisdiction's accountability profile is its federal or unitary structure. Despite competing definitions, leading commentators advise that 'the essential features of a federal constitution are that the central and regional governments have limited powers and that, within those limits, each government is independent of the other'.[64] By corollary, a unitary state is one where 'the legislature of the whole country is the supreme law-making body in the country. It may permit other legislatures to exist and to exercise their powers, but it has the right, in law, to overrule them […]'.[65]

This notion of 'fused' or 'unified' powers is central to our understanding of parliamentary government.[66] While it was customarily thought that Britain was a unitary state, introduction of devolution legislation in 1998 has transferred varying degrees of autonomy to Scotland, Wales, and Northern Ireland.[67] These changes have not only established new democratically elected bodies, but also conferred 'substantial powers on devolved executives'.[68] This has prompted some commentators to propose that the UK has a '*union* constitution', which is 'neither

[59] Strøm, 'Parliamentary Democracy and Delegation' (n 24) 95 (emphasis in original).
[60] Strøm, 'Parliamentary Democracy and Delegation' (n 24) 96.
[61] Strøm, 'Parliamentary Democracy and Delegation' (n 24) 96.
[62] Strøm, 'Parliamentary Democracy and Delegation' (n 24) 96.
[63] Strøm, 'Parliamentary Democracy and Delegation' (n 24) 97.
[64] Turpin and Tomkins (n 25) 211.
[65] Turpin and Tomkins (n 25) 211, quoting KC Wheare, *Modern Constitutions*, 2nd edn (Oxford, Oxford University Press, 1966) 19.
[66] Strøm, 'Delegation and Accountability' (n 24) 263.
[67] See Scotland Act 1998 (UK); Government of Wales Act 1998 (UK); Wales Act 2014 (UK); Northern Ireland (Elections) Act 1998 (UK); Northern Ireland Act 1998 (UK).
[68] Leyland (n 27) 185.

straightforwardly unitary nor systematically federal in character'.[69] For instance, Professor Leyland has argued that devolution has significantly improved accountability mechanisms at the devolved level, advising that the overall process was 'designed to bring government closer to the electorate in the devolved nations by allowing scope for policy preferences to be expressed'.[70] Similar to traditional federal states, it is at least arguable then that devolution has produced 'enhanced levels of democratic and legal accountability' for Scotland, Wales, and Northern Ireland.[71]

Still, despite such regional variances, our prevailing focus on the UK Parliament confirms that Britain 'is clearly recognisable as a state in which a supreme central authority is firmly established on the principle of parliamentary sovereignty'.[72] What is more, notwithstanding devolution and its complexities, '[t]here has never been serious official consideration of a restructuring of the UK on a federal plan'.[73] In Britain's only royal commission into its constitutional structure, the Kilbrandon Commission rejected federalism due to an unacceptable increase in judicial powers and England's dominant position relative to devolved authorities.[74] The Commission concluded:

> A federation consisting of four units—England, Scotland, Wales and Northern Ireland—would be so *unbalanced* as to be *unworkable*. It would be *dominated by the overwhelming political importance and wealth of England*. The English Parliament would rival the United Kingdom federal Parliament; and in the federal Parliament itself the representation of England could hardly be scaled down in such a way as to enable it to be out-voted by Scotland, Wales and Northern Ireland, together representing less than one-fifth of the population.[75]

Confirming the soundness of the Commission's judgment, as of June 2016, England had around 55.2 million inhabitants or just over 84 per cent of the UK's estimated 65.6 million total population.[76] It is not unreasonable to conclude that

[69] Turpin and Tomkins (n 25) 210 (emphasis in original). See also Ferdinand Mount, *The British Constitution Now: Recovery or Decline?* (London, Mandarin, 1993) 199ff; Neil Walker, 'Beyond the Unitary Conception of the United Kingdom Constitution' (2000) *Public Law* 384; Iain McLean, *What's Wrong with the British Constitution?* (Oxford, Oxford University Press, 2010) Ch 8.

[70] Peter Leyland, 'Multi-Layered Constitutional Accountability and the Re-financing of Territorial Governance in the UK' in Nicholas Bamforth and Peter Leyland (eds), *Accountability in the Contemporary Constitution* (Oxford, Oxford University Press, 2013) 310. Leyland notes elsewhere that 'devolution arrangements not only provide the electorate in each nation with the right to vote on the basis of proportional representation, but each piece of legislation introduces its own brand of democratic institutions and processes'. See Leyland (n 27) 188.

[71] Leyland, 'Multi-Layered Constitutional Accountability', ibid 309.

[72] Turpin and Tomkins (n 25) 213.

[73] Turpin and Tomkins (n 25) 214.

[74] Home Office, *Report of the Royal Commission on the Constitution, 1969–1973* (Cmnd 5460, 1973) vol 1, [527]–[532].

[75] ibid [531] (emphasis added).

[76] 'UK population rise of 538,000 is biggest for 70 years' (BBC, 22 June 2017) <www.bbc.com/news/uk-40372533> (last accessed 24 January 2018).

Britain remains in all relevant respects a 'unitary' state for the purposes of establishing its primary accountability profile.

i. Accountability Consequences of Federal/Unitary Structures

Accountability scholars advise that federations like the United States, Canada, and Australia offer considerable benefits over unitary states. Besides offering more avenues of accountability, Mulgan for example instructs that political accountability is enhanced because members at each level are subject to significant public scrutiny and face political damage if they refuse to respond.[77] Although federations may be more susceptible to blame shifting, it appears that unitary states *intensify* the effects of existing transparency concerns, particularly in parliamentary governments where 'single accountability allows for much tighter control of information and makes it easier for those in power to frustrate public accountability'.[78]

At last, the transparency concerns associated with parliamentarism generally are exacerbated by informational scarcity, placing additional pressure on Britain's overall accountability network.

C. Electoral System

The core accountability mechanism in representative democracies is the general election, which in theory can 'provide voters with the means to directly check sitting politicians'.[79] Electoral systems can also affect

> both the 'value' of a vote in terms of its efficacy to secure the election of a preferred representative to Parliament, and also the likelihood that the government elected into power will reflect the interests or policy preferences of the electorate.[80]

The scheme for elections to the UK House of Commons is known as the 'first past the post' (FPTP) system.[81] The FPTP system operates by dividing the UK into 650 approximately equal constituencies in terms of population, each sending a single member to Parliament representing a specific geographical area.[82] A candidate receiving the most votes in a constituency wins the seat. However, unlike 'proportional representation', an FPTP system is not intended to 'produce an elected House which will be a "mirror of the nation" [...]'.[83]

[77] Richard Mulgan, *Holding Power to Account: Accountability in Modern Democracies* (Basingstoke, Palgrave MacMillan 2003) 218.

[78] ibid 196.

[79] Franklin and others (n 24) 389.

[80] Turpin and Tomkins (n 25) 533.

[81] Turpin and Tomkins (n 25) 534. A nationwide referendum in May 2011 resulted in large majority support for preserving the existing 'first past the post' system.

[82] See UK Parliament, 'Parliamentary Constituencies' <www.parliament.uk/about/how/elections-and-voting/constituencies/> (last accessed 24 January 2018). See also Leyland (n 27) 83.

[83] Turpin and Tomkins (n 25) 534.

FPTP electoral systems have many distinctive features. Foremost is their tendency to produce stable, single-party majority governments. As explained by Richard Rose:

> It does this by giving disproportionately more seats to the most successful party. The element of distortion in the ratio of votes to seats is usually considered a small price to pay for the greater advantage of fixing responsibility for government upon a single party with a majority in the House of Commons.[84]

Despite discriminating against third parties without locally concentrated support, an FPTP system promotes accountability because 'a party with a majority can carry through its policies without having to enter into pacts and compromise',[85] as often happens under systems of proportional representation.

i. Accountability Consequences of Electoral Systems

General elections have long been described as a 'very blunt instrument for holding politicians to account'.[86] The recognised limitations of 'electoral accountability' are of course its inefficiency and overall weakness as an accountability mechanism. For example, Warren has cautioned that 'despite its democracy-defining centrality, voting is not a very powerful accountability mechanism, even when differences among institutional arrangements are taken into account'.[87] Manin also warns that '[e]lections are not a sufficient mechanism to insure that governments will do everything they can to maximize citizens' welfare'.[88]

Arguing that elections are too general and undifferentiated to satisfy democratic accountability requirements,[89] Mulgan emphasises three additional concerns. First, since elections are also procedures for selecting political leaders, concerns arise that their multiple functions can overly complicate voter decisions and outcomes.[90] Second, Mulgan reports that only a small percentage of the voting public actually bases their decisions on carefully informed judgments about the future or past performance of governments and politicians.[91] Third, elections also underperform as mechanisms for ensuring informed and constructive political debate.[92] Mulgan laments that political campaigning is too often based on public relations 'spin doctoring' manipulated by political candidates '[...] at the expense of genuine political dialogue [...]'.[93] Likewise, Warren cautions that electoral

[84] Richard Rose, *The Problem of Party Government* (London, MacMillan, 1974) 115.
[85] Leyland (n 27) 85.
[86] Franklin and others (n 24) 389, quoting VO Key, *Public Opinion and American Democracy* (New York, Knopf, 1961) 459.
[87] Warren (n 24) 45.
[88] Manin and others (n 24) 50.
[89] Mulgan (n 77) 45.
[90] Mulgan (n 77) 43–44.
[91] Mulgan (n 77) 44.
[92] Mulgan (n 77) 44.
[93] Mulgan (n 77) 44.

accountability ultimately provides little control over governmental activities, functioning to align policy-making and voter preferences '[...] only over periods of several decades'.[94]

Since FPTP and proportional systems point electoral accountability in two separate directions (ie political party versus individual representative), their effectiveness as accountability mechanisms depends on other institutional factors such as 'party financing, party discipline, legislative procedures, and (in PR systems) the prevalence of pre-electoral pacts that can refocus election campaigns from parties to governments'.[95] Because both systems can diffuse the chain of responsibility—making it harder to hold governments accountable—neither system is clearly superior where electoral accountability is concerned. Overall, while not to be dismissed outright, electoral accountability appears to be a relatively weak mechanism and only a starting point for analysis.

D. Legislative Scrutiny

Many key accountability mechanisms operate through legislatures. Whether considering a parliamentary or presidential system, federal or unitary, 'holding the executive accountable through public inquiry and debate has become the dominant function of all modern legislatures'.[96] As emphasised by leading accountability scholars, legislatures pursue their accountability functions through *four* primary mechanisms, including: official reports and accounts, ministerial responsibility (unique to parliamentarism), committee investigations, and constituency representation.[97]

i. Official Reports

The opening stage of the accountability process involves obtaining maximum information about government matters. Distinct from horizontal mechanisms like the institutional press, '[l]egislatures play an important role in *compelling* governments to publish information about their activities, most notably through the obligation to report regularly to the legislature'.[98] Moreover, besides annual reporting obligations, 'most reports are presented formally to the legislature in open session and thus become public documents'.[99]

This account principally holds true for the UK. As described by the National Audit Office (NAO), '[t]he audited Annual Report and Accounts of each government department, which are presented to Parliament each year, are a fundamental

[94] Warren (n 24) 45.
[95] Franklin and others (n 24) 395–96.
[96] Mulgan (n 77) 45.
[97] Mulgan (n 77) 47.
[98] Mulgan (n 77) 47 (emphasis added).
[99] Mulgan (n 77) 47.

part of the parliamentary accountability cycle'.[100] This 'accountability cycle' commences with each department 'preparing their annual budgets and submitting them to HM Treasury' for review.[101] Once submitted, HM Treasury 'reviews and challenges these, before presenting them to Parliament in the form of the Estimates for each department'.[102] Parliament then authorises each budgetary amount by vote.

The cycle concludes at the end of the fiscal year 'when departments report back to Parliament [...] their actual outturn for the year compared with their authorised amounts'.[103] The Annual Report and Accounts hence purports 'to present a clear picture of the department's aims, activities, functions and performance, linking performance delivered over the past year with expenditure during the same period'.[104] Applying to executive agencies and non-departmental public bodies, official reports would appear to contribute significantly to the UK's accountability profile.

ii. Ministerial Responsibility

Another mechanism of legislative scrutiny is Britain's system of 'ministerial responsibility'. Unique to parliamentarism, this convention is best understood as 'a species of general organisational accountability where the obligations of accountability are located with the person in charge'.[105] That is to say, 'every minister is responsible to Parliament for his or her own official conduct, and a minister who heads a department also has ultimate responsibility for everything done by the department'.[106]

The central delegation relationship for ministerial responsibility—known as the 'singularity principle'—features a single chain of command with each principal delegating to one agent (or several affiliated ones), and where each agent is accountable to one principal.[107] Importantly, this 'principal-agent' model is also associated with Parliament's obligation to *empower* government. Turpin and Tomkins emphasise that '[t]he essence of effective parliamentary control over government is not simply that the House of Commons should stop a government from doing things. It is that the Commons should *positively support* and *sustain* the government of the day [...]'.[108] Parliament in this respect contrasts with the US Congress, which is constitutionally obliged to *check* the executive branch.[109]

100 National Audit Office, 'Understanding Central Government's Accounts: An Introductory Guide for Those with an Oversight Role' (DP Ref: 10242-001, March 2014) 3 <www.nao.org.uk/wp-content/uploads/2014/04/Guide-to-understanding-departmental-accounts.pdf> (last accessed 24 January 2018).

101 ibid 4.

102 ibid.

103 ibid.

104 ibid 6.

105 Mulgan (n 77) 48.

106 Turpin and Tomkins (n 25) 573.

107 Strøm, 'Delegation and Accountability' (n 24) 269.

108 Turpin and Tomkins (n 25) 593 (emphasis added).

109 See generally, US Const art I.

Parliament's control of executive governance therefore 'depends on getting from ministers the relevant facts and explanations'.[110] Underlining the importance of parliamentary debate, Mulgan notes that ministers are obliged to respond to questions about their portfolios, both orally and in writing.[111] While not an especially strong accountability mechanism, parliamentary debates 'are an essential part of the continuous [...] scrutiny of government, compelling it to explain and defend its policies and decisions' publicly on a regular basis.[112]

iii. Committee Investigations

Much legislative scrutiny is also accomplished *outside* the main debating chambers in legislative committees. While the committee system has been strongly associated with American government, '[d]uring the last third of the twentieth century [...] all Westminster systems greatly increased the role of committees in scrutinising government departments and other public agencies'.[113] Britain has relied on a revised system of 'departmental select committees'.[114] As summarised by Professor Leyland:

> Departmental select committees were established in 1979 to oversee the work of the major government departments. There were originally 14 of these committees but there are now 18. The committees consist of between 11 and 17 MPs, with the parties represented according to their relative strength in the House of Commons, which means that *the governing party will have a majority on the committee*. In fact, select committees should be regarded as an important extension of ministerial responsibility, helping to keep track of what ministers do with their responsibility for their departments and other agencies.[115]

Intended to oversee state departments by examining 'expenditure, administration, and policy', these committees were given extensive investigatory capabilities, including powers 'to send for persons, papers, and records,'[116] and the 'limited capacity to employ a staff of expert advisers, mainly on a part-time basis'.[117]

Among their contributions, select committees 'provide MPs with a *countervailing* source of information to that of ministers and the executive departments [...]'.[118] Compared to relying on ministers and officials during parliamentary debates,

[110] Turpin and Tomkins (n 25) 573.
[111] Mulgan (n 77) 50.
[112] Turpin and Tomkins (n 25) 610.
[113] Mulgan (n 77) 53.
[114] See generally Richard Kelly, 'Select Committees: Powers and Functions' in Alexander Horne and others (eds), *Parliament and the Law* (Oxford, Hart Publishing, 2013); House of Commons Information Office, 'Departmental Select Committees' (Revised August 2010) <www.parliament.uk/documents/commons-information-office/p02.pdf> (last accessed 24 January 2018).
[115] Leyland (n 27) 106 (emphasis added).
[116] Turpin and Tomkins (n 25) 620.
[117] Leyland (n 27) 107.
[118] Leyland (n 27) 108 (emphasis added).

departmental select committees provide 'considerable information not available to the mass of individual MPs'.[119] Commentators predictably report that '[g]overnments have not always regarded with enthusiasm the establishment of select committees which can question their policies and investigate the details of administration'.[120]

Select committees also have distinct limitations. Philip Giddings notes that even though '[s]crutiny has been extended, accountability deepened and policy debate widened',[121] Parliament's basic structure remains fundamentally intact. This observation is crucial for interpreting the purpose and effectiveness of select committees. Giddings stresses that

> the Chamber of the House of Commons remains the primary forum for debate and decision; the mode of behaviour and discourse in the House is still that of cohesive, adversarial parties; single party majority government remains the norm; [and] the Executive is still dominant.[122]

Underlining the disparity between select committee powers and the House's work overall, Giddings reports:

> One of the reasons for governments' relatively benign attitude to select committees has been that, if necessary, they can afford to ignore them, at least as far as the dispatch of government business is concerned. Whilst it is helpful for governments to have the support of select committees [...], it is not necessary. Adverse or critical reports from select committees are an irritant or an embarrassment, but no more.[123]

As a result, despite their proliferation and influence, Britain's departmental select committees 'do not have real power over the things that matter to governments—the passage of legislation, the voting of taxation and expenditure, [or] the continuation of ministers in office'.[124] Above all, basic constitutional relations between government and Parliament (including residual transparency concerns) remain unchanged.

iv. Constituency Representation

Finally, it must not be forgotten that legislators function as representatives of their local constituencies.[125] As a measure of electoral influence, '[i]t seems clear enough that governments are not indifferent to public opinion and pay some regard to it in their decision-making'.[126] But even though public grievances reach

[119] Leyland (n 27) 108.
[120] Turpin and Tomkins (n 25) 617.
[121] Philip Giddings, 'Select Committees and Parliamentary Scrutiny: Plus Ça Change' (1994) 47 *Parliamentary Affairs* 669, 684.
[122] ibid 683–84.
[123] ibid 684.
[124] ibid 669.
[125] Mulgan (n 77) 55.
[126] Turpin and Tomkins (n 25) 543.

representatives through traditional means, leading commentators note that '[...] a more reliable source of information about public opinion on particular issues is nowadays provided by *opinion surveys*'.[127] Voter consultation therefore tends to be increasingly conducted as part of larger government efforts to 'carry out research into public reactions to existing and proposed new policies [...]'.[128]

v. Accountability Consequences of Legislative Scrutiny

While legislatures are essential accountability mechanisms, their strengths and weaknesses are challenging to assess. Public accountability scholars maintain that accountability is best secured by adversarial parties operating within an independently powerful legislature.[129] This can be achieved in presidential systems 'if the party lines are clearly defined and the president's party does not control Congress',[130] and in parliamentary systems where legislative scrutiny is provided by 'minority governments where the governing party or parties depend on the votes of other members of Parliament outside the government who are in a position to enforce accountability [...]'.[131]

Summarising legislative accountability mechanisms in a manner consistent with the press' 'watchdog' role, Mulgan has emphasised that 'publicity' and 'public criticism' are their principal means of accountability. Given the legislature's overriding obligations to publicise and debate matters of government action, improving the accountability performance of legislatures should, according to Mulgan, involve '[...] making the executive more *open to legislative investigation* and [...] reducing the capacity of government agencies and officials to conceal their actions'.[132]

This focus on the information and discussion stages of the accountability process greatly assists in evaluating Britain's mechanisms of legislative scrutiny. First, excepting cases of withholding material information or outright misrepresentation, publishing a department's 'Annual Report and Accounts' undeniably augments informational transparency. Second, the obligation of ministers to respond to parliamentary queries also enhances legislative scrutiny, compelling them to publicly explain and defend their policies and decisions. Third, despite concerns with transparency and moral hazard associated with ministerial responsibility, departmental select committees provide Parliament with considerable countervailing sources of government information. Lastly, it is at least arguable that MP accountability has been enhanced by increasing emphasis on public opinion surveys and techniques.

[127] Turpin and Tomkins (n 25) 543 (emphasis added).
[128] Turpin and Tomkins (n 25) 544.
[129] Mulgan (n 77) 60.
[130] Mulgan (n 77) 60.
[131] Mulgan (n 77) 61.
[132] Mulgan (n 77) 63 (emphasis added).

Still, even accepting this generous characterisation of legislative accountability in the UK, it would appear that '*executive dominance* of Parliament remains the most conspicuous feature of the legislative process'.[133] Despite boosts in informational transparency secured through parliamentary debate, the public filing of departmental reports, and the alternative sources of information provided by select committees, the fact remains that even in times of determined opposition, 'it is very unusual for the government not to get a measure passed by Parliament'.[134] This should not be surprising since, alongside Parliament's obligation to empower government, public accountability scholarship reminds us that a principal feature of parliamentarism is its propensity to conduct policy-making behind closed doors.

In the end, whatever virtues might be claimed for legislative scrutiny under Britain's constitutional order, residual transparency concerns and significant accountability deficits persist.

E. Judicial Review

Our final primary accountability mechanism is judicial review. Judicial review through a nation's legal system and courts is in some respects the most powerful form of external review of executive action. Professors Turpin and Tomkins have authoritatively defined judicial review as 'the exercise of an ancient and inherent *supervisory* jurisdiction of the court, by which excess or abuse of public power may be *restrained* or *remedied*'.[135] Rooted in the ultra vires principle that 'powers granted to a public body must not be exceeded',[136] judicial review in Britain is concerned primarily with the legality and process of the decisions of public authorities.[137] That is, '[c]ourts traditionally have seen their role as underpinning the integrity of the legal system and commitments to formal procedural requirements which comprise the rule of law'.[138] Compared to mechanisms of legislative scrutiny, judicial review is widely variable with more determinate effects. Judicial review also impacts all stages of the accountability process, including information gathering, discussion, and rectification.[139]

Although our comparators' constitutions all require judicial review of government action, the extent of the courts' supervisory power varies considerably. For instance, America has long embraced a strong version of judicial review known

133 Leyland (n 27) 114 (emphasis added).
134 Leyland (n 27) 114.
135 Turpin and Tomkins (n 25) 661 (emphasis added).
136 Turpin and Tomkins (n 25) 663.
137 Turpin and Tomkins (n 25) 663.
138 Colin Scott, 'Independent Regulators' in *The Oxford Handbook* (n 24) 479.
139 Mulgan (n 77) 80.

as 'judicial supremacy', which involves the power 'to determine that statutes enacted by Congress and state legislatures are inconsistent with the Constitution and therefore have no legal effect'.[140] Furthermore, Scott observes that American courts 'are seen to have moved somewhat from more formal to more substantive modes of reasoning in addressing issues for decision, with more developed ways for collecting policy evidence, and for evaluating competing claims to efficiency of outcomes'.[141]

By contrast, Britain has no written constitution and embraces parliamentary sovereignty, which largely determines the relationship between courts and Parliament. Parliamentary sovereignty means that 'although the courts have an interpretative function in regard to the application of legislation, it is Parliament, and not the courts, which has the final word in determining the law'.[142] Indeed, Article 9 of the Bill of Rights 1689 provides that '[...] debates or proceedings in Parliament ought not to be impeached or questioned in any court or place out of Parliament'.[143] Besides establishing an absolute privilege for MPs, this assertion has also been taken to mean that statutes passed in proper form cannot be judicially challenged in respect of their validity.[144]

i. Accountability Consequences of Judicial Review

Beyond noting broader differences in judicial review between Britain and America, the precise details of its use and impact are illuminating. Professor Leyland reports that 'between 1982 and 2005 the [total] number of claims for judicial review increased from 685 to over 5,000'.[145] However, as Leyland points out, these figures are misleading. First, only a small fraction of claims advance to a full hearing, many settling out of court or dismissed as unmeritorious.[146] Second, a disproportionate number involve immigration claims and therefore do not represent the entire spectrum of government activity.[147] Third, even though skyrocketing overall, the numbers still represent 'a tiny fraction of decisions taken by public bodies (well under one percent)'.[148] As a result, even if trends continued along established trajectories, Leyland's critique shows that it would take a

[140] Mark Tushnet, *The Constitution of the United States of America: A Contextual Analysis* (Oxford, Hart Publishing, 2009) 134.

[141] Scott (n 138) 479.

[142] Leyland (n 27) 39. On 'hybrid' systems such as Australia and Canada, see Stephen Gardbaum, *The New Commonwealth Model of Constitutionalism: Theory and Practice* (Cambridge, Cambridge University Press, 2013) 204ff.

[143] Bill of Rights 1689, Art 9.

[144] See generally *British Railways Board v Pickin* [1974] AC 765 (HL); *Pepper v Hart* [1993] AC 593 (HL) 638, where Lord Browne-Wilkinson confirmed Article 9 to be 'of the highest constitutional importance'.

[145] Leyland (n 27) 161.

[146] Leyland (n 27) 162.

[147] Leyland (n 27) 162.

[148] Leyland (n 27) 162.

considerably longer amount of time before signalling a dramatic shift from the traditional dominance of the executive and Parliament.

As such, although judicial review must be accepted as 'a fundamental aspect of executive accountability',[149] it seems a relatively weak accountability mechanism in Britain's constitutional order. Given the importance of informational transparency and the supremacy of Britain's legislative and executive branches of government, judicial review can be expected to play only a minor role in checking government overreaching and malfeasance.

F. Conclusion on Primary Accountability Mechanisms

Our opening analysis of primary accountability mechanisms has identified many concerns with Britain's accountability profile. Despite benefitting from significant mechanisms of legislative scrutiny that provide MPs (and the broader public) with important sources of government information, the UK is still beset by transparency concerns associated with its parliamentary-unitary structure and system of ministerial responsibility. With a relatively weak form of judicial review, such concerns expose important accountability deficits relative to other constitutional orders. This places substantial pressures on Britain's secondary and auxiliary accountability mechanisms, including public libel law and the institutional press.

III. Britain's *Secondary* Accountability Mechanisms

Building on our analysis of primary accountability mechanisms, the following secondary mechanisms represent those dynamic institutional features supplementing Britain's basic accountability structure. Combining these various mechanisms establishes the aggregate accountability profile against which public libel doctrine must ultimately be matched.

A. Governmental Auditors

Besides courts and legislatures, government audit institutions are important contributors to political accountability and financial control. As highlighted by Professors Posner and Shahan, '[g]overnmental audits are conducted to provide an *independent assessment* of the extent to which public agencies meet acceptable standards of legal, financial, and performance accountability in implementing public programs'.[150] These audit institutions contribute to accountability by

[149] Mulgan (n 77) 81.
[150] Posner and Shahan (n 24) 488–89 (emphasis added).

scrutinising governmental activities, but 'without having the power to enforce their preferred remedies'.[151] Consequently, while government audits promote information gathering and discussion, they focus narrowly on monitoring budgetary expenditure.

Britain's basic framework of independent auditing dates back to the Public Accounts Committee (PAC) in 1861.[152] Intended to offer ex post facto checks on government expenditures, the PAC's official remit was restricted to 'the audited accounts of government departments'.[153] Besides questioning MPs and departmental accounting officers, the PAC 'works on non-party lines and its reports, which are in practice unanimous, are debated each year in the House of Commons'.[154] Owing to its powers to comment adversely and withhold approval of departmental and agency accounts, the executive is strongly incentivised to respond to the PAC's criticisms through remedial action.

The PAC is also the only parliamentary committee with administrative support from the NAO. The NAO is headed by the Comptroller and Auditor General, which dates back to the Exchequer and Audit Department Act of 1866.[155] The important point from an accountability perspective is that the NAO and the Comptroller and Auditor General are intended to be *independent* entities 'certify[ing] the accounts of all government departments and a wide range of other public sector bodies'.[156] Alongside routine financial auditing, the NAO also 'conducts special investigations during the year into the "economy, efficiency and effectiveness" with which government departments and other public bodies have used their resources', preparing numerous annual 'Value for Money' reports.[157]

i. *Accountability Consequences of Governmental Auditors*

Audit institutions rely mostly on their 'high levels of credibility and legitimacy' compared with other accountability mechanisms. Although lacking enforcement powers, Posner and Shahan explain that their considerable influence 'stems from their *expertise* and *legitimacy*—ministers and civil servants alike, as well as legislators, cannot ignore with impunity the recommendations and findings of auditors'.[158] Moreover, because public officials know that fraud or embezzlement are criminal offences, the PAC has considerable power to hold government agencies and public servants to account.[159] Indeed, Turpin and Tomkins report that '[t]he great majority of the Committee's recommendations are accepted [...]'.[160]

151 Mulgan (n 77) 83.
152 Leyland (n 27) 110.
153 Leyland (n 27) 111.
154 Turpin and Tomkins (n 25) 649; see also Leyland (n 27) 111.
155 Leyland (n 27) 110.
156 Leyland (n 27) 111.
157 Turpin and Tomkins (n 25) 648.
158 Posner and Shahan (n 24) 502–03 (emphasis added).
159 Mulgan (n 77) 89.
160 Turpin and Tomkins (n 25) 649.

Another factor in determining whether audit institutions heighten accountability is 'the *extent of independence* enjoyed by these institutions'.[161] Distinguishing 'financial', 'organisational', 'functional', and 'government' independence, Posner and Shahan also differentiate four audit institution models, namely: (1) court of accounts; (2) collegiate body; (3) government department; and (4) legislative audit office.[162] As expected, the 'government department' model is considered least independent. By contrast, as a 'legislative audit office', the PAC is 'legally and constitutionally separated from the other branches of the government [...]'.[163] Although keeping a complex relationship with Parliament, accountability scholars confirm that 'even though they listen to the requests of [Parliament]' in selecting targets of inquiry, committees like Britain's PAC ultimately '[...] enjoy independence in deciding on their audit activities'.[164]

However, even though the PAC has 'revealed many instances of waste and failure of financial control',[165] its auditing process is wholly *retrospective*. Along with an absence of formal enforcement powers, the entire auditing process over which the PAC presides is defined by this limitation. Leyland relates:

> Although the PAC and the NAO have a crucial part to play in the process of scrutiny, they are concerned only with *past expenditure*, that is, on funds that have *already been allocated*. Essentially, this auditing work, although very important, is Parliament looking over its shoulder at items of expenditure with a paramount concern for the efficient and economical use of public money.[166]

Besides the limits inherent in retroactivity, the above comments signal a deeper limitation of governmental auditing as an accountability mechanism. As Mulgan sharply observes, '[t]he effectiveness of audit accountability depends on the type of issue' under study.[167] Although fraud and misappropriation of public funds are not unknown in Britain (eg UK parliamentary expenses scandal), more subtle transgressions such as '[i]nefficiency, extravagance and waste [...] are less easily detected'.[168] As a result, despite the PAC's successes in identifying inefficiencies in government defence spending,[169] auditors have tended to avoid controversial topics that involve 'evaluations of policy effectiveness where assessments must include judgments about social and political values'.[170]

161 Posner and Shahan (n 24) 496 (emphasis added).
162 Posner and Shahan (n 24) 493ff.
163 Posner and Shahan (n 24) 497.
164 Posner and Shahan (n 24) 497.
165 Turpin and Tomkins (n 25) 648.
166 Leyland (n 27) 112–13 (emphasis added).
167 Mulgan (n 77) 89.
168 Mulgan (n 77) 89.
169 Turpin and Tomkins (n 25) 648–49. The authors reference both the PAC's 1982 report on the Chevaline Project, which concerned massive cost overruns associated with Britain's Polaris missile system, and its 2005 and 2009 investigations of procurement complications associated with the Ministry of Defence's purchase of Chinook Mk3 attack helicopters.
170 Mulgan (n 77) 89.

In the end, rather than criticising audit committees for 'narrowness of focus', a better informed view is that 'a sensible division of labour has emerged, with politicians and legislative committees searching out the more politically contentious issues and auditors concentrating on the more routine areas of bureaucratic behaviour'.[171] Thus, although operating within narrow bandwidths of government information, Britain's PAC is well-organised for its purposes of securing financial savings, raising standards of public services, and improving their quality of delivery.

B. Independent Regulators

Alongside governmental auditors, many investigative and monitoring bodies also investigate public grievances. The first set of independent regulators consists of 'ombudsmen' or 'commissioners'.[172] The second includes 'inspectors' and other regulatory bodies.[173] According to Professor Scott, both groups are responsible for overseeing 'the activities of business, governmental, and third sectors through setting rules or norms and engaging in practices of monitoring and enforcement'.[174] Regulators enforce accountability principally through 'the search for evidence and the publication of reports and recommendations'.[175] Without remedial powers, independent regulators rely instead on 'the moral and political authority of their recommendations to persuade or shame governments into taking remedial action'.[176]

Britain's dominant independent regulator is the Parliamentary Commissioner for Administration (more commonly known as the Parliamentary Ombudsman), whose office was created by the Parliamentary Commissioner Act 1967 to investigate complaints resulting from government 'maladministration' (not defined in the Act).[177] Originally intended 'to plug a manifest gap in dealing with grievances against officialdom',[178] the Ombudsman can (controversially) only undertake investigations at the request of an MP (MP Filter), to whom they report. Also, if the Ombudsman concludes that injustice has transpired, they can only recommend remedial action. Except for nationalised industries and 'contractual and other commercial transactions', the Ombudsman's jurisdiction extends to 'some 350 government departments and agencies and other public bodies'.[179]

[171] Mulgan (n 77) 89–90.
[172] Mulgan (n 77) 90.
[173] Mulgan (n 77) 90.
[174] Scott (n 138) 472 (citation omitted).
[175] Mulgan (n 77) 95.
[176] Mulgan (n 77) 95.
[177] See generally, Turpin and Tomkins (n 25) 627ff.
[178] Leyland (n 27) 113.
[179] Turpin and Tomkins (n 25) 630.

i. Accountability Consequences of Independent Regulators

Independent regulators offer both strengths and weaknesses as accountability mechanisms. A significant strength lies in their dispersal of power. Similar to departmental select committees, '[...] an independent regulator creates an *alternative* source of knowledge and authority through which both government and regulated organizations may be held to account'.[180] Weaknesses include 'the capacity for actors to shift blame on to others for failings, facilitating an avoidance of accountability', or actors being 'caught in an "accountability conspiracy" in which it is against the interests of key actors to blow the whistle on others [...]'.[181]

Perhaps the most controversial feature in Britain's constitutional order is the close relationship of the Ombudsman to Parliament.[182] Criticisms include that 'the "MP filter" has operated in an arbitrary way [...] and is a hindrance to the ordinary citizen in need of a clear and simple remedy for grievances against the administration'.[183] Highlighting the peculiarity of this arrangement, Turpin and Tomkins add that '[d]irect access to the Ombudsman or equivalent officer by members of the public is allowed in almost every other country that has this institution [...]'.[184]

Despite such obvious shortcomings, evidence on the accountability effects of independent regulators is limited. Mulgan observes that their effectiveness 'depends on factors such as the extent of their legal powers and their terms of reference, in addition to the level of their resources'.[185] Scott too insists that successful public sector regulation requires 'political support and acceptance'.[186] Since the accountability effect of independent regulators is contingent upon 'informal rather than formal power', Scott emphasises that it is both difficult to identify, and 'may be highly variable in effects depending on particular contexts'.[187]

At last, perhaps all that can be said about their effectiveness is that 'the existence of independent regulators contributes to the transparency of governmental activities with a tendency to diminish the concentration of power with ministers and their departments'.[188] In the specific context of Britain's constitutional order, retaining the MP Filter restricting access to the Ombudsman significantly diminishes such potential benefits.

180 Scott (n 138) 472 (emphasis added).
181 Scott (n 138) 472–73.
182 Turpin and Tomkins (n 25) 628.
183 Turpin and Tomkins (n 25) 628.
184 Turpin and Tomkins (n 25) 628.
185 Mulgan (n 77) 98.
186 Scott (n 138) 481.
187 Scott (n 138) 484.
188 Scott (n 138) 473.

C. Direct Public Access

Our final secondary mechanism is the influence of transparency and direct public access to government information. Centring on the preliminary 'information gathering' phase of the accountability process, transparency has been defined as 'the *availability of information* about an actor allowing other actors to *monitor* the workings or performance of this actor'.[189] In effect, transparency can be realised 'passively' (freedom of information requests), 'pro-actively' (websites or documents), and through 'forced access' (leaking and whistleblowing).[190]

The most significant route of direct public access in Britain has been statutory freedom of information (FOI) requests. Compared to the US, whose FOI legislation dates back to 1966,[191] the UK has enacted a series of piecemeal reforms culminating in the Freedom of Information Act 2000.[192] Without an established tradition of participatory democracy guaranteeing government information as of right, 'British governments have traditionally maintained a high degree of secrecy about their operations'.[193] Turpin and Tomkins relate:

> British governments have in the past held it to be entirely a matter for their discretion whether and to what extent official information should be made available to the public or to interested organisations. It has been a perennial concern that governments are unduly restrictive in withholding information from the public (and from Parliament) and that secrecy is sometimes maintained not for reasons of the public interest, but to protect the government from criticism or embarrassment.[194]

The authors also insist that ministerial responsibility 'ha[s] contributed to the maintenance of governmental secrecy by enforcing an internal governmental discipline in the control of information'.[195] As a result, if Britain's system of 'responsible government' is to be more than an empty abstraction, then appropriate public access to information is necessary.

The FOI Act 2000 provides a general right of access to information held by public authorities and an obligation to provide requested information within a specified period (usually within 20 working days).[196] As with all FOI legislation, some categories of information are exempt from disclosure.[197] These exemptions fall into two broad categories, depending on whether the requested information enjoys absolute or qualified protection. The first category of 'class' exemptions apply without the need to satisfy any test of harm or prejudice. Such exemptions

[189] Meijer (n 24) 511 (emphasis added).
[190] Meijer (n 24) 511.
[191] Meijer (n 24) 509.
[192] Freedom of Information Act 2000 (UK) (FOI Act 2000); see also Mulgan (n 77) 99.
[193] Turpin and Tomkins (n 25) 557.
[194] Turpin and Tomkins (n 25) 558.
[195] Turpin and Tomkins (n 25) 558.
[196] FOI Act 2000 (n 192) s 10.
[197] See generally FOI Act 2000 (n 192) Part II.

cover a disconcerting breadth of information, including security matters, national security, personal or confidential information, legal privilege, court records, criminal investigations, communications with the Royal Family, other investigations or proceedings conducted by government authorities, and, most controversially, information relating to 'the formulation or development of government policy'.[198] By contrast, the second category of exemptions relies on a prejudice test or proof of other harmful consequences of disclosure. These potential exemptions are available for matters relating to national defence, domestic and international relations, health and safety, economic interests, domestic law enforcement, and commercial interests.[199]

At last, despite intending for 'a more extensive scheme for making information publicly available and [to cover] a much wider range of public authorities',[200] Britain's FOI Act 2000 provides 23 separate exemptions from its general disclosure obligations.

i. Accountability Consequences of Direct Access Mechanisms

There is considerable disagreement amongst scholars regarding the accountability effects of Britain's FOI legislation. For instance, despite criticising the Act's exemption regime in permitting 'public authorities to withhold much information of a factual nature not manifestly requiring to be kept secret in the public interest',[201] Turpin and Tomkins conclude optimistically that '[d]espite its limitations, the Freedom of Information Act has provided a valuable reinforcement of governmental accountability and a worthwhile extension of the rights of the individual'.[202] Similarly, while sharing concerns that its exemption regime places 'many legitimate areas of scrutiny [...] beyond its scope',[203] Professor Leyland concludes vaguely that Britain's FOI legislation is 'having an important impact in delivering accountability in many areas'.[204]

Public accountability scholars are much less confident. Although there is some evidence that FOI legislation enhances political accountability in states with *weak* accountability mechanisms, evidence in states with more developed accountability networks (like the UK) is quite limited. Since government information requires handling and interpretation, accountability scholars have learned that, even if they *can* obtain it, 'only very few citizens use [such] information to call public organizations to account'.[205] Citizens typically rely instead on specialist organisations, 'such as Parliament, the municipal council, the Court of Audit, the Ombudsman, and

198 FOI Act 2000 (n 192) ss 23, 24, 30, 32, 35, 37, 40, 41, 42.
199 FOI Act 2000 (n 192) ss 26, 27, 28, 29, 31, 38, 43.
200 Explanatory Notes to the FOI Act 2000 [6].
201 Turpin and Tomkins (n 25) 561.
202 Turpin and Tomkins (n 25) 564.
203 Leyland (n 27) 143.
204 Leyland (n 27) 138.
205 Meijer (n 24) 514.

also the media'.[206] Mulgan also derides the wide-ranging exemption opportunities under FOI legislation, concluding that it has 'not fundamentally altered the information imbalance between governments and citizens'.[207]

Furthermore, Mulgan reminds us that despite Britain's FOI legislation, political accountability can still be seriously impeded through traditional government channels. Not only can governments conceal information, invoke statutory exemptions, withhold information, or manipulate and manage information, but their considerable advantages in resources and size allow them to outpace the capacity of primary and secondary accountability mechanisms to monitor and scrutinise government activities.[208] Tunis Wortman's forewarnings on the dangers of governmental power remain as enduring as ever.[209]

D. Conclusion on Secondary Accountability Mechanisms

Our examination of secondary mechanisms also reveals significant concerns with Britain's accountability profile. First, due to limitations associated with retroactivity, a singular focus on financial auditing and public expenditures, and the insensitivities of forensic auditing to instances of extravagance and waste, Britain's main audit institutions operate within a narrow bandwidth of accountability input and effectiveness.

Second, as Britain's main independent regulator, the Parliamentary Ombudsman is hindered by the MP Filter, which restricts individual citizens' access to the office. Third, due to extensive exemptions under Britain's FOI legislation, and that very few individuals other than journalists routinely use it, the effectiveness of Britain's direct public access legislation is very likely not to have altered the information imbalance between citizens and government.

IV. Chapter Conclusion

Chapter eight has demonstrated that the UK is beset by significant transparency concerns associated with its parliamentary-unitary structure and system of ministerial responsibility. This informational discrepancy between government and citizens is not fundamentally altered by Britain's independent auditors, regulators, or direct public access mechanisms. It is against these aggregated accountability deficits that public libel doctrine must be matched to mitigate such concerns in our next and final chapter.

[206] Meijer (n 24) 514 (citations omitted).

[207] Mulgan (n 77) 103.

[208] Mulgan (n 77) 113–14.

[209] Tunis Wortman, *A Treatise, Concerning Political Enquiry, and the Liberty of the Press* (New York, 1800) 175.

9

Reinstating the Checking Function in Britain's Constitutional Context

I. Law Reform Recommendations

A. Rationale for Britain's Public Libel Doctrine

Before proceeding to our specific law reform proposals, a brief recapitulation of the UK's public libel jurisprudence is necessary. As shown in chapters four and five, Britain's public libel doctrine is significantly undertheorised. Whether considering the *Reynolds* test or the UK Parliament's new defence of 'Publication on Matter of Public Interest', British authorities have enlisted remarkably little support from free expression rationales. Where efforts are made, judges and legislators have appealed vaguely to 'democratic' theory, overlooking or conflating the checking function and accountability concerns in favour of interpretations more consistent with notions of deliberative democracy. Meiklejohn, not Blasi, plays first fiddle.

This undertheorising of course began with attempts to liberalise media defamation principles in *Reynolds v Times Newspapers Ltd.*[1] Adjudicating upon material facts involving investigative reporting of political misconduct at the highest levels of executive governance, the House of Lords overwhelmingly rejected a generic qualified privilege for publications on political matters. The Law Lords based their preference for an ad hoc 'responsible journalism' defence on the perceived absence of a 'convincing rationale' for greater protection for political speech.

A remarkable succession of theoretical imprecision began with Lord Nicholls' leading opinion in *Reynolds*. Reassuring Britons that there '[...] was no need to elaborate on the importance of the role discharged by the media in the expression and communication of information and comment on political matters',[2] he nonetheless reasoned that '[t]he interest of a democratic society in ensuring a free press weighs heavily in the balance [...]'.[3] Without identifying this allegedly vital

[1] [2001] 2 AC 127 (HL).
[2] ibid 200.
[3] ibid.

interest, the checking function was effectively excluded by Lord Nicholls' conviction that 'it would be *unsound in principle* to distinguish political discussion from discussion of other matters of serious public concern'.[4] Not surprising then that the defendants' more modest, negligence-based alternative was rejected since applying it to political information '[...] would *lack a coherent rationale*'.[5] Displaying similar predilections, Lord Cooke put matters most bluntly, concluding that '[...] there is in my opinion no good reason why politicians should be subjected to a greater risk [...] of false allegations of fact in the media'.[6] Combined with perfunctory and misleading use of Strasbourg jurisprudence (which, we will recall, contains many of the clearest articulations of the checking function), it beggars belief how accountability concerns *could* have influenced the Law Lords' reasoning.

Similar complications have beset Britain's legislative law reforms.[7] In replacing *Reynolds* with a statutory defence intended to enhance freedom of expression, the UK Parliament sought to 'optimally balance' its defamation principles whilst disregarding free speech justifications and distorting categorical approaches. These difficulties originated in the Act's pre-legislative background. Despite conceding that '[t]he law governing defamation is crucial to the proper functioning of any democratic society',[8] the Joint Committee on the Draft Defamation Bill rejected a categorical defence for political speech because it would 'offer insufficient protection to people whose reputation is harmed by untruths and *overly focus on the mind of the publisher* [...]'.[9]

The grounds for the Joint Committee's curious position were eventually revealed in parliamentary debates. While The Lord Chancellor and Secretary of State for Justice Mr Kenneth Clarke emphasised 'striking the right balance' in Britain's defamation laws, the nearest anyone came to justifying stronger commitments to freedom of expression was his passing explanation that '[t]hat is how power is held to account, abuses of authority are uncovered and truth is advanced'.[10] Even if such stock phrases constituted clear representations of the checking function (which they do not), debate in the House of Lords abruptly side-tracked selection of suitable public libel doctrine by sanctioning a radically flawed interpretation of the 'actual malice' rule. An authority no less than Lord Lester (the draft Defamation Bill's original sponsor and defence counsel in *Reynolds*) stated that

> [t]he reason why the American position does not make much sense [...] is that it focuses on the identity of the publisher and not the content of the publication. It asks: is the publisher a public figure? That is the wrong question.[11]

[4] ibid 204 (emphasis added).
[5] ibid 203 (emphasis added).
[6] ibid 219.
[7] Defamation Act 2013 (UK) c 26, s 4.
[8] Joint Committee on the Draft Defamation Bill, *Session 2010–12: Report, together with formal minutes* (HC 930–I, 19 October 2011) 15.
[9] ibid 28 [35] (emphasis added).
[10] HC Deb 12 June 2012 col 177.
[11] HL Deb 19 December 2012 col GC538.

But as we have seen, the US Supreme Court asked no such question. Rather, it endorsed a generic qualified privilege for defamatory statements of fact directed at *public officials* and *figures*. The overriding concern was not the identity of the publisher, but the identity of the *plaintiff*. By focussing on the latter, concerns more resonant with the checking function's aims to enhance informational transparency and hold power to account are prioritised. This mischaracterisation thus demonstrates the powerful influence of deficient free expression theorising on doctrine selection. As a result, rather than seeking adequate measures of institutional accountability, only ancillary concerns with 'litigation expenses' and 'discovery complications' were highlighted by British parliamentarians. By so profoundly misrepresenting 'America's' categorical, plaintiff-centric approach, whatever possibility existed for aligning doctrinal options with relevant free speech justifications—let alone institutional and constitutional demands—was quickly lost. In effect, an entire bandwidth of public libel law's most liberal alternatives was excluded due to misinterpreting a doctrinal approach that ironically originated on English soil scarcely a century earlier.

In sum, along with obfuscating accountability concerns in its leading decisions, Britain's public libel doctrine is typified by a reluctance to privilege political speech and recurrent mischaracterisations of categorical defences. By doing so, British authorities have marginalised the most relevant theoretical and institutional concerns in public libel jurisprudence—democratic accountability and the 'watchdog' role of the press.

B. Specific Law Reform Proposals

i. Rationale for a Categorical Approach

Returning then to Britain's specific accountability profile, our revised framework exposed significant accountability deficits attributable to the following factors. First, despite profiting from alternative sources of information generated by its mechanisms of legislative scrutiny, the UK remains beset by widespread transparency concerns associated with its parliamentary-unitary structure and convention of ministerial responsibility. Second, this informational disparity between government and citizens is not fundamentally altered by Britain's independent auditors, regulators, or direct public access mechanisms. Given the restrictions on citizen access to the Parliamentary Ombudsman, and the substantial number of exemptions undermining access to information under Britain's Freedom of Information Act 2000 (FOI Act 2000) legislation, there remains considerable need for supplemental, horizontal accountability mechanisms. Moreover, our law reform proposals must be informed by the more general deficiency in protection for political speech exposed by chapter four's doctrinal analysis of UK public libel law.

In view of the foregoing, the most appropriate doctrinal solution for Britain's accountability profile seems to require, at a minimum, a generic qualified privilege similar in operation and effect to the 'actual malice' rule. What is more, in the absence of a more comprehensive analysis of media structure, etc (discussed below), an absolute privilege for political speech cannot be ruled out as a suitable accommodation. While this may seem surprising, the inescapable lesson of our present enquiry is not that Britain's recent defamation law reforms have gone too far, but, rather, that they have *not gone far enough*.

Therefore, until UK judges and legislators begin scrutinising parliamentarism's unique accountability requirements and dysfunctions, we are left with the sobering realisation that Britain's public libel law may only be aggravating one of its most challenging structural weaknesses as a representative democracy.

ii. Implications for Britain's Existing Defence

The value of our revised framework can also be demonstrated by using it to adapt Britain's new statutory defence. Since there is no ultimate connection between the form of public libel doctrine and the degree of protection afforded to freedom of expression, our concern to reinstate the checking function must also apply to ad hoc balancing approaches like the UK's defence of 'Publication on Matter of Public Interest'. However, to provide an effective foothold for the checking function to address broader concerns with democratic accountability, a few plaintiff-centric amendments are required.

First, rather than leave the balancing exercise open-ended as in *Reynolds*, rebuttable presumptions of 'public interest' and 'reasonable belief' should apply to public libel cases involving plaintiff politicians, public officials, and influential public figures and corporations. As highlighted by American public libel jurisprudence and the Strasbourg Court, these are the plaintiffs who most clearly engage the checking function's underlying premises and concerns. To secure an advantage for press publications in such cases, the standard of proof required to rebut these presumptions should be 'clear and convincing' evidence, a suitably firmer (but not insurmountable) challenge compared with the customary civil standard of 'balance of probabilities'. The overall benefits of this approach would be considerable. Besides allowing the checking function to do its job when most relevant on the facts, it would still permit plaintiffs to adduce evidence restricting application of the defence where clearly unwarranted. For example, plaintiffs could adduce evidence of 'irresponsible journalism'; that an offending publication was not in the 'public interest'; or, relatedly, that a defamatory statement was not relevant to a plaintiff's official duties or public character. Compared to a categorical approach like the 'actual malice' rule, the chief advantage would be preserving a substantially similar protection for the institutional press to investigate and report widely on public malfeasance, while also permitting an unrestricted examination of all relevant circumstances. In short, more routes to establishing liability are preserved, but only for highly deserving cases.

Second, this enhanced protection for investigating and reporting on matters relating to political and public misconduct must also be harmonised with Britain's efforts to establish a system of 'voluntary' press regulation. Since Lord Justice Leveson's report was presented to Parliament on 29 November 2012,[12] British authorities have agreed to a Royal Charter on Self-Regulation of the Press to implement the Leveson Report's principal recommendations, alongside the associated Crime and Courts Act 2013 and the Enterprise and Regulatory Reform Act 2013.[13] Of particular concern, Schedule 3 of the Royal Charter allows any external 'recognised regulator' to exercise significant powers over newspaper organisations, including the use of arbitration, the power to direct apologies, and the discretion to impose fines for contraventions of established press standards.[14]

Furthermore, sections 34 to 42 of the Crime and Courts Act 2013 provide for exemplary damages and discriminatory costs provisions under which non-member publishers could be forced to pay both sides' litigation costs, even if successful in defending their case. While intended as an incentive to join the Royal Charter's regulatory scheme, Lara Fielden of the University of Oxford's Reuters Institute for the Study of Journalism cautions that globally '[n]o other press council [...] makes this direct link between financial sanctions in the courts and membership of the press council'.[15] Alongside concerns with thwarting 'voluntary' participation, safeguarding the intended operation of the checking function would seem to require exempting newspaper organisations from such potentially chilling provisions when defending defamatory publications on matters of political and public wrongdoing. That is, exemptions for journalistic reports focussing on the same plaintiff politicians, public officials, and influential public figures and corporations would seem necessary. Therefore, in formerly disregarding the close relationship between defamation law reform and press regulation, Lord Justice Leveson's earlier view that it would 'not [...] be valuable either to go over that ground or to postulate what might be the effect of any legislation eventually enacted',[16] would seem to have been misplaced.

iii. Application to Reynolds, Jameel, *and* Flood

The value of our proposed amendments to Britain's new statutory defence is most convincingly shown by considering their impact on the three public libel decisions that British authorities have selected to guide its interpretation and use. As we shall see, adding rebuttable presumptions to section 4 of the Defamation Act 2013

12 The Right Honourable Lord Justice Leveson, *An Inquiry into the Culture, Practices and Ethics of the Press: Report* (29 November 2012, HC 780) (Leveson Report).

13 'Royal Charter on Self-Regulation of the Press' (Final Draft, 11 October 2013) (Royal Charter) <www.gov.uk/government/uploads/system/uploads/attachment_data/file/254116/Final_Royal_Charter_25_October_2013_clean__Final_.pdf> (last accessed 25 January 2018); Crime and Courts Act 2013 (UK); Enterprise and Regulatory Reform Act 2013 (UK).

14 Royal Charter, ibid Sch 3.

15 Lara Fielden, 'A Royal Charter for the Press: How does it Measure up to Regulation Overseas?' (Oxford, Reuters Institute, 2013) 2.

16 Leveson Report (n 12) Vol 4, 1508.

would make possible more theoretically consistent and defensible results than achieved previously in *Reynolds*,[17] *Jameel v Wall Street Journal Europe*,[18] and *Flood v Times Newspapers Ltd.*[19] This is accomplished by extending support to media defendants in precisely those cases raising concerns with the checking function's primary aim of holding power to account. It would also provide stronger guidance to lower courts, which have been least likely to properly theorise and apply the checking function in the past.

An especially persuasive demonstration of our law reform proposals flows from their application to *Reynolds*. As we know, *Reynolds* involved investigative reporting of political malfeasance at the highest levels of governance. With statutory protection for 'editorial judgment' and presumptions of 'public interest' and 'reasonable belief' rebuttable only on 'clear and convincing' evidence,[20] it would be exceedingly difficult to endorse the House of Lords' original disposition to dismiss the newspaper defendants' appeal. In particular, *The Sunday Times* journalist's evidence that he had omitted the plaintiff's explanation from his article 'because he rejected Mr Reynolds's version of the events and concluded that Mr Reynolds had been deliberately misleading',[21] would have been amply supported under our modified approach. More precisely, this evidence would not have succumbed to concerns with 'responsible journalism' quite so easily. Recognising that the checking function was the overriding free expression justification, it would be easier to conclude that the writer, editor, and newspaper defendants in *Reynolds* were well within their protected spheres of journalistic activity when reporting on the Irish Prime Minister's troubles in appointing a new President of the High Court. Similarly, Lord Nicholls' reasoning that the statements of fact in *The Sunday Times* article (such as they were) 'were not information the public had a right to know', would simply not stand under our proposed strengthening of Britain's new defence.

Greater attention on the press' 'watchdog' role in *Reynolds* might also have prompted sharper recognition of the prevailing support for the checking function in Strasbourg jurisprudence. By reorienting legal analysis around facilitating the generation and reporting of 'accountability news', it would have been just as improbable for Lord Nicholls to conclude (mistakenly) that special recognition for political speech 'lacks a coherent rationale', as it would be for Lord Cooke to believe that 'no trace is to be found' in Strasbourg jurisprudence of *any* support for stronger media defamation protections for political speech. Again, embedding the checking function in rebuttable presumptions of 'public interest' and 'reasonable belief' can be expected to keep courts focussed on providing stronger protections for press independence and investigative journalism as a doctrinal corrective to Britain's accountability deficits exposed in chapter eight.

[17] *Reynolds* (n 1).
[18] [2007] 1 AC 359 (HL).
[19] [2012] UKSC 11.
[20] Defamation Act 2013 (n 7) s 4(4).
[21] *Reynolds* (n 1) 206 (Lord Nicholls).

Jameel also validates our law reform recommendations. Unlike *Reynolds*, the leading plaintiff in *Jameel* was not a politician or public official, but a prominent foreign businessman. Although a slim majority of the House of Lords gave proper effect to the importance of editorial judgment by concluding that the newspaper's failure to obtain the plaintiff's side of the story was insufficient to deny application of the *Reynolds* defence, the real confusion was found in their treatment of the second plaintiff, a corporate trading company. Importantly, a majority of the Law Lords failed to recognise a basis for treating non-governmental corporations differently by requiring proof of special damages. This difficulty was attributable to undertheorising accountability concerns and disregarding the powerful influence of commercial interests. For instance, in equating corporate reputational interests with those of natural persons, Lord Bingham instructively concluded, 'I find nothing repugnant in the notion that this is a value which the law should protect'.[22]

Only Lord Hoffmann and Baroness Hale (dissenting in part) made any connection to concerns with democratic accountability and the checking function rationale. In supporting a different damages rule for corporate defamation plaintiffs, Baroness Hale reasoned sharply:

> My Lords, in my view such a requirement would achieve a proper balance between the right of a company to protect its reputation and the right of the press and public to be critical of it. These days, the dividing line between governmental and non-governmental organisations is increasingly difficult to draw. The power wielded by the major multinational corporations is enormous and growing. *The freedom to criticise them may be at least as important in a democratic society as the freedom to criticise the government.*[23]

Rather than risk neglecting the vast influence and social importance of corporate defamation plaintiffs, a rebuttable presumption in cases involving corporations and influential public figures would go a long way towards realising Baroness Hale's perceptive dicta. That is, fixing the Court's attention on the special relevance of the checking function to public libel cases would provide a more principled basis for expanding the reach of Britain's new statutory defence. This would surely narrow the possibilities for similar confusion taking root in future public libel cases involving non-governmental plaintiffs, whether natural persons, or corporations.

Lastly, our modifications to Britain's defence of 'Publication on Matter of Public Interest' would have avoided much confusion in *Flood*. As in *Reynolds* and *Jameel*, Britain's highest court faced significant challenges reconciling public libel plaintiffs to a shared free expression rationale. Specifically, in yet another case involving investigative journalism of government and official wrongdoing, Lord Phillips P encountered difficulties applying the 'public interest' test from *Reynolds*, reasoning that since Sergeant Flood was not a 'public figure', '[p]ublication of his name can have meant nothing to most readers [...]'.[24] As noted in chapter four,

[22] *Jameel* (n 18) [26]. Lord Hoffmann acceded to Baroness Hale's judgment on this point (at [90]).
[23] *Jameel* (n 18) [158] (emphasis added).
[24] *Flood* (n 19) [73].

this reasoning generated needless confusion and sidestepped application of the checking function. For however else one wished to characterise Detective Sergeant Flood's terms of employment, he was clearly a 'public official' falling within the categories of individuals to whom the checking function classically applies.

Lord Phillips P also expressed concerns with revealing Sergeant Flood's identity and inviting suspicion among his fellow officers, two considerations that would have been disposed of quickly and convincingly under our revised statutory defence. As we know, compared to overriding concerns with exposing official misconduct, proponents of the checking function view such reputationally-sensitive matters as of meaningful, but *secondary* importance. Incorporating rebuttable presumptions of 'public interest' and 'reasonable belief' based on the checking function rationale would arguably have calmed Lord Phillips P's apprehensions and might more reliably mitigate possibilities of courts denying media defendants protection from defamation liability in similar cases. In essence, by reinforcing the checking function through rebuttable presumptions and a heightened standard of proof, it is easier for courts to acknowledge the *functional equivalence* of plaintiff politicians, public officials, and influential public figures and corporations for the purposes of keeping tabs on what society's powerful are doing. Applying our modified section 4 defence to *Reynolds*, *Jameel*, and *Flood* thus handles a sufficiently diverse spectrum of public libel plaintiffs to illustrate its overall effectiveness and consistency of approach.

In the end, besides acting as a general reminder to marshal all relevant freedom of expression justifications in public libel cases, our rebuttable presumptions and elevated standard of proof provide more direct assurances for media defendants by triggering enhanced doctrinal protections for investigative journalism when the subjects of their public interest publications engage pivotal accountability concerns characteristic of the checking function of the press.

II. Discussion

At this stage we must proceed to critically evaluate and reflect upon what has been discovered and achieved. A significant part of this process is considering all reasoned options and remaining candid about any relevant restrictions on the overall analysis.

A. Methodological Constraints and Further Research

Despite the contributions of our revised framework, its analysis and prescriptions are inescapably preliminary. As highlighted by media scholars and 'systems-theories' of accountability, a more comprehensive evaluation must also consider a jurisdiction's media structure and any contextual developments affecting the checking function of the press. As indicated in chapter seven, our accountability analysis might be usefully expanded over time to include the following factors.

First, an important component for evaluating doctrinal approaches is weighing each jurisdiction's 'traditions and power of the press',[25] to borrow Lord Nicholls' suggestive phrase from *Reynolds*. As implied by the formulations of 'censorial power' by eighteenth-century radical Whigs, securing the press' role as 'the Attorney General of the People'[26] and 'that vigilant guardian of Public Liberty'[27] requires, above all, that it be *independent* and *adversarial* in interest to government. This, we will recall, was emphasised strongly by Professor Blasi. As a result, differences in function, ownership, and structure of newspaper organisations invite careful analysis as to whether and how they impact the press' role as an institutional check and accountability mechanism,[28] not to mention their implications for public libel doctrine.

Second, account must also be taken of *contextual* factors affecting the press' 'watchdog' role. As recognised by the Chang study and the University of Oxford's Reuters Institute for the Study of Journalism, '[t]he business of journalism is widely held to be in serious crisis today, in particular because of the rise of the internet'.[29] Although the crisis has seemed 'more closely connected with the relative degree of dependence on volatile revenue sources like advertising and on the differential impact of the global recession [...]',[30] the effect of such industry-wide shifts in news generation and investigative reporting remains an important factor when evaluating press institutions and their embodiment of the checking function.[31]

Finally, it is easily forgotten that an expanded accountability analysis must sooner or later consider a jurisdiction's commitment to protecting *reputation*.[32] Inevitably, we must return to Blackstone's original formulation pitting reputational

25 *Reynolds* (n 1) 202.

26 Capel Lofft, *An Essay on the Law of Libels* (London, 1785) 60.

27 Tunis Wortman, *A Treatise, Concerning Political Enquiry, and the Liberty of the Press* (New York, 1800) 246.

28 C Edwin Baker long argued that media ownership concentration has important implications for press independence and democratic legitimacy. See C Edwin Baker, *Media Concentration and Democracy: Why Ownership Matters* (Cambridge, Cambridge University Press, 2007).

29 David AL Levy and Rasmus Kleis Nielsen (eds), *The Changing Business of Journalism and Its Implications for Democracy* (Reuters Institute, 2010) 1. See also Robert W McChesney and John Nichols, *The Death and Life of American Journalism: The Media Revolution That Will Begin the World Again* (Philadelphia, Nation Books, 2010). See also Alex S Jones, *Losing the News: The Future of the News that Feeds Democracy* (Oxford, Oxford University Press, 2009); Lee C Bollinger, *Uninhibited, Robust, and Wide-Open: A Free Press for a New Century* (Oxford, Oxford University Press, 2010) Ch 3; Robert W McChesney and Victor Pickard (eds), *Will the Last Reporter Please Turn out the Lights: The Collapse of Journalism and What can be Done to Fix It* (New York, New Press, 2011).

30 Levy and Nielsen, ibid.

31 McChesney and Nichols (n 29) Ch 1; Jones (n 29) Ch 8.

32 See Robert C Post, 'The Social Foundations of Defamation Law: Reputation and the Constitution' (1986) 74 *California Law Review* 691. See also Lawrence McNamara, *Reputation and Defamation* (Oxford, Oxford University Press, 2007); Bob Tarantino, 'Chasing Reputation: The Argument for Differential Treatment of "Public Figures" in Canadian Defamation Law' (2010) 48 *Osgoode Hall Law Journal* 595.

interests against freedom of expression. As captured more recently by Judge Edgerton of the Court of Appeals for the District of Columbia Circuit, '[w]hatever is added to the field of libel is taken from the field of free debate'.[33] It is to be expected then that the results of any wide-ranging accountability assessment might shift significantly depending on the degree of support for protecting reputation. For instance, in his leading article on reputation analysis, Professor Robert Post has shown that different concepts of reputation (eg dignity, honour, property) have pushed defamation doctrine in 'diverse and divergent directions' in the past, and that 'each weighs very differently in the balance against our constitutional interest in freedom of expression'.[34] As we have known all along, free expression and accountability concerns represent only one side of defamation law's theoretical equation.

Overall, while much work remains before achieving a definitive public libel methodology, the theoretical repositioning required by our revised framework provides a long overdue and appropriate basis for embarking upon this challenging methodological process. With these restrictions in mind, the foremost lessons of our comparative enquiry are more realistically and convincingly shown.

B. Comparative Law Reflections

i. Equivalence Functionalism

'Functionalist' scholars have long known that '[o]ne can speak of comparative law only if there are *specific comparative reflections* on the problem to which the work is devoted'.[35] As explained by Zweigert and Kötz, comparatists are in the 'best position' to do this because, having employed a comparative law methodology, they 'have more material at [their] disposal, [are] aware of solutions which would not occur to the homespun lawyer, however imaginative, and [are] not blinded by faith in the superiority of [their] own system'.[36] As plausibly the only legal method consistent with legitimate scientific aspirations, comparative law achieves its unique prescriptive force by 'show[ing] the way to a better mastery of the legal material, to deeper insights into it, and thus, in the end, to better law'.[37] Since this process is always 'affected by the peculiarities of the particular problem' under study,[38]

[33] *Sweeney v Patterson* 128 F2d 457, 458 (1942).

[34] Post (n 32) 693.

[35] Konrad Zweigert and Hein Kötz, *Introduction to Comparative Law* (Oxford, Oxford University Press, 2011) 6 (emphasis added).

[36] ibid 47. The concept of 'functionalism' advanced here draws heavily on 'equivalence functionalism', which is premised on notions that not only can similar institutions fulfil different functions at different times, but that similar functional needs can be fulfilled by different institutions. See Ralf Michaels, 'The Functional Method of Comparative Law' in Mathias Reimann and Reinhard Zimmermann, *The Oxford Handbook of Comparative Law* (Oxford, Oxford University Press, 2008) 356–59.

[37] Zweigert and Kötz (n 35) 34.

[38] Zweigert and Kötz (n 35) 43.

'taking stock' of our principal findings requires a brief recap of our underlying problem and comparative approach.

First, following selection of our five comparators—which sensibly included the main contributors to public libel law's recent liberalisation—the second stage in our process involved 'summarising the law' by providing specifics of our five doctrinal regimes. After reviewing this 'basic material' in chapter one, our opening chapter concluded by offering a 'new point of view' from which to consider this doctrinal heterogeneity—namely, a widespread undertheorising of 'democratic' free speech justifications. Part B then satisfied the third stage by uncovering a 'new perspective' with which to *critique* our comparators' doctrinal approaches. Specifically, public libel law is beset generally by a collective disregard of accountability concerns and the checking function of the press.

The fourth and penultimate stage of our enquiry involved an elaborate course of 'system-building', which established the *special syntax* and *vocabulary* 'necessary for comparative researches on particular topics'.[39] Our primary objective in Part C was freeing domestic solutions from their conceptual context and stripping them of their doctrinal overtones 'so that they may be seen purely in the light of their *function*, as an attempt to satisfy a particular legal need'.[40] As it turned out, our new framework required us to adjust press regulation (via public libel doctrine) to a jurisdiction's broader accountability profile, precisely the sort of 'loose structure' that Zweigert and Kötz anticipated we might initially find.[41] According to the esteemed authors, any new conceptual framework must 'cast a wider net than those of national systems [...] because the functional approach of comparative law concentrates on the *real live problem* which often lurks unseen behind the concepts of the national systems'.[42] The 'hidden problem' in our case was our comparators' tendency to overlook democratic accountability concerns and, by corollary, missing opportunities to adjust press regulation to suit a jurisdiction's broader accountability dynamics—difficulties which we now see more clearly through our revised analytical framework and its supporting analysis.

Finally, Part D demonstrated the effectiveness of our proposed new systems by applying our revised framework to Britain and its newly-adopted public libel doctrine. This required novel law reform proposals, in some cases departing sharply from conventional doctrinal approaches.

ii. 'Systematising' Contributions

With such prefatory steps in hand, our final stage involves 'critically evaluating' what we have learned. Since the 'results' of our enquiry are largely determined by its methodological constraints, we must be careful to avoid overreaching

39 Zweigert and Kötz (n 35) 44.
40 Zweigert and Kötz (n 35) 44 (emphasis added).
41 Zweigert and Kötz (n 35) 45.
42 Zweigert and Kötz (n 35) 45 (emphasis added).

when reporting on 'best outcomes'. As explained in chapter seven, the soundness and reliability of our results is ultimately contingent on applying a *fully articulated* version of our revised framework. Therefore, due to potential impacts of differences in media structure and context—not to mention commitments to 'reputation'—any recommendations beyond exposing *broader inconsistencies* or *untenable positions* must be approached with caution. Ironically, due to the methodological need and challenges of formulating a new 'functionalist' framework, its maiden application to Britain has provided us with precious little by way of prescriptive results.

This can be better appreciated by reviewing our study's main contributions, which consist of: (1) accurately describing public libel law's doctrinal heterogeneity, widespread undertheorising, and missing 'selection theory'; (2) reformulating public libel law within the combined syntax and structure of public accountability scholarship and general systems theory, facilitating *diagnosis* of the underlying problem; and (3) formulating a new analytical framework for matching public libel doctrine to a jurisdiction's *actual* accountability profile. Our comparative enquiry has necessarily been focussed on establishing the new 'systems' and 'perspectives' through which to view the traditionally confounding technicalities of public libel law. This inevitably alters the ratio of information/analysis to prescription, requiring a greater focus on 'systems-building' to place public libel doctrine on a more relevant and principled foundation. Of necessity, this 'systematising function' is our enquiry's most vital contribution to the problem of public libel law. It represents a critical first step towards achieving a comprehensive and *contextually-sensitive* 'selection theory' for public libels. In the end, these 'systematising' contributions are both a valued and expected result of 'functionalist' legal scholarship, as Professor Ralf Michaels relates:

> The system created by equivalence functionalism is a construction, and as such it is open to criticism like any other system. But it may be a *better, more appropriate* system than others, it may provide *new angles* on the legal systems we compare, and it may thereby help us both *understand* and *critique* those systems.[43]

iii. Theoretical Implications

In the meantime, our revised framework or 'functionalist construction' *does* help us better 'understand and critique' public libel law, not only by confirming the nature and source of its undertheorising, but by yielding important theoretical and doctrinal lessons. Reflecting on the former provides the following more abstract assurances.

First, despite the Privy Council's conviction that comparative analysis helps to 'clarify and refine the issues and the available options' in public libel law,[44] our

[43] Michaels (n 36) 373 (emphasis added).
[44] *Lange v Atkinson* [2000] 1 NZLR 257 (PC) 263 (Lord Nicholls).

enquiry has demonstrated that only by *reformulating* and *contextually reinstating* the checking function can such well-intentioned guidance translate into a practicable methodology. For example, by undertheorising the checking function and accountability concerns in *Lange No 1* and *Lange No 2*,[45] the New Zealand Court of Appeal's attempts to compare the UK's electoral system, FOI legislation, domestic human rights protections, and media structure were bound to raise more questions than answers. Without arranging these mechanisms *systematically*, it was impossible to determine how they were meant to steer judges or legislators towards 'optimal' doctrinal solutions. Although accountability concerns were arguably implicit throughout, without explicit reference to accountability theory, the Court of Appeal was unable to identify all applicable accountability mechanisms, and, most crucially, how they might *interrelate*. This is confirmed by probing the uneasy relationship between the Court's reasoning and doctrine.

While easy to overlook, an unstated premise of the Court of Appeal's analysis was that New Zealand required more liberal public libel doctrine than England or Australia precisely because its accountability mechanisms were in fact *stronger*. By contrast, our revised framework both provides a more complete inventory of accountability mechanisms, and a clear criterion by which doctrinal adjustments should be made using Dunsire's balance-restoring 'collibration' model. Had it distinguished accountability *deficits* and *overloads* using this method, the New Zealand Court of Appeal's analysis would have led to the opposite result—namely, a *less* liberal doctrinal alternative. Careful assessment of the effects of accountability mechanisms at multiple levels of abstraction seems to have been the missing piece of the puzzle all along.

Second, we can still obtain important preliminary data on accountability dynamics and institutional design by applying our provisional framework. As explained in chapter eight, the contrast between 'parliamentary' and 'presidential' governments is likely to have the most significant impact on a jurisdiction's general accountability limits and potentials for political monitoring and control. Equally, our British case study suggests that the mechanism of 'judicial review' is likely to have a correspondingly dominant influence on accountability dynamics and design. We can expect these effects to be most extensive where a jurisdiction employs an especially *weak* or *strong* version of judicial review.

Third, despite the potential impact of 'reputation' on free expression principles in the context of *private* libels, its effect on public libel doctrine is ultimately limited by overriding concerns to ensure minimal efficacy for the checking function of the press. That is, the whole point of developing a 'plaintiff-centric' approach to public libels is to maximise possibilities for fine-tuning the press' 'watchdog' function to mitigate institutional accountability needs and dysfunctions. At least prima facie, it is difficult to imagine a situation where reputational interests might trump

[45] *Lange v Atkinson* (1998) 3 NZLR 424 (CA) 468 (*Lange No 1*); *Lange v Atkinson* (2000) 3 NZLR 385 (CA) (*Lange No 2*).

accountability concerns in public libel cases. After all, the principal objective in these scenarios must be to minimise institutional or contextual *threats* to the press' checking function role, not to disregard it in favour of safeguarding the reputational sensitivities of society's privileged and powerful.

Finally, our revised framework and its underlying reliance on public accountability theory help clarify the relationship between Meiklejohnian theory and the checking function rationale. For instance, where chapter two demonstrated that Professor Meiklejohn's democratic 'self-governance' theory focusses disproportionately on deliberative/electoral concerns at the expense of democratic accountability, Part C revealed that Professor Blasi's 'checking value' was just *one* accountability mechanism (albeit an important *horizontal* one) in a jurisdiction's overall network. Also, Meiklejohn's construal of elected representatives as mere 'agents of the collective political will' raises a broader concern with 'descriptive representation', which Pitkin noted, 'has no room for representation *as* accountability'.[46] Other than 'reflect[ing] his constituents as truly and accurately as possible', it makes little sense to speak of holding to account such representatives where 'there is no room within such a concept [...] for leadership, initiative, or creative action'.[47]

It is therefore not only erroneous for courts and legislatures to overlook or to conflate Meiklejohn's and Blasi's models but, even when taken together, both do not address the full spectrum of accountability concerns at stake in public libel cases. Therefore, despite the dominance of Meiklejohnian theory in constitutional free speech litigation, it would be a mistake to assume that public libel jurisprudence can be adequately supported by only one or both of these models. We can only fully appreciate their contributions and limitations as free expression justifications and democratic theories by interpreting them in the light of broader notions of public accountability.

iv. Doctrinal Implications

Alongside these more abstract lessons, our comparative study also has important doctrinal repercussions. Specifically, besides mishandling 'democratic' theory and demonstrating a collective aversion to free expression theorising, our comparators' misconception of 'categoricalism' is perhaps its most troublesome feature. If sanctuary was intended to be found in ad hoc balancing, the primary lesson of our enquiry is of course that it *cannot*. As we have seen, ad hoc balancing *requires* recourse to a *complete* inventory of free expression justifications, especially accountability concerns and the checking function of the press. As illustrated by Canadian and British courts, it is easier to succumb to institutional 'forgetfulness' with ad hoc balancing than when consistently applying established rules designed to achieve the checking function's principal objectives.

[46] Hanna Fenichel Pitkin, *The Concept of Representation* (California, University of California Press, 1967) 89 (emphasis added).

[47] ibid 90.

Similarly, British authorities have been adverse to categorical approaches as being invariably 'too protective' of freedom of expression. However, our study demonstrates that the checking function is fundamentally *contextual* in nature, such that greater nuance in public libel jurisprudence is both possible and necessary. Building on Professor Schauer's insight that '[…] there is no necessary correlation between the approach employed and the strength of the first amendment protection',[48] our revised framework expands the uses and implications of public libel doctrine, confirming its critical role in tailoring the checking function to a jurisdiction's broader accountability requirements. Furthermore, we can only untangle the checking function's improper identification with categoricalism and bright-line rules by *contextualising* it as part of a jurisdiction's broader accountability network. The prevailing question is never 'whether or not' the checking function, but always *how much* or *how little*. By employing a *multi*-dimensional, accountability-based methodology for formulating and adapting public libel doctrine, our law reform proposals rise above existing methodological confusion and substantive errors.[49]

The primary doctrinal implications of our comparative study then are as follows. First, because of their shared disregard of accountability concerns, 'responsible journalism' defences have not and arguably *cannot* reliably determine whether and how public libels should be protected. Without orientating ad hoc balancing around the free speech theory most relevant to public libel cases (ie the checking function), courts risk downplaying the press' role in investigating and reporting political misconduct, either by failing to appreciate the press' vital 'watchdog' role, or by insisting on a rigidly-applied criterion of 'responsible journalism' at odds with investigative journalism. Contrary to Lord Nicholls' predictions, our comparators' public libel decisions demonstrate that ad hoc balancing does *not* in fact guarantee 'greater flexibility and adaptability'.

Second, even if accountability and the checking function *were* properly theorised, ad hoc 'responsible journalism' defences alone would be insufficient to satisfy the broad accountability assessments required by our revised framework. In this respect, it is debatable whether such doctrinal approaches even ask the right questions. By focussing on the defendant's behaviour and whether a statement of fact is in the 'public interest', important considerations unique to defamation plaintiffs cannot easily be aligned with relevant free speech justifications. For instance, by disregarding the plaintiff's status as a *politician* or *public official*, the

[48] Frederick Schauer, 'Categories and the First Amendment: A Play in Three Acts' (1981) 34 *Vanderbilt Law Review* 265, 303.

[49] For example, disregarding accountability and the checking function has enhanced the appeal of overly-technical interpretations of constitutional sources of free expression. As indicated in chapter three at n 2, British scholars have commonly and erroneously tied categoricalism to the unqualified wording of the First Amendment. But once the US Supreme Court endorsed the 'actual malice' rule instead of an absolute privilege in *New York Times v Sullivan* 376 US 254 (1964), the Court was immediately offside the First Amendment's strictures. Something *other* than consistency with statutory language had to account for doctrine selection.

analytical foothold for the checking function (and accountability concerns more broadly) fails to present itself squarely for analysis. These concerns are serious enough to raise doubts as to whether these defences can be considered 'ad hoc' at all. After all, British judges have consistently undertheorised 'democratic' free speech justifications and have interpreted the test of 'responsible journalism' very restrictively. These two problems are inextricably linked.

Finally, by contextualising the checking function as a subcomponent of broader, interrelated networks of accountability mechanisms under our revised framework, it is essential that both categorical and 'responsible journalism' defences be questioned and set aside, at least temporarily. This is not to suggest that the checking function or a concern for greater accountability must involve categorical approaches, or that 'responsible journalism' defences cannot be adapted to suit diverse institutional settings. Rather, as a matter of methodological necessity, doctrinal approaches must be principally *determined* by the accountability profile associated with a nation's institutional background. Otherwise, we are not taking seriously the potential impact and internal logic of our revised framework.

C. Institutional Competence

As a final and related point, although our revised analytical framework benefits public libel law by placing the defamation inquiry on a more sophisticated and reliable footing, it is crucial to entrust the demanding tasks of accountability assessment and the selection of suitable doctrine to a jurisdiction's most capable institutional body.[50]

These implications of our revised model can be examined along two paths. First, as demonstrated in chapter nine, a greater attention to the checking function and accountability concerns can be used to enhance the effectiveness of Britain's new statutory defence. Specifically, in public libel cases involving plaintiff politicians, public officials, and influential public figures and corporations, UK authorities would be well advised to substitute the defendant's existing legal burdens with presumptions of 'public interest' and 'reasonable belief' rebuttable only on 'clear and convincing' evidence to the contrary. In this way, the 'reasonableness' of a newspaper organisation's conduct is presumed and protected in a manner similar to the effect of a categorical rule, but with the added flexibility possible under ad hoc balancing.

The second path involves examining judicial competence to adopt categorical approaches of any sort. Continuing with our UK example, while obviously precluded by section 4 of the Defamation Act 2013, merely considering this possibility

[50] See generally Neil K Komesar, *Imperfect Alternatives: Choosing Institutions in Law, Economics, and Public Policy* (Chicago, University of Chicago Press, 1996). See also Richard White, 'Separation of Powers and Legislative Supremacy' (2011) 127 *Law Quarterly Review* 456.

highlights important institutional limitations of judiciaries. Aside from obvious conflicts with the principle of parliamentary sovereignty, any restriction on a judge's discretion must be preceded by extensive accountability assessments across multiple levels of abstraction. While greater attentiveness to the checking function can be built into Britain's existing defence, the inescapable upshot of our revised framework is that a much larger problem is afoot. Public libel doctrine then must *follow* assessment of a jurisdiction's accountability profile; not precede it. Particularly in the context of adversarial litigation, the judiciary would seem to be fundamentally incapable of the substantial investigatory tasks involved in fleshing out our new methodology, even in its current preliminary state. Therefore, even if judges could consistently consider all relevant free expression justifications or properly apply rebuttable presumptions under a revised public interest defence, without sufficient investigatory resources, it is perhaps implausible to expect that '[o]ver time, a valuable corpus of case law will be built up',[51] as Lord Nicholls originally expected.

As a result, given the comparatively broad powers and resources of legislative bodies, Britain's public libel doctrine seems best advanced by a formal process of parliamentary inquiry. After all, the more probative and thorough the accountability analysis, the more confidently public libel doctrine can be matched to Britain's *actual* institutional background. Since formulating and adapting public libel doctrine is fundamentally about matters of Britain's constitutional structure, some form of select committee inquiry or royal commission might be best suited to undertake this challenging but necessary assignment.

III. Chapter Conclusion

Part D explored the implications of our revised framework by applying it to Britain and its newly-updated public libel doctrine.

Having selected the UK as our law reform candidate in chapter eight, our investigation of Britain's primary and secondary accountability mechanisms revealed significant deficits in government transparency and accountability. When judged against the undertheorised basis for its public libel regime, we determined in chapter nine that the most appropriate doctrinal match for its accountability profile requires, at a minimum, the adoption of a generic qualified privilege. What is more, we could not rule out the prospect of an absolute privilege for political speech. This is deeply ironic since, alongside discounting accountability concerns in leading cases, Britain's public libel jurisprudence exhibits both a firm reluctance to privilege political speech and deeply-rooted misconceptions about categorical defences. Alternatively, Britain's existing statutory defence can be adapted

[51] *Reynolds* (n 1) 205.

by introducing presumptions of 'public interest' and 'reasonable belief' rebuttable on 'clear and convincing' evidence to the contrary in cases involving plaintiff politicians, public officials, and influential public figures and corporations. Such plaintiff-centric amendments are vital for ensuring an effective foothold for the checking function in addressing accountability concerns in free speech litigation involving media defendants.

Still, despite their prescriptive force, these law reform recommendations raise significant concerns with institutional competence and the need for methodological refinement. Although analysing public libel doctrine along the lines suggested places the defamation inquiry on a more sophisticated and reliable foundation, the increased resources and enlarged scope of review characteristic of legislative bodies argues in favour of reserving selection of Britain's public libel doctrine to some form of parliamentary inquiry. After all, the more granular and extensive the evidence and analysis of accountability dynamics, the more effectively public libel doctrine can be matched to institutional settings.

Similarly, although our revised framework can identify gross mismanagement of public libel doctrine and establish justifiable ranges of possible alternatives, the analysis proposed here is unavoidably preliminary. As indicated in chapter seven, a comprehensive accountability assessment must also consider a jurisdiction's media structure and any contextual factors affecting its accountability profile and embodiments of the checking function. Above all, an accountability assessment along such lines must still be balanced against a jurisdiction's commitment to protecting reputation. With the possible exception of reputational interests, these factors will invariably affect the required form of public libel doctrine in potentially drastic ways.

Finally, our revised analytical framework has also given rise to many unforeseen theoretical and doctrinal consequences. Besides clarifying the relationship between Meiklejohnian theory and the checking function rationale, it has also demonstrated the disproportionate impact of judicial review and parliamentary/presidential structures to jurisdictional accountability dynamics. Doctrinal concerns with the overall aptness of ad hoc balancing defences for public libels have also been raised.

In the end, while much work remains for refining our methodology for formulating public libel doctrine, the theoretical repositioning required by our revised framework provides a long overdue and promising foundation for this very process.

Conclusion—Prospective Challenges to Public Libel Law Reform

We conclude by momentarily broadening our analytical focus to situate the role of the institutional press within the present-day 'crisis of journalism'.[1] As recognised within several academic disciplines, over the last two decades an unsettling picture of contemporary news media has emerged. Among the more disturbing trends, news organisations have witnessed the proliferation of digital media and the decline of the daily newspaper industry; increased media ownership concentration; massively reduced circulation and advertising revenues; record lay-offs of journalists and reporters; the near elimination of investigative reporting, science journalism, and local news coverage; and the rise of government public relations.[2] Perhaps most troubling, these trends have occasioned significant losses in the manufacture and reporting of 'accountability news', the most expensive and crucial news product for sustaining a well-informed electorate and holding power to account.[3]

The most perspicacious commentators have recognised that these trends not only signal a crisis for newspaper organisations and journalism; at core, they present a crisis for democracy. Alongside the Chang study and research from the Reuters Institute for the Study of Journalism,[4] noted media and journalism scholars Robert McChesney and John Nichols have detailed the collapse of the institutions, practices, and resources necessary for democratic governance in their *Death and Life of American Journalism*.[5] Although focussing principally on its origins

[1] See Robert W McChesney and John Nichols, *The Death and Life of American Journalism: The Media Revolution That Will Begin the World Again* (Philadelphia, Nation Books 2010). See also Alex S Jones, *Losing the News: The Future of the News that Feeds Democracy* (Oxford, Oxford University Press, 2009); Lee C Bollinger, *Uninhibited, Robust, and Wide-Open: A Free Press for a New Century* (Oxford, Oxford University Press, 2010) Ch 3; Robert W McChesney and Victor Pickard (eds), *Will the Last Reporter Please Turn out the Lights: The Collapse of Journalism and What can be Done to Fix It* (New York, New Press 2011). For an excellent discussion of media ownership concentration, see C Edwin Baker, *Media Concentration and Democracy: Why Ownership Matters* (Cambridge, Cambridge University Press, 2007).

[2] McChesney and Nichols, ibid Ch 1.

[3] See Jones, ibid Ch 1.

[4] See Eric CC Chang and others, 'Legislative Malfeasance and Political Accountability' (2010) 62(2) *World Politics* 177; David AL Levy and Rasmus Kleis Nielsen (eds), *The Changing Business of Journalism and Its Implications for Democracy* (Oxford, Reuters Institute, 2010).

[5] McChesney and Nichols (n 1).

and impact in America, their description of the present crisis and its wider implications for democracy is compelling:

> By the end of this first decade of the 21st century, the crisis of journalism is obvious to all. Daily newspapers are in free-fall collapse. The entire commercial news-media system is disintegrating. Wall Street and Madison Avenue are abandoning the production of journalism en masse. Our nation faces the absurd and untenable prospect of attempting what James Madison characterized as impossible: to be a self-governing constitutional republic without a functioning news media.[6]

This transformation of newspaper organisations and professional journalism is of particular significance to public libel law not only because it threatens the constitutional role of the press, but, more precisely, because it diminishes its impact as an accountability mechanism and heightens its sensitivity to legal regulation. Introduced as a 'contextual' factor in chapter seven, the crisis of journalism effectively requires law reform authorities to consider more liberal public libel doctrine than might otherwise have seemed appropriate. This intensifies the importance of the theoretical bases for freedom of expression and the press, particularly the checking function rationale. Since political accountability is arguably more important than ever due to the reported decline in accountability news production, this study has been premised on the firm conviction that, without proper theoretical and comparative law analysis, the checking function will continue to be inconsistently applied and ignored, or even worse, lost entirely as an independent free speech justification.

Building on prior scholarship documenting the failure of the checking function to gain a proper foothold in constitutional theory, our efforts to determine its current status have involved a broad comparative law analysis of public libel doctrine in Canada, the United States, Britain, Australia, and New Zealand. Confirming trends first observed by leading jurists in the 1970s, our doctrinal critique has revealed that the foremost deficiency in public libel jurisprudence is a persistent and widespread disregard of accountability concerns and the checking function of the press. Whether overlooking clear references to political accountability and the checking function in Strasbourg jurisprudence, conflating the checking function with Meiklejohnian theory, or rejecting free expression theorising altogether, leading common law jurisdictions have referred vaguely to democratic theory and have otherwise not taken seriously vital notions of democratic accountability when seeking to 'optimally' balance freedom of expression and reputation.

Rather than continue blindly down the prevailing path of habitually rejecting the 'actual malice' rule when selecting doctrinal alternatives, we have instead proposed a new approach to correct such juridical shortcomings. Based on recent advances in public accountability theory, we formulated a reliable framework for analysis by combining two sets of accountability mechanisms essential to supporting adequate measures of government control. As we have seen, the combined

[6] McChesney and Nichols (n 1) 3.

effect of these accountability mechanisms provides the principal background against which public libel doctrine must be coordinated. Although inspired by the comparative law deliberations of the Privy Council and New Zealand Court of Appeal, our application of this revised framework confirmed that suitable doctrinal options can only be identified by theoretically recasting and contextually reinstating the checking function of the press. In simplest terms, a comprehensive assessment of the effects of accountability mechanisms at multiple levels of abstraction is essential. Due to this highly contextualised analysis, a 'one-size-fits-all' approach cannot be sustained, whether arguing for or against specific doctrinal options.

Looking forward, the need for our revised framework has been intensified by leading free speech commentators who endorse international 'harmonisation' of internet, defamation, and media laws based on US First Amendment doctrine.[7] Recognising the widespread effects of digital media on news organisations and the reality that '[t]here are many different views about the proper role of the press in a society',[8] Columbia University President Lee C Bollinger advises that 'we are just at the beginning of a clash of philosophies about the structure of societies and the global society and, in particular, about the nature of expression in the world community'.[9] Confident that 'a central challenge of the twenty-first century will be to create a *global* system of a free press for the emerging global society',[10] Bollinger foresees 'a global public forum that is uninhibited, robust, and wide-open and a press that serves that forum' based on American legal principles.[11]

But if our present study demonstrates anything, it is that such blanket prescriptions are incompatible with the enhanced studies of accountability mechanisms and institutional settings required by our revised framework. More to the point, our examination of public libel jurisprudence suggests that Bollinger's proposals would never work. Our comparative doctrinal analysis not only established that appropriate accountability measures can be attained by employing different rules, institutions, and constitutional structures,[12] but even limited application of our revised framework reveals that any workable international order could only be achieved through a dynamic understanding of how these differences *interrelate*. Compared to applying our framework domestically, its complexities on an international scale would be staggering. As our analysis currently stands then, there is no reason to think that Professor Bollinger's universalised approach is either desirable or realistic. In essence, his law reform proposals either imply (dubiously) that

[7] Bollinger (n 1).
[8] Bollinger (n 1) 92.
[9] Bollinger (n 1) 92.
[10] Bollinger (n 1) 112 (emphasis in original).
[11] Bollinger (n 1) 112.
[12] See John Bell, 'Legal Research and the Distinctiveness of Comparative Law' in Mark Van Hoecke (ed), *Methodologies of Legal Research: Which Kind of Method for What Kind of Discipline?* (Oxford, Hart Publishing 2011) 158.

accountability dynamics and dysfunctions are the same worldwide, or are simply not worth considering at all.

Finally, for those sceptical whether the highpoint of the checking function was *The New York Times'* decision to publish a selection of documents (some classified)—in defiance of President Nixon—detailing the federal government's lies and misdirection regarding the Vietnam War, there is abundant evidence that its symbolic and discursive value is stronger than ever. Following the largest leak of confidential documents in history by WikiLeaks commencing 28 November 2010, *Guardian* journalists David Leigh and Luke Harding reported on a surprising inventory of incidents of abuse of political power on an unprecedented international scale. Remarking on human rights abuses, corruption, spying on fellow United Nations members, dubious financial ties between G8 leaders, corporate espionage, dirty tricks, and hidden bank accounts documented in leaked diplomatic cables, Leigh and Harding observed:

> Sifting through this huge database of diplomatic documents, it was hard not to come away with a depressing view of human nature. Mankind, the world over, seemed revealed as a base, grasping species. Many political leaders showed remarkable greed and venality.[13]

Considered alongside the most recent Panama Papers revelations, the UK parliamentary expenses scandal, and various 'cash for influence' wrongdoings—to name only a few of the dozens of political indiscretions and offences reported in Britain over the past 20 years—Professor Blasi's insistence that the checking function must be based on 'an essentially pessimistic view of human nature and human institutions'[14] is more appropriate now than ever. By corollary, so too must be the necessity for guaranteeing acceptable accountability measures through effective modifications to democratic institutional designs.

As a result, applying our framework to contemporary public libel jurisprudence would appear to be especially urgent. At stake is the prospect of unravelling the uncertain relationships between representative democracy, press freedom, and constitutional structure that captured the interest and imagination of scholars like Van Vechten Veeder over a century earlier. Until then, as a 'measure of the culture, liberality, and practical ability' of our own age, we are well advised to seek meaningful accountability by deploying the checking function of the press through public libel defences tailored to differences in each jurisdiction's accountability profile and institutional milieu—preferably before the erosion of journalism's print-based model threatens to diminish its accountability effects altogether.

[13] David Leigh and Luke Harding, *WikiLeaks: Inside Julian Assange's War on Secrecy* (London, Guardian Books, 2011) 212, 222.

[14] Vincent Blasi, 'The Checking Value in First Amendment Theory' (1977) *American Bar Foundation Research Journal* 521, 541.

INDEX

www.ingramcontent.com/pod-product-compliance
Lightning Source LLC
Chambersburg PA
CBHW071300180926
51613CB00001B/82
* 9 7 8 1 5 0 9 9 2 0 8 1 5 *